UNDERSTANDING DIVERSITY

UNDERSTANDING DIVERSITY

READINGS, CASES, AND EXERCISES

Carol P. Harvey

Assumption College

M. June Allard

Worcester State College

HarperCollins*College*Publishers

Cover and Text Design: Initial Graphic Systems, Inc.
Electronic Production Manager: Eric Jorgensen
Publishing Services: Interactive Production Services
Electronic Page Makeup: Interactive Composition Corporation
Printer and Binder: R.R. Donnelley Crawfordsville
Cover Printer: Coral Graphic Services, Inc.

Understanding Diversity: Readings, Cases, and Exercises

Library of Congress Cataloging-in-Publication Data
Harvey, Carol P.
   Understanding diversity : readings, cases and exercises / Carol P.
   Harvey and M. June Allard.
      p. cm.
     Includes bibliographical references and index.
     ISBN 0-673-46996-4 : $$20.00
    1. Minorities—Employment—United States. 2. Multiculturalism—
United States. 3. Personnel management—United States.
I. Allard, M. June. II. Title.
HF5549.5.M5H37 1995
658.3'041—dc20   94-26136
                              CIP

95 96 97 9 8 7 6 5 4 3 2

To those who have suffered because of their differences and to those who have helped us to understand their differences.

C O N T E N T S

Chapter Three
On the Dimensions of Diversity 107

Chapter Four
On Experiencing Diversity: Cases   159

Chapter Five
On Experiencing Diversity: Exercises   223

P R E F A C E

Recent changes in the demographic composition of the workforce, the influence of new values and lifestyles, the shift to a global rather than a national marketplace, and the emphasis on team rather than individual management models has made understanding how to work with and manage diverse workers a strategic imperative. This book presents an anthology of readings, cases, and exercises that are designed to help individuals examine their own perspectives on diversity and improve their understanding of how organizations must change in order to manage effectively in the twenty-first century.

Understanding Diversity: Readings, Cases, and Exercises can be used in three different ways. First, in an introductory management of diversity course, this book can either be used alone as a reader and source of applied and skill building activities or in conjunction with a theoretical text. Second, in organizational behavior, human resource, or organizational change courses, this book can supplement the basic text when the instructor wants to provide the students with a diversity perspective by adding selected readings, cases, and exercises to the course material. Third, this book can be used as a source of basic workplace training material for consulting work in organizations.

OBJECTIVES OF THIS BOOK

1. *To meet the needs of both students and faculty for readings, cases, and experiential material to use in classes that involve issues of workforce diversity.*

We found that after several years of teaching a course in workforce diversity, we are still unable to find a book that our students like, that we feel addresses both the important cultural and workforce issues, that presents diversity from multiple perspectives, and that includes cases and exercises suitable for the college classroom. Although some books present theoretical perspectives, there is yet no universally accepted paradigm for understanding diversity. Other books are narrow in scope and focus primarily on one type of diversity such as race or gender and ignore too many others, like sexual orientation, that affect working relationships.

Although most of these books have some merit, our experience in using them in the classroom is that they leave a void. Consequently, we find ourselves and many of the colleagues whom we surveyed, supplementing these texts with many handouts from a variety of sources.

As we studied the sample syllabi sent to us by experienced instructors, we discovered that although many of them used a core of common reading materials, there were great differences in their theoretical perspectives and consequently in how they structured their courses. This is understandable because workforce diversity is an emerging field without a commonly accepted theoretical basis.

However, in the syllabi a strong preference is evident for the use of experienced-based models of learning. This makes sense to us because understanding diversity involves systemic changes in the way individuals think, groups interact, and organizations manage. Consequently, the most effective teaching and learning about diversity requires an experiential component as part of the learning process.

2. *To present students with multiple perspectives and viewpoints on under-standing diversity.*

Because diversity is such a complex, developing, and multifaceted topic, we think that students need to read works by many researchers, scholars, and practitioners who have specialized in particular aspects of this subject. To truly understand diversity, it is as important to understand the perspective and contribution of the white male as it is of the physically challenged female, etc. As a result, we feel that there is a need to combine together in one volume some of the more popular writings on diversity with some newer unpublished material developed by those who teach and train in this area.

In addition, our work in this area has led us to the conclusion that many of the roots of understanding diversity lie within the social sciences. Although diversity is a major issue in business today, social scientists have been researching and working in this field for quite some time. Through classroom experience, we learned that beginning the study with a basic understanding of cultural differences provides a foundation for understanding the need for organizational change to meet the needs of the new workforce.

3. *To provide a highly readable anthology that allows instructors flexibility in utilizing material in the most effective format for their courses.*

Consequently, we have chosen material written in the student voice rather than in the researcher's. There are many books on the market that can be used in conjunction with this book to provide additional theoretical perspectives. In addition, since college classes vary in size, length of time, and student composition, we have attempted to accommodate these variations by including material appropriate for different situations. We have chosen a mixture of experiential material that is adaptable for small groups as well as for larger classes, and exercises that can take 5–10 minutes of a 50 minute class as well as more complex exercises that require a two-and-a-half to a three-hour block of time. Another consideration is that group dynamics are different based on class composition, so we have chosen to include exercises that are suitable for different situations. Details on the use of the exercises are provided in the instructor's manual.

ORGANIZATION OF THE BOOK

The material for this book is divided into readings, cases, and exercises that progress from a macro to a micro level. We have purposefully separated readings from cases and exercises so that the instructor may structure the course according to his/her needs and teaching style.

Chapter One begins with a definition of the meaning of diversity, a discussion of cultural differences, and an exploration of theoretical models. The accompanying readings consider diversity from a broad cultural perspective. They were selected to give the reader a foundation from which to explore the macro influences on his/her own perceptions that cut across individual differences in gender, race, ethnicity, and other dimensions of diversity.

Chapter Two focuses on the implications of managing differences at the organizational level. The articles in this part were chosen to explain the differences between Equal Employment Opportunity/Affirmative Action legislation and valuing differences as a strategic imperative.

Chapter Three features readings about groups that represent unchangeable aspects of diversity: gender, race/ethnicity, physical challenge, and sexual orientation. Because of space constraints, it was not possible to explore all dimensions of diversity in the readings. Our coverage of other important but more changeable aspects of differences such as age, religion, social class, marital status, and physical appearance, etc. are included in the cases and exercises that supplement the readings.

Chapters Four and Five are the applied section of this book and contain the cases and exercises. These sections bring issues of difference down to the micro level by requiring the individual student to participate more actively in his/her own learning process.

The cases in Chapter Four, the majority of which are from clearly identified real companies, allow students to apply material from the readings to deal with the diversity problems that are becoming a part of today's management experience. Many of the cases address multiple issues from the readings such as understanding individual differences, stereotypes, Equal Employment Opportunity/Affirmative Action, organizational change, managing diversity, and aspects of individual differences.

The exercises in Chapter Five are designed to help students progress from simply acquiring information about differences, to understanding the sources of their perspectives, to applying this learning to improve their understanding of the impact of working and managing in a diverse workplace.

This book is accompanied by an instructor's manual that explains how the readings, cases, and exercises can be selected and scheduled. It provides details on the key points of each reading, answers to all discussion and case questions, detailed guidelines for the administration and use of each exercise, and sources of supplementary reading and video material.

Understanding Diversity: Readings, Cases, and Exercises was written to meet the need for easily accessible readings and experiential material for college level business courses involving issues of diversity. The intention is to provide an anthology of foundational readings and a selection of cases and exercises that will allow the instructor flexibility in assigning material according to the structure and theoretical orientation of the course. It should be noted that many of the articles in this text are classics that do not use inclusive language; however, they are included here as originally written.

ACKNOWLEDGMENTS

This book benefits from the contributions and efforts of many people. First and foremost, we wish to thank all of the contributing authors for sharing their expertise. Without them, this book would not be possible.

We are grateful to our reviewers for their many thoughtful comments and constructive suggestions that improved both the text and the Instructor's Manual. Our thanks to Karen Golden–Biddle, Emory University, Kathleen Powers, Willamette University (Salem, OR), Marilyn Harris, Central Michigan University, Sandra Johnson, University of Minnesota, Saroj Parasuraman, Drexel University, Laverne Hairston Higgins, University of Oregon, Sonja Delgado, New York City Diversity Consultant, and Ellen Ernst Kossek, Michigan State University.

In addition we wish to thank our colleagues who so generously shared syllabi, reading lists, and suggested articles for inclusion.

It has been a privilege to work with the publishing staff at HarperCollins. We are particularly indebted to Mike Roche, Executive Editor, Lois Lombardo, Freelance Project Manager, Eric Jorgensen, Electronic Production Manager, Melissa Rosati, Management Editor, for her vision, guidance, and support of this project, and Pamela Wilkie, Editorial Assistant.

Each of us wishes to thank our academic institutions for their support and encouragement. They provided us with a sabbatical, a grant for reduced workload, resources, and facilities. We also want to thank Pamela McKay of the Worcester State College Library, Priscilla Berthiaume, Jean Hayes, and Larry Spongberg of the Assumption College Library, and Janet Lambert of the Business Studies Department of the Assumption College for their assistance.

Let us also extend our thanks to Francis Harvey Jr. for his continuing support, to David and Kevin Harvey, Joseph Dunn, and the workstudy students at Assumption College for proofreading the manuscript and especially to Carmella Murphy for her technical assistance in compiling the manuscript.

Carol P. Harvey
M. June Allard

C H A P T E R

ONE

On Culture and Diversity

Americans eat oysters but not snails. The French eat snails but not locusts. The Zulus eat locusts but not fish. The Jews eat fish but not pork. The Hindus eat pork but not beef. The Russians eat beef but not snakes. The Chinese eat snakes but not people. The Jalé of New Guinea find people delicious.[1]

What a menu it takes to feed the world! The charming diversity of practices cited by sociologist Robertson is not limited to cafeteria choices, however. It is echoed across a multitude of other behaviors and beliefs as well.

Popular belief once viewed America as the melting pot for diversity. But even on this there is diversity of opinion: there are those who argue that the melting pot only existed outside the organization gates while inside the white male culture dominated. Still others argue that there never was a melting pot at all.

> There *never* was a melting pot; there is not *now* a melting pot; there never will *be* a melting pot; and if there ever was, it would be such a tasteless soup that we would have to go back and start all over![2]

In any event, the melting pot concept in America is itself melting away. Where once we talked of acculturation, today we talk of accommodation and even of appreciation. No longer do we think in terms of assimilation; instead we think of "managing" diversity.

Just what is diversity? There is no easy answer because there is no real consensus of usage. For some it refers to racial, ethnic, and gender differences, and for others it includes a much broader range of differences among people.

In this book, we have consciously defined diversity very broadly to include the multitude of social, cultural, physical, and environmental differences among people that affect the way they behave. Diversity for us includes race, ethnicity, gender, physical abilities, sexual orientation, age, and many other dimensions.

We are in accord with Loden and Rosener who see it as ". . . this vast array of physical and cultural differences that constitute the spectrum of human diversity,"[3] and with R. Roosevelt Thomas ". . . I mean the whole nature of the modern workforce—in terms of age, educational differences, background, language, nationality, and a multitude of other factors."[4]

To better grasp the breadth and complexity of diversity, it is helpful to view it through the eyes of the social modelers.

DIVERSITY MODELS

Diversity models are like snapshots taken from different angles and distances and at different times. We have found no single comprehensive model of diversity, no single picture or perspective, that adequately depicts its multifaceted character.

Diversity models differ in focus and scope. For purposes of discussion, we have clustered the models into three groups: those that focus on the individual, those concerned with the process of developing sensitivity, and those centering on the organization.

Models of the Individual

A sample of models that concentrate mainly on the individual is shown in Figure 1.1. In spite of differences in focus among them, all these models provide still pictures; they describe static aspects of diversity.

Type	Focus	Theorists
Static	Individuals: dimensions on which they differ from each other	Loden and Rosener
Static	Individuals: major group memberships	Szapocznik and Kurtines
Static	Individuals: incompatible cultural values	Rivera

Figure 1.1 Diversity models centering on the individual.

Some of the social modelers examine the principal ways in which individuals differ from each other. Loden and Rosener, for example, distinguish between primary dimensions, that is, characteristics of people that do not change, and secondary characteristics, that is, dimensions that can change. Figure 1.2 displays the relationship between the central or primary characteristics and those that are secondary in nature.[5]

Szaponcznik and Kurtines also focus on the individual, but from a broader perspective. Theirs is a panoramic photograph that depicts the individual within a family embedded within an environment comprised of diverse cultures. This model recognizes that the individual faces the pulls of diverse generations as well as the pulls of a diverse nonfamilial environment.[6]

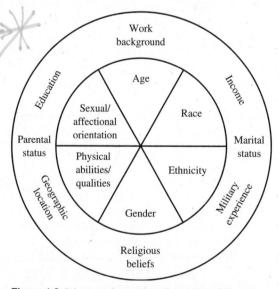

Figure 1.2 Primary and secondary dimensions of diversity.
Source: Marilyn Loden and Judy Rosener. *Workforce America! Managing Employee Diversity as a Vital Resource.* Copyright © 1991 by Irwin: Business One. Reprinted with permission from Richard D. Irwin, Inc.

Still other writers focus on the conflict faced by individuals living in cultures with conflicting values. Rivera, for example, describes the conflicts in values and behaviors faced by Hispanics who are born into a traditional group culture but who must also live and work in the more individualistic contemporary culture.

Models of Sensitivity Learning

A different type of diversity model is concerned with learning to increase sensitivity toward other cultures. One approach provides a still photograph by examining the personal and cultural elements in sensitivity learning. Another is more concerned with change, and it traces the sequence of steps in the learning process. See Figure 1.3.

Type	Focus		Theorists
Static	Sensitivity:	elements in development (individual) of cultural sensitivity	Locke
Static/ Dynamic	Sensitivity:	stages in sensitivity learning	Hoopes, Bennett

Figure 1.3 Diversity models centering on sensitivity.

Locke constructed a framework for organizing the factors to be considered in assessing cultural sensitivity. His model first places the individual in a series of widening contexts (family, community, cultural, and global) that influence sensitivity, and then the model describes elements to explore for an understanding of other cultures.[7]

Other cultural photographers, such as Hoopes and Bennett, offer a somewhat more dynamic approach with time lapse pictures of the stages in sensitivity learning. Modifying the stages originally described by Hoopes, Bennett identified the six stages in the learning continuum shown in Figure 1.4.[8]

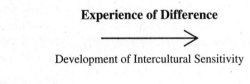

Experience of Difference

Development of Intercultural Sensitivity

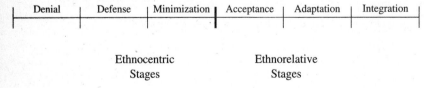

| Denial | Defense | Minimization | Acceptance | Adaptation | Integration |

Ethnocentric Stages   Ethnorelative Stages

Figure 1.4 Stages of development in experiencing differences.
Source: Reprinted from *International Journal of Intercultural Relations*, 10, Milton Bennett. "A Developmental Approach to Training for Intercultural Sensitivitry." p. 182 Copyright © 1986, with kind permission from Pergamon Press Ltd, Headington Hill Hall, Oxford 0X3 0BW, UK.

Models of Organizational Diversity

As the kaleidoscopic nature of American society is increasingly reflected in the workplace, that is, as the physical and cultural make-up of the workforce changes, the *social culture* of the workplace is taking on new importance. It is not surprising that theorists have turned their attention to constructing models by which managers in organizations can cope with diversity.

Although social scientists have addressed cultural diversity issues for a long time, attempts to model organizational diversity are relatively recent. As Harris notes, ". . . it is only in the past decade that executives and scholars really began to appreciate how culture impacts behavior, morale, and productivity at work".[9]

Diversity models for organizations focus on a variety of aspects of organization life. Some are static in nature, focusing on the elements in diversity management; others are more dynamic, focusing on action plans for change. See Figure 1.5.

Cox, for instance, has devised an Interactional Model of Cultural Diversity for the workplace, which examines in detail the individual, intergroup, and organizational factors that together "collectively define the *diversity climate* of an organization."[10]

Thomas points out the futility of sporadic isolated attempts at diversity management and focuses on the systemic changing of organizational climate. He offers an action plan that essentially examines the culture of the organization, identifies the fundamental elements (roots) of the culture, assesses their impact on diversity, and then plans changes in those roots identified as hindering diversity management.[11]

The flex-management model of Jamieson and O'Mara relates the policies, systems, and practices of an organization to strategies for individualizing, that is, for matching management needs to individual needs. The aim is to manage by "accommodating differences and providing choices."[12]

A few far-thinking planners and agents of change have been experimenting with the management of worker diversity in corporations for several years. Palmer has studied these corporate approaches and finds that they differ widely and often conflict, because they are based on differing views of the world and of diversity. In essence, some approaches turn a blind eye to all differences and seek to treat everyone the same, others are concerned with rectifying injustices to particular groups, and still others seek to recognize and appreciate group as well as individual differences.[13]

Whatever the definition, whatever the model of diversity, it is clear that understanding, or valuing, or managing diversity requires some insight into its cultural underpinnings.

Type	Focus		Theorist
Static	Organization:	Individual, intergroup and organizational factors	Cox
Dynamic	Organization:	Action plan for changing organization climate	Thomas
Dynamic	Organization:	Organizational factors matched to individual needs	Jamieson and O'Mara
Dynamic	Organization:	Corporate approaches to managing diversity	Palmer

Figure 1.5 Diversity models centering on organizations.

CULTURE

To provide such insights, we have chosen to begin this book on diversity with a brief discussion, followed by readings, on culture. We hope, thereby, to provide a broad background against which to examine more specific diversity dimensions and issues in society in general and in corporate and other organizations as well.

Culture defines how we look at life in general, and it guides how we respond to characteristics such as race, ethnicity, physical attributes, age, social class, education, and a host of other factors. It shapes our responses to these qualities both within ourselves and in other people.

At the broad social level, culture tells us who we are (what groups we belong to), how we should behave and ". . . gives us attitudes about 'them,' the people who are different from us. It tells us what should be important as well as how to act in various situations."[14]

Culture envelopes us so completely that often we do not realize that there are other ways of dealing with the world, that others may have a *different* outlook on life, a *different* logic, a *different* way of responding to people and situations.

Culture permeates diversity issues in the organization. Organizations themselves have cultures, organizational managers behave in terms of both organizational and personal cultural backgrounds, and workers bring diverse cultural backgrounds to their organizations. In corporate and nonprofit organizations, the culture of the consumer is of key importance to marketing considerations. In multinational organizations, successful operation *depends* upon compatibility with host-country cultures.

Organizational cultures are reflected in the way they manage people, that is, in who they hire, how they evaluate the people they hire, and who they promote. Some organizations do not value nationalities unaccustomed to looking managers in the eye, or older workers, or women who do not act assertive enough, or cultural deviations in dress styles running counter to organizational dress codes. Too, some corporations reflect the cultures of their industries. For example, women find far less acceptance in the manufacturing sector than in the services sector, whereas males are less welcome in nursing than in manufacturing; gays and lesbians are more accepted in fashion, advertising, and the arts than in many other industries.

For organizations now coping with a plurality of identity-conscious groups, the management of diversity not only involves moral considerations, but it influences corporate profitability.

In managing cultural diversity, cultural complexity, cultural change, and cultural judgments (stereotypes) are very important facets of cultural influence to be considered.

Cultural Complexity

The complexity of our cultural backgrounds vastly increases the difficulty of managing a diverse workforce. Not only are there differences in values among cultures, there are vast differences within cultures as well. Culture is not the same for every

member of any single group. We all belong to many groups that influence our behavior and beliefs. Certainly not all blacks behave the same way nor do they have
identical values; neither do all women, all Latinos, all members of the upper middle
class, nor all members of any other group.

We are born with gender, race, and ethnicity memberships and we acquire
even more identities as we go through life. The values and beliefs of our groups are
not always consistent with each other, and the relative importance of each of these
group memberships to us is not the same for everyone. For example, family is a far
more important membership for some than it is for others, as is religious affiliation.
The importance to us of particular memberships affects not only our own behavior
in the workplace, but it affects how we interpret the behavior of others.

Cultural Change

Perhaps because of the completeness of its influence in our lives, we tend to think of
culture as an object or a thing. But culture is neither concrete nor stable. Rather, it is
a state or condition that changes and evolves.[15, 16, 17] One has only to think of how
often our country's international friends and enemies change or of the things that
have changed between our parent's generation and our own or even within our own
lifetime to realize this.

The fact that cultures change in what they value and the behaviors they pre-
scribe compounds the difficulty in understanding members of other cultural groups
on one hand, but on the other, makes it clear that insensitivity, bias, and intolerance
can be unlearned, that is, replaced with understanding and acceptance. This is a
welcome note for all types of organizations struggling to better deal with diversity
issues.

Cultural Judgments (Stereotypes)

Among the most important aspects of our cultural backgrounds are the dimensions
or criteria of judgment provided for assessing others. For those groups with whom
we have little contact, our culture provides us with a predetermined set of attitudes
and a prescription for interacting. It provides us with stereotypes, those labels by
which we typecast all members of a group as though they were clones from an in-
flexible mold. Stereotypes organize the unknown world for us, but at the same time
they give us tunnel vision. They encourage us to perceive all members of one group
as welfare cheats, of another group as lazy, of another as musical, and another as
gifted mechanically. Individual differences and character are lost.

In the workplace, even the manager of good will who relies on stereotypes in
dealing with others runs the risk of making incorrect assessments of people and their
behavior, of creating misunderstanding and conflict, and of blocking opportunities
for others. The results are lower morale, lower productivity, and ultimately lower
profitability.

Society and organizations are faced with major social change. It is far more than a social cause, a moral or ethical issue, or even an economic issue. It is a *reality*.

To deal with diversity we need to understand ourselves, and our cultural blinders (stereotypes and dimensions of judgment) in order to go beyond thinking of our way as the only way and to develop appreciation for other viewpoints. We need, too, to be able to put ourselves in the shoes of others to understand how they view us and interpret our actions.

To accomplish these ends, the readings in Chapter One were selected to provide insights and perspectives on culture. The opening article on the Nacerima jolts the reader with a striking and memorable description of American culture. Americans are used to thinking of their culture as superior, the standard against which to compare other cultures. This article provides an "out-of-culture" experience to discourage the notion of cultural superiority and it provides a view of how others may be judging our culture.

The Sowell article furthers the process of placing one's cultural background in perspective and reducing cultural vanity by providing an historical, worldwide perspective of cultural diversity and interrelatedness. It illustrates with example after example of cultural borrowing that cultures that advance are dynamic, changing, and interdependent, and that cultural inferiority or superiority in any domain is transitory.

The tunnel vision resulting from reliance upon the stereotypes supplied by our culture is examined in the article by Sawin and in *Mental Maps*. The abstract concept of stereotypic thinking becomes more concrete through the analogy of mental maps developed by Sawin.

Sometimes a picture is worth a thousand words. The mental map drawings, intended as a companion piece to the Sawin article, graphically increase the concreteness of Sawin's mental maps analogy. The drawings are not a theoretical invention, but are pictures constructed from actual research data of how people see the world depending on their place in society (ethnic and social class memberships). Finally, they show how limiting our perspective on the world can be.

The application of cultural background to the workplace is provided in the Rivera article, a sensitive account of the clash of general cultural values with application to the workplace. The contrast is drawn between the behavior and attitudes fostered by a background in a traditional group-oriented culture and one from a background in the more individualistic contemporary culture.

In addition to providing perspective, the readings in the opening chapter were selected to be as experiential as possible. It has been our observation that merely reading about diversity does little to sensitize anyone to it or to suggest approaches for dealing with divergent perspectives in society or in organizations. Many of the readings contain experiential elements and all have discussion questions designed to stimulate dialogues which will evoke dissenting opinions and differing perspectives on issues.

As the opening quotation illustrates, there is enormous diversity among peoples. It is not possible to learn everything about every type of diversity or every cultural group, but it is possible to develop radar antennae tuned to social sensitivity. In the words of Bennett

> The critical element in the expansion of intercultural learning is not the fullness with which one knows each culture, but the degree to which the process of cross-cultural learning, communication and human relations have been mastered.[18]

NOTES

1. Robertson, I. *Sociology*. New York: Worth, 1987, p. 67.
2. Thernstrom, Stephan. "Ethnic Groups in American History." *Ethnic Relations in America*. Englewood Cliffs, NJ: Prentice-Hall, 1982, p. 3.
3. Loden, Marilyn, and Rosener, Judy. *Workforce America: Managing Employee Diversity as a Vital Resource*. Homewood, Ill: Business One Irwin, 1991, p. 18.
4. "Teaching Diversity: Business Schools Search for Model Approaches." *AACSB* 23 (1992): p. 3.
5. Loden and Rosener, *op. cit*, p. 20.
6. Szapocznik, Jose, and Kurtines, William. "Family Psychology and Cultural Diversity Opportunities for Theory, Research & Applications." *American Psychologist* 48 (1993): pp. 400–407.
7. Locke, Don. *Increasing Multicultural Understanding: A Comprehensive Model*. Newbury Park, CA: Sage, 1992, pp. 1–13.
8. Bennett, Milton. "A Developmental Approach to Training for Intercultural Sensitivity." *International Journal of Intercultural Relations* 10 (1986): pp. 179–196.
9. Harris, Philip and Moran, Robert. *Managing Cultural Differences: High Performance Strategies for a New World of Business*. 3rd. ed. Houston, TX: Gulf Publishing, 1991, p. 12.
10. Cox, Taylor, Jr. Cultural Diversity in Organizations: Theory, Research & Practice. San Francisco, CA: Berrett-Koehler, 1993, p. 9.
11. Thomas, R. Roosevelt, Jr. *Beyond Race and Gender: Unleashing the Power of Your Total Work Force by Managing Diversity*. New York: AMACON, 1991, pp. 50–71.
12. Jamieson, David, and O'Mara, Julie. *Managing Workforce 2000: Gaining the Diversity Advantage*. San Francisco: Jossey-Bass, 1991, pp. 36–37.
13. Palmer, Judith D. "Three Paradigms for Diversity Change Leaders." *OD Practitioner* 21 (1989): pp. 15–18.
14. Simons, George. *Working Together: How to Become More Effective in a Multicultural Organization*. Los Altos, CA: Crisp Publications, 1989, p. 5.
15. Sowell, Thomas. "A World View of Cultural Diversity." *Society* 29 (1991): p. 38.
16. Kessler-Harris, Alice. "Multiculturalism Can Strengthen, Not Undermine, a Common Culture." *The Chronicle of Higher Education*. Oct. 21, 1992, p. B3.
17. Samuels, Warren. "Dynamics of Cultural Change." *Society* 29 (1991): pp. 23–26.
18. Bennett, *op. cit.*, p. 181.

An anthropologist takes the role of an observer from a culture more developed than our own and describes features of our civilization in the same manner as we describe cultures we view as primitive.

Body Ritual Among the Nacirema

Horace Miner

The anthropologist has become so familiar with the diversity of ways in which different peoples behave in similar situations that he is not apt to be surprised by even the most exotic customs. In fact, if all of the logically possible combinations of behavior have not been found somewhere in the world, he is apt to suspect that they must be present in some yet undescribed tribe. This point has, in fact, been expressed with respect to clan organization by Murdock (1949:71). In this light, the magical beliefs and practices of the Nacirema present such unusual aspects that it seems desirable to describe them as an example of the extremes to which human behavior can go.

Professor Linton first brought the ritual of the Nacirema to the attention of anthropologists twenty years ago (1936:326), but the culture of this people is still very poorly understood. They are a North American group living in the territory between the Canadian Cree, the Yaqui and Tarahumare of Mexico, and the Carib and Arawak of the Antilles. Little is known of their origin, although tradition states that they came from the east. According to Nacirema mythology, their nation was originated by a culture hero, Notgnihsaw, who is otherwise known for two great feats of strength—the throwing of a piece of wampum across the river Pa-To-Mac and the chopping down of a cherry tree in which the Spirit of Truth resided.

Nacirema culture is characterized by a highly developed market economy which has evolved in a rich natural habitat. While much of the people's time is devoted to economic pursuits, a large part of the fruits of these labors and a considerable portion of the day are spent in ritual activity. The focus of this activity is the human body, the appearance and health of which loom as a dominant concern in the ethos of the people. While such concern is certainly not unusual, its ceremonial aspects and associated philosophy are unique.

The fundamental belief underlying the whole system appears to be that the human body is ugly and that its natural tendency is to debility and disease. Incarcerated in such a body, man's only hope is to avert these characteristics through the use of the powerful influences of ritual and ceremony. Every household has one or more shrines devoted to this purpose. The more powerful individuals in the society have several shrines in their houses and, in fact, the opulence of a house is often referred to in terms of the number of such ritual centers it possesses. Most houses are of wattle and daub construction, but the shrine rooms of the wealthy are walled with stone. Poorer families imitate the rich by applying pottery plaques to their shrine walls.

Reproduced by permission of the American Anthropological Association from *American Anthropologist*, vol. 58, June 1956. Not for sale or further reproduction.

While each family has at least one shrine, the rituals associated with it are not family ceremonies but are private and secret. The rites are normally only discussed with children, and then only during the period when they are being initiated into these mysteries. I was able, however, to establish sufficient rapport with the natives to examine these shrines and to have the rituals described to me.

The focal point of the shrine is a box or chest which is built into the wall. In this chest are kept the many charms and magical potions without which no native believes he could live.

These preparations are secured from a variety of specialized practitioners. The most powerful of these are the medicine men, whose assistance must be rewarded with substantial gifts. However, the medicine men do not provide the curative potions for their clients, but decide what the ingredients should be and then write them down in an ancient and secret language. This writing is understood only by the medicine men and by the herbalists who, for another gift, provide the required charm.

The charm is not disposed of after it has served its purpose, but is placed in the charm-box of the household shrine. As these magical materials are specific for certain ills, and the real or imagined maladies of the people are many, the charm-box is usually full to overflowing. The magical packets are so numerous that the people forget what their purposes were and fear to use them again. While the natives are very vague on this point, we can only assume that the idea in retaining all the old magical materials is that their presence in the charm-box, before which the body rituals are conducted, will in some way protect the worshipper.

Beneath the charm-box is a small font. Each day every member of the family, in succession, enters the shrine room, bows his head before the charm-box, mingles different sorts of holy waters in the font, and proceeds with a brief ritual of ablution. The holy waters are secured from the Water Temple of the community, where the priests conduct elaborate ceremonies to make the liquid ritually pure.

In the hierarchy of magical practitioners, and below the medicine men in prestige, are specialists whose designation is best translated "holy-mouth-men." The Nacirema have an almost pathological horror of and fascination with the mouth, the condition of which is believed to have a supernatural influence on all social relationships. Were it not for the rituals of the mouth, they believe that their teeth would fall out, their gums bleed, their jaws shrink, their friends desert them, and their lovers reject them. They also believe that a strong relationship exists between oral and moral characteristics. For example, there is a ritual ablution of the mouth for children which is supposed to improve their moral fiber.

The daily body ritual performed by everyone includes a mouth-rite. Despite the fact that these people are so punctilious about care of the mouth, this rite involves a practice which strikes the uninitiated stranger as revolting. It was reported to me that the ritual consists of inserting a magic bundle of hog hairs into the mouth, along with certain magical powder, and then moving the bundle in a highly formalized series of gestures.

In addition to the private mouth-rite, the people seek out the holy-mouth-man once or twice a year. These practitioners have an impressive set of paraphernalia, consisting of a variety of augers, awls, probes, and prods. The use of these objects in the exorcism of the evils of the mouth involves almost unbelievable ritual torture of the client. The holy-mouth-man opens the clients's mouth and, using the above mentioned tools, enlarges any holes which may of been created in the teeth. Magical materials are put into these holes. If there are no naturally occurring holes in the teeth, large sections of one or more teeth are gouged out so that the supernatural substance can be applied. In the client's view, the purpose of the ministrations is to arrest decay and to draw friends. The extremely sacred and traditional character of the rite is evident in the fact that the natives return to the holy-mouth-man, despite the fact that their teeth continue to decay.

It is to be hoped that, when a thorough study of the Nacirema is made, there will be careful inquiry into the personality structure of these people. One has but to watch the gleam in the eye of a holy-mouth-man, as he jabs an awl into an exposed nerve, to suspect that a certain amount of sadism is involved. If this can be established, a very interesting pattern emerges, for most of the population shows definite masochistic tendencies. It was to these that Professor Linton referred in discussing a distinctive part of the daily body ritual which was performed only by men. This part of the rite involves scraping and lacerating the surface of the face with a sharp instrument. Special women's rites are performed only four times during each lunar month, but what they lack in frequency is made up for in barbarity. As part of this ceremony, women bake their heads in small ovens for about an hour. The theoretically interesting point is that what seems to be a preponderantly masochistic people have developed sadistic specialists.

The medicine men have an imposing temple or latipso, in every community of any size. The more elaborate ceremonies required to treat very sick patients can only be performed at this temple. These ceremonies involve not only the thaumaturge but a permanent group of vestal maidens who move sedately about the temple chambers in distinctive costume and headdress.

The latipso ceremonies are so harsh that it is phenomenal that a fair proportion of the really sick natives who enter the temple ever recover. Small children whose indoctrination is still incomplete have been known to resist attempts to take them to the temple because "that is where you go to die." Despite this fact, sick adults are not only willing but eager to undergo the protracted ritual purification, if they can afford to do so. No matter how ill the supplicant or how grave the emergency, the guardians of many temples will not admit a client if he cannot give a rich gift to the custodian. Even after one has gained admission and survived the ceremonies, the guardians will not permit the neophyte to leave until he makes still another gift.

The supplicant entering the temple is first stripped of all his or her clothes. In everyday life the Nacirema avoids exposure of his body and its natural functions. Bathing and excretory acts are performed only in secrecy of the household shrine, where they are ritualized as part of the body-rites. Psychological shock results from the fact that body secrecy is suddenly lost upon entry into the latipso. This sort of ceremonial treatment is necessitated by the fact that the excreta are used by a diviner to ascertain the course and nature of the client's sickness. Female clients, on the other hand, find their naked bodies are subjected to the scrutiny, manipulation and prodding of the medicine men.

Few supplicants in the temple are well enough to do anything but lie on their hard beds. The daily ceremonies, like the rites of the holy-mouth-men, involve discomfort and torture. With ritual precision, the vestals awaken their miserable charges each dawn and roll them about on their beds of pain while performing ablutions, in the formal movements of which the maidens are highly trained. At other times they insert magic wands in the supplicant's mouth or force him to eat substances which are supposed to be healing. From time to time the medicine men come to their clients and jab magically treated needles into their flesh. The fact that these ceremonies may not cure, and may even kill the neophyte, in no way decreases the people's faith in the medicine men.

There remains one other kind of practitioner, known as a "listener." This witch-doctor has the power to exorcise the devils that lodge in the heads of people who have been bewitched. The Nacirema believe that parents bewitched their own children. Mothers are particularly suspected of putting a curse on children while teaching them the secret body rituals. The counter-magic of the witch-doctor is unusual in its lack of ritual. The patient simply tells the "listener" all his troubles and fears, beginning with the earliest difficulties he can remember. The memory displayed by the Nacirema in these exorcism sessions is truly remarkable. It is not uncommon for the patient to bemoan the rejection he felt upon being weaned as a babe, and a few individuals even see their troubles going back to the traumatic effects of their own birth.

In conclusion, mention must be made of certain practices which have their base in native esthetics but which depend upon the pervasive aversion to the natural body and its functions. There are ritual fasts to make fat people thin and ceremonial feasts to make thin people fat. Still other rites are used to make women's breasts larger if they are small, and smaller if they are large. General dissatisfaction with breast shape is symbolized in the fact that the ideal form is virtually outside the range of human variation. A few women afflicted with almost inhuman hypermammary development are so idolized that they make a handsome living by simply going from village to village and permitting the natives to stare at them for a fee.

Reference has already been made to the fact that excretory functions are ritualized, routinized, and relegated to secrecy. Natural reproduction functions are similarly distorted. Intercourse is taboo as a topic and scheduled as an act. Efforts are made to avoid pregnancy by the use of magical materials or by limiting intercourse to certain phases of the moon. Conception is actually very infrequent. When pregnant, women dress so as to hide their condition. Parturition takes place in secret, without friends or relatives to assist, and the majority of women do not nurse their infants.

Our review of the ritual life of the Nacirema has certainly shown them to be a magic-ridden people. It is hard to understand how they have managed to exist so long under the burdens which they have imposed upon themselves. But even such exotic customs as these take on real meaning when they are viewed with the insight provided by Malinowski when he wrote (1948:70)

> Looking from far and above, from our high places of safety in developed civilization, it is easy to see all the crudity and irrelevance of magic. But without its power and guidance early man could not have advanced to the higher stages of civilization.

REFERENCES CITED

Linton, Ralph. *The Study of Man*. New York, D. Appleton-Century Co., 1936.

Malinowski, Bronislaw. *Magic, Science and Religion*. Glencoe, The Free Press, 1948.

Murdock, George P. *Social Structure*. New York, The MacMillan Co., 1949.

DISCUSSION QUESTIONS

1. What general message do you think the author was trying to convey in this de
   scription of one aspect of American culture?
2. Why are some behaviors described as "magic"?
3. Why are some behaviors described as "rituals"? Do you think this is a fair label?
4. Does the humorous approach to our culture bother you? Do you feel that the de
   scription is belittling or sarcastic in tone?
5. Imagine that you are a member of the author's culture. What kinds of stereotypes
   could you have of the American culture and its people if this reading is your only
   source of information?

A view of cultural diversity from a worldwide perspective showing that throughout history, diverse civilizations have progressed by sharing their unique features and advances with each other.

A World View of Cultural Diversity

Thomas Sowell

Diversity has become one of the most often used words of our time—and a word almost never defined. Diversity is invoked in discussions of everything from employment policy to curriculum reform and from entertainment to politics. Nor is the word merely a description of the long-known fact that the American population is made up of people from many countries, many races, and many cultural backgrounds. All this was well known long before the word "diversity" became an insistent part of our vocabulary, an invocation, an imperative, or a bludgeon in ideological conflicts.

The very motto of the country, *E Pluribus Unum*, recognizes the diversity of the American people. For generations, this diversity has been celebrated, whether in comedies like *Abie's Irish Rose* (the famous play featuring a Jewish boy and an Irish girl) or in patriotic speeches on the Fourth of July. Yet one senses something very different in today's crusades for "diversity"; certainly not a patriotic celebration of America and often a sweeping criticism of the United States, or even a condemnation of Western civilization as a whole.

At the very least, we need to separate the issue of the general importance of cultural diversity—not only in the United States but in the world at large—from the more specific, more parochial, and more ideological agendas that have become associated with this word in recent years. I would like to talk about the worldwide importance of cultural diversity over centuries of human history before returning to the narrower issues of our time.

The entire history of the human race, the rise of man from the caves, has been marked by transfers of cultural advances from one group to another and from one civilization to another. Paper and printing, for example, are today vital parts of Western civilization, but they originated in China centuries before they made their way to Europe. So did the magnetic compass, which made possible the great ages of exploration that put the Western hemisphere in touch with the rest of mankind. Mathematical concepts likewise migrated from one culture to another: trigonometry from ancient Egypt, and the whole numbering system now used throughout the world originated among the Hindus of India, though Europeans called this system Arabic numerals because it was the Arabs who were the intermediaries through which these numbers reached medieval Europe. Indeed, much of the philosophy of ancient Greece first reached Western Europe in Arabic translations, which were then retranslated into Latin or into the vernacular languages of the West Europeans.

Reprinted with permission of Transaction Publishers from *Society*, vol. 29, no. 1, 1991, pp. 37–44.

Much that became part of the culture of Western civilization originated outside that civilization, often in the Middle East or Asia. The game of chess came from India, gunpowder from China, and various mathematical concepts from the Islamic world, for example. The conquest of Spain by Moslems in the eighth century A.D. made Spain a center for the diffusion into Western Europe of the more advanced knowledge of the Mediterranean world and of the Orient in astronomy, medicine, optics, and geometry.

The later rise of Western Europe to world preeminence in science and technology built upon these foundations, and then the science and technology of European civilization began to spread around the world, not only to European offshoot societies such as the United States or Australia, but also to non-European cultures, of which Japan is perhaps the most striking example.

The historic sharing of cultural advances, until they became the common inheritance of the human race, implied much more than cultural diversity. It implied that some cultural features were not only different from others but better than others. The very fact that people—all people, whether Europeans, Africans, Asians, or others—have repeatedly chosen to abandon some feature of their own culture in order to replace it with something from another culture implies that the replacement served their purposes more effectively. Arabic numerals are not simply different from Roman numerals, they are better than Roman numerals. This is shown by their replacing Roman numerals in many countries whose own cultures derived from Rome, as well as in other countries whose respective numbering systems were likewise superseded by so-called Arabic numerals.

It is virtually inconceivable today that the distances in astronomy or the complexities of higher mathematics should be expressed in Roman numerals. Merely to express the year of the declaration of American independence as MDCCLXXVI requires more than twice as many Roman numerals as Arabic numerals. Moreover, Roman numerals offer more opportunities for errors, as the same digit may be either added or subtracted, depending on its place in sequence. Roman numerals are good for numbering kings or Super Bowls, but they cannot match the efficiency of Arabic numerals in most mathematical operations—and that is, after all, why we have numbers at all. Cultural features do not exist merely as badges of identity to which we have some emotional attachment. They exist to meet the necessities and to forward the purposes of human life. When they are surpassed by features of other cultures, they tend to fall by the wayside or to survive only as marginal curiosities, like Roman numerals today.

Not only concepts, information, products, and technologies transfer from one culture to another. The natural produce of the earth does the same. Malaysia is the world's leading grower of rubber trees—but those trees are indigenous to Brazil. Most of rice grown in Africa today originated in Asia, and its tobacco originated in the Western hemisphere. Even a great wheat-exporting nation like Argentina once imported wheat, which was not an indigenous crop to that country. Cultural diversity, viewed internationally and historically, is not a static picture of differentness but a dynamic picture of competition in which what serves human purposes more effectively survives while what does not tends to decline or disappear.

Manuscript scrolls once preserved the precious records, knowledge, and thought of European or Middle Eastern cultures. But once paper and printing from China became known in these cultures, books were clearly far faster and cheaper to produce and drove scrolls virtually into extinction. Books were not simply different from scrolls; they were better than scrolls. The point that some cultural features are better than others must be insisted on today because so many among the intelligentsia either evade or deny this plain reality. The intelligentsia often use words like "perceptions" and "values" as they argue in effect that it is all a matter of how you choose to look at it.

They may have a point in such things as music, art, and literature from different cultures, but there are many human purposes common to peoples of all cultures. They want to live rather than die, for example. When Europeans first ventured into the arid interior of Australia, they often died of thirst or hunger in a land where the Australian aborigines had no trouble finding food or water, within that particular setting, at least, the aboriginal culture enabled people to do what both the aborigines and Europeans wanted to do—survive. A given culture may not be superior for all things in all settings, much less remain superior over time, but particular cultural features may nevertheless be clearly better for some purposes—not just different.

Why is there any such argument in the first place? Perhaps it is because we are still living in the long, grim shadow of the Nazi Holocaust and are, therefore, understandably reluctant to label anything or anyone "superior" or "inferior." But we do not need to. We need only recognize that particular products, skills, technologies, agricultural crops, or intellectual concepts accomplish particular purposes better than their alternatives. It is not necessary to rank one whole culture over another in all things, much less to claim that they remain in that same ranking throughout history. They do not.

Clearly, cultural leadership in various fields has changed hands many times. China was far in advance of any country in Europe in a large number of fields for at least a thousand years and, as late as the sixteenth century, had the highest standard of living in the world. Equally clearly, China today is one of the poorer nations of the world and is having great difficulty trying to catch up to the technological level of Japan and the West, with no real hope of regaining its former world preeminence in the foreseeable future.

Similar rises and falls of nations and empires have been common over long stretches of human history—for example, the rise and fall of the Roman Empire, the "golden age" of medieval Spain and its decline to the level of one of the poorest nations in Europe today, the centuries-long triumphs of the Ottoman Empire intellectually as well as on the battlefields of Europe and the Middle East, and then its long decline to become known as "the sick man of Europe." Yet, while cultural leadership has changed hands many times, that leadership has been real at given times, and much of what was achieved in the process has contributed enormously to our well-being and opportunities today. Cultural competition is not a zero-sum game. It is what advances the human race.

If nations and civilizations differ in their effectiveness in different fields of endeavor, so do social groups. Here is especially strong resistance to accepting the reality of different levels and kinds of skills, interests, habits, and orientations among different groups of people. One academic writer, for example, said that nineteenth-century Jewish immigrants to the United States were fortunate to arrive just as the garment industry in New York began to develop. I could not help thinking that Hank

Aaron was similarly fortunate that he often came to bat just as a home run was due to be hit. It might be possible to believe that these Jewish immigrants just happened to be in the right place at the right time if you restricted yourself to their history in the United States. But, again taking a world view, we find Jews prominent, often predominant, and usually prospering, in the apparel industry in medieval Spain, in the Ottoman Empire, in the Russian Empire, in Argentina, in Australia, and in Brazil. How surprised should we be to find them predominant in the same industry in America?

Other groups have excelled in other special occupations and industries. Indeed, virtually every group excels at something. Germans, for example, have been prominent as pioneers in the piano industry. American piano brands like Steinway and Knabe, not to mention the Wurlitzer organ, are signs of the long prominence of Germans in this industry, where they produced the first pianos in Colonial America. Germans also pioneered in piano-building in Czarist Russia, Australia, France, and England. Chinese immigrants have, at one period of history or another, run more than half the grocery stores in Kingston, Jamaica, and Panama City and conducted more than half of all retail trade in Malaysia, the Philippines, Vietnam, and Cambodia. Other groups have dominated the retail trade in other parts of the world—the Gujaratis from India in East Africa and in Fiji or the Lebanese in parts of West Africa, for example.

Nothing has been more common than for particular groups—often a minority—to dominate particular occupations or industries. Seldom do they have any ability to keep out others and certainly not to keep out the majority population. They are simply better at the particular skills required in that occupation or industry. Sometimes we can see why. When Italians have made wine in Italy for centuries, it is hardly surprising that they should become prominent among winemakers in Argentina and in California's Napa Valley. Similarly, when Germans in Germany have been for centuries renowned for their beermaking, how surprised should we be that in Argentina they became as prominent among brewers as Italians among winemakers? How surprised should we be that beermaking in the United States arose where there were concentrations of German immigrants in Milwaukee and St. Louis, for example? Or that the leading beer producers to this day have German names like Anheuser-Busch or Coors, among many other German names?

Just as cultural leadership in a particular field is not permanent for nations or civilizations, neither is it permanent for given racial, ethnic, or religious groups. By the time the Jews were expelled from Spain in 1492, Europe had overtaken the Islamic world in medical science, so that Jewish physicians who sought refuge in the Ottoman Empire found themselves in great demand in that Moslem country. By the early sixteenth century, the sultan of the Ottoman Empire had on his palace medical staff forty-two Jewish physicians and twenty-one Moslem physicians.

With the passage of time, however, the source of the Jews' advantage—their knowledge of Western medicine—eroded as successive generations of Ottoman Jews lost contact with the West and its further progress. Christian minorities within the Ottoman Empire began to replace the Jews, not only in medicine but also in international trade and even in the theater, once dominated by Jews. The difference was that these Christian minorities—notably Greeks and Armenians—maintained their ties in Christian Europe and often sent their sons there to be educated. It was not race or ethnicity as such that was crucial but maintaining contacts with the ongoing progress of Western civilization. By contrast, the Ottoman Jews became a declining people in a declining empire. Many, if not most, were Sephardic Jews from Spain, once the elite of world Jewry. But by the time the state of Israel was formed in the twentieth century, those Sephardic Jews who had settled for centuries in the Islamic world now lagged painfully behind the Ashkenazic Jews of the Western world—notably in income and education. To get some idea what a historic reversal that has been in the relative positions of Sephardic Jews and Ashkenazic Jews, one need only note that Sephardic Jews in colonial America sometimes disinherited their own children for marrying Ashkenazic Jews.

Why do some groups, subgroups, nations, or whole civilizations excel in some particular fields rather than others? All too often, the answer to this question must be: Nobody really knows. It is an unanswered question largely because it is an unasked question. There is an uphill struggle merely to get acceptance of the fact that large differences exist among peoples, not just in specific skills in the narrow sense (computer science, basketball, or brewing beer) but more fundamentally in different interests, orientations, and values that determine which particular skills they seek to develop and with what degree of success. Merely to suggest that these internal cultural factors play a significant role in various economic, educational, or social outcomes is to invite charges of "blaming the victim." It is much more widely acceptable to blame surrounding social conditions or institutional policies.

But if we look at cultural diversity internationally and historically, there is a more basic question whether blame is the real issue. Surely, no human being should be blamed for the way his culture evolved for centuries before he was born. Blame has nothing to do with it. Another explanation that has had varying amounts of acceptance at different times and places is the biological or genetic theory of differences among peoples. I have argued against this theory in many places but will not take the time to go into these lengthy arguments here. A world view of cultural differences over the centuries undermines the genetic theory as well. Europeans and Chinese, for example, are clearly genetically different. Equally clearly, China was a more advanced civilization than Europe in many ways, scientific, technological, and organizational, for at least a thousand years. Yet over the past few centuries, Europe has moved ahead of China in many of these same ways. If those cultural differences were due to genes, how could these two races have changed positions so radically from one epoch in history to another?

All explanations of differences between groups can be broken down into heredity and environment. Yet a world view of the history of cultural diversity seems, on the surface at least, to deny both. One reason for this is that we have thought of environment too narrowly, as the immediate surrounding circumstances or differing institutional policies toward different groups. Environment in that narrow sense may explain some group differences, but the histories of many groups completely contradict that particular version of environment as an explanation. Let us take just two examples out of many that are available.

Jewish immigrants from Eastern Europe and Italian immigrants from southern Italy began arriving in the United States in large numbers at about the same time in the late nineteenth century, and their large-scale immigration also ended at the same time, when restrictive immigration laws were passed in the 1920s. The two groups arrived here in virtually the same economic condition—namely, destitute. They often lived in the same neighborhoods and their children attended the same schools, sitting side by side in the same classrooms. Their environments, in the narrow sense in which the term is commonly used, were virtually identical. Yet their social histories in the United States have been very different.

Over the generations, both groups rose, but they rose at different rates, through different means, and in a very different mixture of occupations and industries. Even wealthy Jews and wealthy Italians tended to become rich in different sectors of the economy. The California wine industry, for example, is full of Italian names like Mondavi, Gallo, and Rossi but the only prominent Jewish winemaker, Manishewitz, makes an entirely different kind of wine, and no one would compare Jewish winemakers with Italian winemakers in the United States. When we look at Jews and Italians in the very different environmental setting of Argentina, we see the same general pattern of differences between them. The same is true if we look at the differences between Jews and Italians in Australia, or Canada, or Western Europe.

Jews are not Italians and Italians are not Jews. Anyone familiar with their very different histories over many centuries should not be surprised. Their fate in America was not determined solely by their surrounding social conditions in America or by how they were treated by American society. They were different before they got on the boats to cross the ocean, and those differences crossed the ocean with them.

We can take it a step further. Even Ashkenazic Jews, those originating in Eastern Europe, have had significantly different economic and social histories from those originating in Germanic Central Europe, including Austria as well as Germany itself. These differences have persisted among their descendants not only in New York and Chicago but as far away as Melbourne and Sydney. In Australia, Jews from Eastern Europe have tended to cluster in and around Melbourne, while Germanic Jews have settled in and around Sydney. They even have a saying among themselves that Melbourne is a cold city with warm Jews while Sydney is a warm city with cold Jews.

A second and very different example of persistent cultural differences involves immigrants from Japan. As everyone knows, many Japanese-Americans were interned during the Second World War. What is less well known is that there is and has been an even larger Japanese population in Brazil than in the United States. These Japanese, incidentally, own approximately three-quarters as much land in Brazil as there is in Japan. (The Japanese almost certainly own more agricultural land in Brazil than in Japan.) In any event, very few Japanese in Brazil were interned during the Second World War. Moreover, the Japanese in Brazil were never subjected to the discrimination suffered by Japanese-Americans in the decades before the Second World War.

Yet, during the war, Japanese-Americans overwhelmingly remained loyal to the United States and Japanese-American soldiers won more than their share of medals in combat. But in Brazil, the Japanese were overwhelmingly and even fanatically loyal to Japan. You cannot explain the difference by anything in the environment of the United States or the environment of Brazil. But if you know something about the history of those Japanese who settled in these two countries, you know that they were culturally different in Japan before they ever got on the boats to take them across the Pacific Ocean and they were still different decades later. These two groups of immigrants left Japan during very different periods in the cultural evolution of Japan itself. A modern Japanese scholar has said: "If you want to see Japan of the Meiji era, go to the United States. If you want to see Japan of the Taisho era, go to Brazil." The Meiji era was a more cosmopolitan, pro-American era; the Taisho era was one of fanatical Japanese nationalism.

If the narrow concept of environment fails to explain many profound differences between groups and subgroups; it likewise fails to explain many very large differences in the economic and social performances of nations and civilizations. An eighteenth-century writer in Chile described that country's many natural advantages in climate, soil, and natural resources and then asked in complete bewilderment why it was such a poverty-stricken country. The same question could be asked of many countries today.

Conversely, we could ask why Japan and Switzerland are so prosperous when they are both almost totally lacking in natural resources. Both are rich in what economists call "human capital"—the skills of their people. No doubt there is a long and complicated history behind the different skill levels of different peoples and nations. The point here is that the immediate environment—whether social or geographic—is only part of the story.

Geography may well have a significant role in the history of peoples, but perhaps not simply by presenting them with more or less natural resources. Geography shapes or limits peoples' opportunities for cultural interaction and the mutual development that comes out of this. Small, isolated islands in the sea have seldom been sources of new scientific advances of technological breakthroughs, regardless of where such islands were located and regardless of the race of people on these islands. There are islands on land as well. Where soil, fertile enough to support human life, exists only in isolated patches, widely separated, there tend to be isolate cultures (often with different languages or dialects) in a culturally fragmented region. Isolated highlands often produce insular cultures, lagging in many ways behind the cultures of the lowlanders of the same race—whether we are talking about medieval Scotland, colonial Ceylon, or the contemporary montagnards of Vietnam.

With geographical environments as with social environments, we are talking about long-run effects not simply the effects of immediate surroundings. When Scottish highlanders, for example, immigrated to North Carolina in colonial times, they had a very different history from that of Scottish lowlanders who settled in North Carolina. For one thing, the lowlanders spoke English while the highlanders spoke Gaelic on into the nineteenth century. Obviously, speaking only Gaelic in an English-speaking country affects a group's whole economic and social progress.

Geographical conditions vary as radically in terms of how well they facilitate or impede large-scale cultural interactions as they do in their distribution of natural resources. We are not even close to being able to explain how all these geographical influences have operated throughout history. This too is an unanswered question largely because it is an unasked question, and it is an unasked question because many are seeking answers in terms of immediate social environment or are vehemently insistent that they have already found the answer in those terms.

How radically do geographic environments differ, not just in terms of tropical versus arctic climates, but also in the very configuration of the land and how this helps or hinders large-scale interactions among peoples? Consider one statistic: Africa is more than twice the size of Europe, and yet Africa has a shorter coastline than Europe. This seems almost impossible. But the reason is that Europe's coastline is far more convoluted, with many harbors and inlets being formed all around the continent. Much of the coastline of Africa is smooth, which is to say, lacking in the harbors that make large-scale maritime trade possible by sheltering the ships at anchor from the rough waters of the open sea.

Waterways of all sorts have played a major role in the evolution of cultures and nations around the world. Harbors on the sea are not the only waterways. Rivers are also very important. Virtually every major city on earth is located either on a river or a harbor. Whether it is such great harbors as those in Sydney, Singapore, or San Francisco; or London on the Thames, Paris on the Seine, or numerous other European cities on the Danube, waterways have been the lifeblood of urban centers for centuries. Only very recently has man-made, self-powered transportation, like automobiles and airplanes, made it possible to produce an exception to the rule like Los Angeles. (There is a Los Angeles River, but you do not have to be Moses to walk across it in the summertime.) New York has both a long and deep river and a huge sheltered harbor.

None of these geographical features in themselves create a great city or develop an urban culture. Human beings do that. But geography sets the limits within which people can operate and in some places it sets those limits much wider than in others. Returning to our comparison of the continents of Europe and Africa, we find that they differ as radically in rivers as they do in harbors. There are entire nations in Africa without a single navigable river—Libya and South Africa, for example.

"Navigable" is the crucial word. Some African rivers are navigable only during the rainy season. Some are navigable only between numerous cataracts and waterfalls. Even the Zaire River, which is longer than any river in North America and carries a larger volume of water, has too many waterfalls too close to the ocean for it to become a major artery of international commerce. Such commerce is facilitated in Europe not only by numerous navigable rivers but also by the fact that no spot on the continent, outside of Russia, is more than 500 miles from the sea. Many places in Africa are more than 500 miles from the sea, including the entire nation of Uganda.

Against this background, how surprised should we be to find that Europe is the most urbanized of all inhabited continents and Africa the least urbanized? Urbanization is not the be-all and end-all of life, but certainly an urban culture is bound to differ substantially from non-urban cultures, and the skills peculiar to an urban culture are far more likely to be found among groups from an urban civilization. Conversely, an interesting history could be written about the failures of urbanized groups in agricultural settlements.

Looking within Africa, the influence of geography seems equally clear. The most famous ancient civilization on the continent arose within a few miles on either side of Africa's longest navigable river, the Nile, and even today the two largest cities on the continent, Cairo and Alexandria, are on that river. The great West African kingdoms in the region served by the Niger River and the long-flourishing

East African economy based around the great natural harbor on the island of Zanzibar are further evidences of the role of geography. Again, geography is not all-determining—the economy of Zanzibar has been ruined by government policy in recent decades—but nevertheless, geography is an important long-run influence on the shaping of cultures as well as in narrow economic terms.

What are the implications of a world view of cultural diversity on the narrower issues being debated under that label in the United States today? Although "diversity" is used in so many different ways in so many different contexts that it seems to mean all things to all people, there are a few themes that appear again and again. One of these broad themes is that diversity implies organized efforts at the preservation of cultural differences, perhaps governmental efforts, perhaps government subsidies to various programs run by the advocates of diversity.

This approach raises questions as to what the purpose of culture is. If what is important about cultures is that they are emotionally symbolic, and if differentness is cherished for the sake of differentness, then this particular version of cultural diversity might make some sense. But cultures exist even in isolated societies where there are no other cultures around—where there is no one else and nothing else from which to be different. Cultures exist to serve the vital, practical requirements of human life—to structure a society so as to perpetuate the species, to pass on the hard-earned knowledge and experience of generations past and centuries past to the young and inexperienced in order to spare the next generation the costly and dangerous process of learning everything all over again from scratch through trial and error—including fatal errors. Cultures exist so that people can know how to get food and put a roof over their head, how to cure the sick, how to cope with the death of loved ones, and how to get along with the living. Cultures are not bumper stickers. They are living, changing ways of doing all the things that have to be done in life.

Every culture discards over time the things that no longer do the job or which do not do the job as well as things borrowed from other cultures. Each individual does this, consciously or not, on a day-to-day basis. Languages take words from other languages, so that Spanish as spoken in Spain includes words taken from Arabic, and Spanish as spoken in Argentina has Italian words taken from the large Italian immigrant population there. People eat Kentucky Fried Chicken in Singapore and stay in Hilton Hotels in Cairo. This is not what some of the advocates of diversity have in mind. They seem to want to preserve cultures in their purity, almost like butterflies preserved in amber. Decisions about change, if any, seem to be regarded as collective decisions, political decisions. But this is not how cultures have arrived where they are. Individuals have decided for themselves how much of the old they wished to retain, how much of the new they found useful in their own lives.

In this way, cultures have enriched each other in all the great civilizations of the world. In this way, great port cities and other crossroads of cultures have become centers of progress all across the planet. No culture has grown great in isolation—but a number of cultures have made historic and even astonishing advances when their isolation was ended, usually by events beyond their control.

Japan was a classic example in the nineteenth century, but a similar story could be told of Scotland in an earlier era, when a country where once even the nobility were illiterate became, within a short time as history is measured, a country that produced world pioneers in field after field: David Hume in philosophy, Adam Smith in economics, Joseph Black in chemistry, Robert Adam in architecture, and James Watt, whose steam engine revolutionized modern industry and transport. In the process, the Scots lost their language but gained world preeminence in many fields. Then a whole society moved to higher standards of living than anyone ever dreamed of in their poverty-stricken past.

There were higher standards in other ways as well. As late as the eighteenth century, it was considered noteworthy that pedestrians in Edinburgh no longer had to be on the alert for sewage being thrown out the windows of people's homes or apartments. The more considerate Scots yelled a warning, but they threw out the sewage anyway. Perhaps it was worth losing a little of the indigenous culture to be rid of that problem. Those who use the term "cultural diversity" to promote a multiplicity of segregated ethnic enclaves are doing an enormous harm to the people in those enclaves. However they live socially, the people in those enclaves are going to have to compete economically for a livelihood. Even if they were not disadvantaged before, they will be very disadvantaged if their competitors from the general population are free to tap the knowledge, skills, and analytical techniques Western civilization has drawn from all the other civilizations of the world, while those in the enclaves are restricted to what exists in the subculture immediately around them.

We need also to recognize that many great thinkers of the past—whether in medicine or philosophy, science or economics—labored not simply to advance whatever particular group they happened to have come from but to advance the human race. Their legacies, whether cures for deadly diseases or dramatic increases in crop yields to fight the scourge of hunger, belong to all people—and all people need to claim that legacy, not seal themselves off in a dead-end of tribalism or in an emotional orgy of cultural vanity.

DISCUSSION QUESTIONS

1. Most Americans have grown up with the U.S. leading the world in many areas such as technology, standard of living, medicine, and education. Is it important that we always lead in these areas? How can diversity in the workforce help us advance? Have we made good use of our peoplepower resources in the past? Why or why not?
2. The U.S. regularly exchanges scientists, business and industry leaders, and technology with countries all over the world. Would the author think this is a good idea or will this just help other countries get ahead of us?
3. In America, the management of workers by "assimilation into the workforce" is being replaced by the "integration of diversity." How would the author explain this shift in approach?
4. The author states that "What serves human purposes more effectively survives, while what does not, tends to decline or disappear." What aspects of American

culture in general do you think may decline? What aspects of American business culture may decline?

5. List objects that we have now or the ways things are done now that differ markedly from your parents' generation.

6. It has been said that English is the international language of business; Italian is the international language of music; French is the international language of diplomacy. What explanation would the author give for this? Might this change?

An analogy is drawn between maps and stereotypes in which stereotypes are depicted as mental maps.

How Stereotypes Influence Opinions About Individuals

Gregory Sawin

Stereotyping is a way of thinking. It means that someone already has made up his or her mind about what a stranger is really like based only on the stranger's race, age, sex, etc. Having a stereotype about other people can lead you to having an opinion about them before you get to know them. Basically, a stereotype is a belief that all people of a certain type have some common quality—for example, "All old people are politically conservative." Someone who has this stereotypical belief will be inclined to expect a conservative attitude in the next old person he sees.

In everyday life, a map we use when traveling is most useful to us when it is up-to-date and is a good match to the territory. We can rely on a new map of California to tell us how to get from one place to another. The layout of the cities and roads on the map is a close match to the actual layout of the cities and roads in the territory of California. The stereotype "All old people are politically conservative" serves as a kind of mental map a person has inside her head that supposedly tells her about a part of the territory of the outside world called "all old people." Such a mental map influences a person's perception and judgment; so a person with this stereotype may say, "I **know** that old man over there is politically conservative because **all** old people are conservative."

One theory of stereotyping, complexity-extremity, seems to support the idea that good mental maps are based on reliable knowledge of the territory.[1] One way of acquiring reliable knowledge is first-hand experience. The more experience we have with certain things, the more reliable is our knowledge about them. This theory says that someone is likely to stereotype another person inaccurately when he has had little direct experience with people who are "like" the other person. For example, a teenager is more likely to have a more inaccurate stereotype about "all old people" than about "all teenagers" because the teenager knows more teenagers than old people. The teenager would have a more accurate, more detailed mental map of "all teenagers" compared to his mental map of "all old people." So his answer to the question "What are teenagers like?" probably would be more specific and detailed than his answer to the question "What are old people like?" Knowing first-hand that there are many kinds of teenagers would prevent him from saying that all teenagers are alike. But his few experiences with old people may have resulted in a simple

Reprinted with permission of International Society for General Semantics from *Et Cetera*, vol. 48, no. 2, Summer 1991, pp. 210–212.

mental map of old people that leads him to believe that all old people are more alike than all teenagers; so he might say that all old people are politically conservative.

Most people are not concerned about the map-territory idea as it relates to everyday thinking and living. They just automatically **assume** that their beliefs, attitudes, and opinions are the right ones to have. But no one is born with beliefs; they are learned. So each person learns many mental maps (beliefs, opinions, and knowledge in general) in the course of a lifetime.

Realizing that stereotyping is a way of thinking that is learned leads to the question "What does the map-territory idea tell us about stereotypes?" The map-territory idea points out that maps that don't match the territory are often useless and sometimes even harmful. Such bad maps may lead us to jump to conclusions that will result in an unnecessary bad experience for someone. For example, the stereotype "All old people are politically conservative" may lead a nonconservative young person to automatically dislike an old person. That dislike may lead to making hostile remarks to the old person, who, in fact, may agree with many of the youth's political ideas. This whole chain of events, from stereotype to dislike to hostile remarks, is based on a fantasy—an inaccurate mental map.

But creating and using mental maps that are a good match to the territory of the outside world can help us avoid bad experiences and even have more successful experiences in life. A good mental map doesn't just happen; it is carefully built on reliable knowledge of the territory. This is an important point—what we observe about the nature of the territory tells us how to create the map. The map should not come first and tell us how to judge the territory, especially in terms of what attitudes to have regarding other people. We can't have a good match between mental maps and the territory of the outside world when we try to "warp the territory to fit the map."[2] We should observe the territory, then create a map to match it. If we use this approach in dealing with old people, for example, we will observe and listen to many old people **before** creating a mental map about them. If we do this, we can never say, "All old people are politically conservative," because we will never meet **all** old people.

Observing the territory before we create the map should lead us to choose our words carefully in forming our map. If we tried to observe and meet as many old people as possible, we would find that no two old people are exactly alike and some old people are not conservative. Since we would have no use for the term "all," our mental map would be something on the order of "Some old people are conservative, while some are liberal, some are middle-of-the-road, etc." That "etc." is important because it indicates that even this more accurate mental map does not tell us everything about old people—just as a real map doesn't tell us about every detail in a territory. Any map must leave out some details of the actual territory it is supposed to represent. When we realize that our mental maps also must leave out some details, then we are less absolute and simpleminded in our attitudes and statements about the territory of the world around us.

If we have this kind of **awareness** of the limitations of our mental maps plus the desire to make our statements correspond more accurately to the facts, we can reduce the chance of jumping to wrong conclusions about other people.

NOTES AND REFERENCES

1. L. Jussim, L. M. Coleman, and L. Lerch, "The Nature of Stereotypes: A Comparison and Integration of Three Theories," *Journal of Personality and Social Psychology* 52, no. 3 (1987), 536–546.
2. Harry L. Weinberg, *Levels of Knowing and Existence* (New York: Harper, 1959), 76.

DISCUSSION QUESTIONS

1. Give an example of a time in your life when your "mental map" of someone incorrectly influenced your perceptions and judgments about that person.
2. What inaccurate perceptions may people have about you, due to your membership in some demographic group? How correct or incorrect are these perceptions?
3. Can you cite a specific example of a change in one of your "mental maps" since you began this course? To what do you attribute this change?
4. How can people's "mental maps" cause problems in organizations, in personal relationships, and in international business?

A graphic depiction of how different ethnic and racial groups hold vastly different views of the world.

Mental Maps

The figures that follow represent perceptions of Los Angeles by upper middle class whites (Figure 1.6a), black residents of Avalon (Figure 1.6b), and Spanish-speaking residents in Boyle Heights (Figure 1.6c).

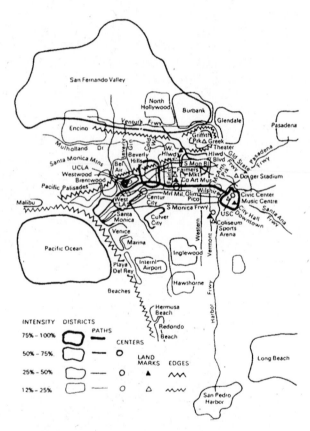

Figure 1.6(a) Los Angeles perceived through the eyes of upper middle class whites in Westwood

From P. Orleans, "Differential Cognition of Urban Residents: Effects of Social Scale on Mapping," orinally published in *Science, Engineering and the City*, National Academy of Engineering, 1967. Reprinted with permission from the National Academy of Engineering.

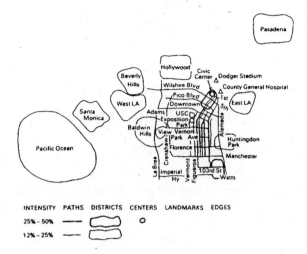

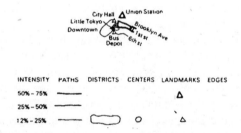

Figure 1.6(b) Los Angeles through the eyes of black residents in Avalon

Figure 1.6(c) Los Angeles through the eyes of Spanish-speaking residents in Boyle Heights

DISCUSSION QUESTIONS

1. Explain why these drawings are so different from each other. To what factors do you attribute these differences?
2. How do these groups' perceptions of their neighborhoods relate to the Sawin article on the development of stereotypes from our own "mental maps"?

A contrast of traditional with contemporary cultural values shows how their differences lead to differences in behavior which can be disadvantageous for the minority professional when not understood, but which can also become assets if balanced well.

Understanding Cultural Diversity
Miquela Rivera

Cultural values play a key role in how you view the world and how you learn to succeed in it. While individual background, talents and training contribute to each individual's unique experiences, this conceptual framework provides a base from which to begin understanding the differences—subtle and striking—that minority professionals face and the assets they bring with them.

THE DILEMMA

The diagram shows a comparison between a set of "traditional" cultural values and a set of "contemporary" cultural values. While you could argue that these values could apply to many groups of people, it's important to consider how it reflects your experiences, your upbringing, and your current attitudes toward home and work.

The list in the circle shows a set of traditional values. The sense of "we" or "us" is crucial to this set of values. For example, when you're born into a Hispanic family, you're born into a group. The family is the core of survival and success. Ask a Hispanic living near his family what he's doing on the weekend and he might tell you he's having a barbecue. Inquire about the guest list and you might get a vague answer. He doesn't need to issue formal invitations. Somehow, people will show up

Traditional Values   **Contemporary Values**

From *The Minority Career Book* by Miquela Rivera, Ph.D. Copyright 1991. Reprinted with permission from Bob Adams, Inc.

to eat and there'll be enough food, too. Activities are not usually conducted alone or in a vacuum in a traditional culture. What "we" are going to do is often more important than what "I" want to do.

The contemporary culture, on the other hand, concerns itself with "I," with individual preferences and "doing your thing." The focus is on how "I" will get ahead, regardless of the cost.

Cooperation is central to traditional culture, as typified by the circle in the diagram. Anthropologist Carlos Velez describes the Mexican culture, for instance, as "mutualistic and reciprocal." If one member of the group helps another with childcare, the other might return the favor by assisting with home repairs. The sharing or exchange of labor, money, and goods is often seen, even among professionals who have been raised traditionally.

Competition, on the other hand, is crucial in a contemporary culture. Getting ahead and getting there quickly matters. If you have help along the way, great. But you're mainly on your own.

In a traditional culture, the common good is considered important. How will it affect a family if a young Navajo moves hundreds of miles away from the reservation? Decisions are made with consideration of everyone else in the circle.

Individual advancement is the name of the game in a contemporary set of values. You do what you need to do to get ahead.

Modesty is a central value of traditional cultures. You can do well professionally, academically and economically but you don't need to tell everyone about it. When you return home, you'll resume the position you've always held there, even way back when. A Superior Court Judge might still be "Inky" to the neighborhood gang. The family will remember the troubles their now-successful relative had while she was going through medical school. You might be enjoying where you are now but don't forget where you came from.

In a contemporary culture, it's crucial to know how to toot your own horn. If *you* don't, no one else will. Get ahead by being noticed; that's the key.

The traditional set of cultural values promotes a *continual interchange* between people, as shown by the circle. A contemporary culture promotes individualism (doing it on your own), illustrated by the ladder. The arrow between the two indicates the tightrope that many minority professionals walk between the two cultures—balancing, choosing, weighing, deciding and balancing again.

CROSS-CULTURAL CONFLICT AND STRESS

The first time a person from a traditional background experiences the stress of cultural conflict is typically when he or she starts school. To come from a circle of exchange, talking and sharing, to be forced into a mold of independent thinking, solitary work and quiet attention is a dramatic transition for anyone, especially someone who is only five or six years old. No wonder teachers or supervisors who don't understand the traditional cultural experience become frustrated with the continual talking between minority students or employees. The traditional minorities are only doing what they've been doing for years—interacting—but it isn't always accept-able in a classroom or boardroom.

Competition and the contemporary set of values are introduced when the mi-nority starts school. Team sports, academic requirements and social organizations teach the child how to depend on himself to survive and get ahead. That's a far cry from the circle in which he's been raised.

The minority professional faces a stressful challenge each time she must walk between the two sets of values. Feeling perhaps more comfortable in one than the other, the minority professional might end up feeling as if she belongs fully to neither.

It might seem unnatural to speak up for yourself and get recognized but if you don't do it, you'll never get ahead. It might matter to you as a minority professional how your career affects your extended family but to the corporation, your dedication must lie with the company.

The hardest part for you may be the continual feeling you might experience of being alone, on your own, with loved ones out of reach and coworkers even more distant. But that's the price you have to pay. The challenge is to pick the best of both and minimize the cost.

ADVANTAGES OF BEING A MINORITY

The good news is that minority professionals bring a wonderful richness of personal experience and resources to the world of work. The Japanese have a tightly knit cul-ture that promotes modesty, cooperation and concern for others. They've gotten ahead in technical production because they have promoted the same concept on the job; the corporation becomes the family or circle in which the worker lives. The combination of technical expertise and good human relations results in well-made, highly competitive goods.

If minority professionals can combine their ability to get along well with oth-ers and promote cooperation and teamwork while mastering the technical skills to compete and get ahead, they will be able to solve problems resourcefully, efficiently and creatively. They will be at the cutting edge of managing a diverse workforce in a dynamic economy. That's a position of strength.

Miquela Rivera, Ph.D., is a psychologist in private practice and past chair of the Arizona Board of Psychologist Examiners. She is a contrib-utor to a variety of career publications and is also the author of the *Mi-nority Career Book*, published by Bob Adams, Inc.

DISCUSSION QUESTIONS

1. With which set of values, traditional or contemporary, were you raised? Why might some people report that they were raised with contemporary values and not the traditional values described by the author?
2. There is a trend today toward the team approach in organizations. Discuss what this means in terms of the traditional and contemporary values described by the author.
3. There is also a trend in today's organizations toward more participative management styles. Discuss how this might affect someone from a traditional values background.
4. Do you think all organizations have identical contemporary cultures? What does this mean for any worker?

CHAPTER

TWO

On Organizations and Diversity

Understand that over the long term, the successful manager is going to deal with large numbers of minorities and women in business, and I presume most managers want to be successful, want their company to be successful. Therefore, don't walk away from it; walk up to it.[1]

Four factors have given organizations reason to identify the need to understand and manage diversity: the changing composition of the workforce, the influence of new values and lifestyles, a change in the way that business is conducted from a national to a global economy, and a trend away from hierarchical command and control models towards more decentralized team-based management.

In the past, management primarily meant white middle-aged native-born males, who were willing to work long hours, relocate at the whim of their organizations, and manage primarily domestic organizations through a command/control model. Today's typical worker is more apt to be nonwhite or female, have child care responsibilities, and work in a team configuration for an international company. The challenge is to manage these new employees in ways that maximize productivity and quality, while minimizing interpersonal conflict and additional cost.

Since demographic data clearly establish the changing nature of the workforce in terms of gender, race, ethnicity, and age, it becomes a strategic imperative for organizations to learn how to manage today's new workforce.

Consider the following facts:

- More than one-half of the American workforce is currently composed of women, minorities, and immigrants.
- Only 15 percent of the new entrants to the workforce through the year 2000 will be white males.[2]
- Women are expected to account for three-fifths of the labor force growth in the 1990's.[3]
- Approximately 84 percent of the immigrants to the United States are now coming from Asian and Latin American countries.[4]
- By the year 2000 almost one-half of the U.S. workforce will be between the ages of 35–54.

Although demographic shifts may change the composition of the workforce as a whole, they have not necessarily produced proportionate changes in the way organizations are managed. For example, at a time when women account for 46 percent of the workforce, they represent less than 3 percent of the officers and 4.5 percent of the directors of the Fortune 500 companies.[5]

Almost 30 years of Equal Employment Opportunity (EEO) and Affirmative Action (AA) legislation helped protected groups get into the lower levels of organizations. However, EEO/AA also hurt these groups because of the backlash effect created when some misdirected managers hired and promoted less qualified people simply to fill quotas. These practices set up employees and their organizations for failure.

Clearly, there are other factors that prevented women, racial/ethnic minorities, and other groups from gaining positions at the highest levels of their organizations.

ACT	PROVISIONS
Equal Pay Act (1963)	Equal pay for men and women performing the same work
Title VII - Civil Rights Act (1964)	Prohibits discrimination on the basis of race, sex, color, or national origin
Age Discrimination in Employment Act (1967) (amended in 1978 & 1986)	Prohibits discrimination against people over 40 and restricts mandatory retirement except if age is a "bona fide occupational qualification"
Vocational Rehabilitation Act (1974)	Prohibits employers with Federal Contracts over $2500 from discriminating against the handicapped
Pregnancy Discrimination Act (1978)	Prohibits discrimination against pregnant women; requires that they be treated as all other employees for work related proposes including benefits
Immigration Reform and Control Act (1986)	Established penalties for employers who knowingly hire illegal aliens; prohibits employment on the basis of national origin or citizenship
Americans with Disabilities Act (1990)	Requires employer to accommodate disabled persons

Figure 2.1 Major federal laws related to Equal Employment Opportunity.

Glass ceilings and walls, which prevented both vertical and horizontal career movements, were built by stereotypes, lack of understanding of the pervasiveness of existing norms and values, prejudices, and differences in communication styles.

Equal Employment Opportunity, Affirmative Action, and managing diversity are not synonyms. Equal Employment Opportunity legislation is designed to guarantee equal treatment in employment practices such as hiring, training, promotion, and termination etc., regardless of the employee's gender, color, race, religion, age, physical ability, or ethnic group origins (see Figure 2.1). Affirmative Action is a detailed plan that goes beyond discontinuing discriminatory practices because it involves the proactive recruitment and promotion of protected group members.

In contrast, managing diversity means that the organization realizes that difference can add value in terms of new perspectives, creativity, and better understanding of customers and markets. Differences in gender, race, ethnicity, age, physical ability, and sexual orientation, etc. were seen as liabilities to managing in the old models, but as assets to be utilized in newer models.

In addition to population shifts, a second change is in worker attitudes and values. A generation ago we could be quite sure that most Americans' grandfathers were white, had immigrated from western Europe, and wanted to become americanized. The title of a 1909 Israel Zangwill play, *The Melting Pot*,[6] has often been used as a metaphor to describe the phenomenon of people changing their names, learning a new language, and adapting their culture to better blend into American life.

Although today the validity of that metaphor is often questioned in terms of adaptations to life outside of work, in the workplace there are norms, values, and a culture usually based on the white male experience that dominates. Many of today's workers come from Latin American and Asian countries, have English as a second language, and retain names that may be difficult to pronounce and spell. In addition to ethnic differences, many of today's workers could never blend in, even if they wanted to. Nearly half often wear skirts, over 10 percent are black, and an increasing number are physically challenged. They not only look different but they think differently, have different styles of communication, and are less interested in giving up their ways even if this were an option.[7]

Whereas our grandfathers would have probably worked for the same company most of their lives, tolerated ethnic prejudices and jokes, been the sole breadwinner for the family, and expected little more than a paycheck for long hours of work, members of today's workforce have very different attitudes. Unlike grandpa, because of differences in lifestyles, today's diverse workforce is often interested in spousal benefits for lesbian and gay partners, flextime, family leave policies, and support networks.

Turnover rates of the most valuable diverse employees escalate when people think that they are not accepted, are cut out of the information loop, cannot be candid, and are not valued for their differences. When diverse employees are subject to sexual harassment, ethnic jokes, homophobic attitudes, and organizational policies and practices that do not support them, they either leave, sue, or stay but contribute less to the organization.

> Or consider an organization with 10,000 employees, 35% of whom are likely to be women and minorities. If the turnover rate for these employees is double that of white males, and it costs $25,000 to recruit and train each person, an average annual savings of $3.5 million accrues from reducing their turnover rate to that of white males.[8]

The third reason that diversity has become such an important topic is that the way we do business has changed dramatically in the past few years. Organizations are now global rather than domestic; they are leaner and more collaborative rather than hierarchial and controlling. Today nearly 40 percent of U.S. corporate profits result from overseas investments.[9] By the year 2000 it is estimated that one-half of the world's investments will be controlled by multinational corporations.[10] Approximately 70 percent of all U.S. businesses are in direct competition with companies overseas.[11]

Certainly, it is an asset to a business when they have employees who speak several languages and understand other cultures and markets. However, global opportunities also bring increased complications to managing diverse employees on international assignments.

The fourth reason that diversity has become a major issue is that American business is currently undergoing major structural and organizational changes. In response to the challenges of increased emphasis on quality and productivity, companies are downsizing, decreasing layers of middle management, and frequently reorganizing into team configurations. Currently, more than half the Fortune 500 companies utilize participative work teams.[12]

Such changes bring particular challenges and conflicts to managing diversity. Equal Opportunity and Affirmative Action legislation may complicate reassignments or dismissals and create unproductive backlash. Prejudice, mistrust, lack of understanding and poor communication between diverse workers can only detract from worker productivity.

The readings in Chapter Two were chosen to further expand these four factors; to help the reader to understand the differences between EEO/AA as programs that value diversity as a strategic imperative; and to illustrate the challenges and benefits a diverse workforce brings to the organization.

Although teams work best when they are cohesive and their members accept the organizational goals as their own, the challenge for management in today's multicultural organizations is to encourage and support diverse employees' participation so that they contribute a multiplicity of perspectives. Parker's *Distinguishing Difference and Conflict* opens this section because it presents a foundation for the organizational changes that are needed to truly manage diversity. The article explores the need to see differences in terms of their potential contribution rather than in terms of disruption to the traditional way of doing business. Understanding change in a positive light is fundamental to any discussion of managing diversity in a meaningful way.

For the type of changes we are talking about here to occur, one must realize that the process of managing diversity is very different from the process of managing government mandated programs. In Thomas' *From Affirmative Action to Affirming Diversity*, he clearly explains these differences and outlines a cyclical six step process with which organizations become entangled when they attempt to manage diverse workers but are really dealing with EEO/AA programs. As a result, these companies not only fall far short of managing diversity, but they also fail to see the advantages of a diverse workforce. Thomas takes a positive proactive approach by offering ten specific guidelines to beginning the managing diversity process and by presenting cases that illustrate successful high profile organizations that have managed to break out of this cycle.

As a follow-up, Cox and Blake, in *Managing Cultural Diversity—Implications for Organizational Competitiveness*, review the research data and expand the idea that managing diversity programs is a source of competitive advantage both inside and outside of an organization.

When different types of people are hired, the value that they bring to the organization is frequently negated by backlash. People from the majority culture often find it difficult to accept those who may have received a slight hiring advantage because of government mandates. The following two articles offer fresh perspectives on this problem. *Moving Forward on Reverse Discrimination* by Kubasek and Giapetro takes a different approach to the defense of Equal Employment Opportunity and Affirmative Action programs. Their arguments provide a philosophical/ethical approach to understanding why people who are different may require different treatment in the workplace. In contrast, Nazario's article, *Many Minorities Feel Torn by the Experience of Affirmative Action*, examines EEO/AA from the often ignored minority viewpoint and offers suggestions for more effective management of Equal Employment Opportunity legislation in the organization.

The last two articles involve the implications and application of working with strategic changes and diversity. Feltes, Robinson, and Fink's *Equal Employment Responsibilities of Multinational Corporations* explores the economic, legal, and ethical complications of diversity when U.S. corporations operate in other countries.

Lastly, Butterfield's *Xerox Makes It Work* ties together all the ideas explored in this chapter. This reading illustrates how one corporation has experienced both successes and failures in its attempt to operationalize diversity as a strategic imperative and progress beyond a EEO/AA mode towards a goal of managing diversity. In the opening quotation for this section, David Kearns, former president and chairman of Xerox, challenges managers to face up to the changing workforce in a positive way. This will be one of the most important challenges of managing in the twenty-first century.

NOTES

1. Copeland, Lenny. "Valuing Diversity, Part II: Pioneers and Champions of Change." *Personnel*, July 1988: 49.
2. Johnson W. B., and Packer, A. H. *Workforce 2000*. Hudson Institute: Indianapolis, Indiana, 1987, p. xiii.
3. *Occupational Outlook Handbook*, U.S. Bureau of Labor Statistics, Washington, D. C. 1992–93, pp. 8–9.
4. Johnson and Packer, *op. cit.* pp. 93–94.
5. Lubin, Joan S. "Rights Law to Spur Shifts in Promotions." *Wall Street Journal*, December 30, 1991.
6. Thernstrom, Stephen. "Ethnic Groups in American History." *Ethnic Relations in America*, Lance Liebman, ed. Englewood Cliffs, NJ: Prentice-Hall, 1982, p. 12.
7. Fine, M., Johnson, F. and Ryan, M. S. "Cultural Diversity in the Workforce," *Public Personnel Management*, 19 (1990), pp. 305–319.
8. Daft, Richard L. *Management,* 3rd. ed. Ft. Worth, TX: Dryden, 1993, p. 464.
9. Taoka, George M., and Dan R. Beeman. *International Business: Environments, Institutions and Operations*. New York: HarperCollins, 1991, p. 4.
10. Feltes, P. R., Robinson, K., and Fink, R. L. "Employee Responsibilities of Multinational Corporations." *Business Forum*, Summer, 1992: pp. 18–21.
11. Daft, *op. cit.,* p. 441.
12. Lawler, Edward E. III. "Let the Workers Make the White Knuckle Decisions." *Fortune*, March 26, 1990: pp. 49–50.

A discussion of diversity in organizations in terms of factors in the treatment of difference and ways of addressing diversity and including the positive aspects and the escalation into conflict.

Distinguishing Difference and Conflict

Carole G. Parker
Saint Michael's College

In recent years, diversity in organizations has been an exciting, stimulating, and intriguing topic. What happens in organizations to influence either the discounting or appreciation of individual differences?

Smart managers today realize the importance of balance in work groups and are moving to incorporate differences—age, gender, race, culture, sexual preference, styles of being—in their organizations to capitalize on the potential that diversity offers.

In order to manage differences, the interest, energy, and commitment of the various parties involved must be shared. Because differences among people are not inherently good or bad, there is no "right" way to deal with differences. Although differences are sometimes disruptive, they can also lead to very important benefits, both to individuals and organizations.

HOW DIFFERENCES ARE OFTEN MANAGED

What action and factors must be uppermost in selecting the most appropriate approach to addressing differences? Differences are often managed by avoidance or repression. The avoidance of differences too often takes the form of associating mostly with individuals with similar backgrounds, experiences, beliefs, and values. Usually this allows an environment of mutual support and predictability. Another avoidance strategy is to separate individuals who create sparks between each other.

The repression of differences occurs when disagreements are not allowed to emerge. This happens frequently in team activities or by emphasizing behavior focusing on cooperation, collaboration, and loyalty.

Repression is quite costly. Resistances develop that have both organizational and individual consequences. The process of blocking strong feelings and repressing differences may result in desensitization and a loss of productivity. When individuals with differences come together managers must exert self-control to reduce unnecessary conflict.

There are both appropriate times and dangers associated with the use of avoidance and repression in managing differences. Teams or work groups faced with tight deadlines may want to limit the number and type of ideas generated. Avoidance may

---

This reading is a companion piece intended to be read after the completion of the Transcendus Exercise found in Chapter Five of this text.

be an appropriate interim strategy for dealing with differences by enabling an individual to learn more about a person or situation before declaring a stance. The challenge to management is to decide when to use these approaches. For example, the **Bay of Pigs** incident during the Kennedy administration in the early 1960s was the result of an avoidance of differences. Such avoidance of difference can lead to groupthink, which occurs when everyone in a group agrees with everyone else, although there are different opinions. The space shuttle **Challenger** disaster is another example of groupthink. Groupthink is the result of a lack of challenge for ideas, opinions, values, or beliefs.

Still another danger in avoiding differences is overcompatibility. When overcompatibility exists in an organization, it may be due to a strong need for support, reassurance, security, or a need to reduce a threat. In an organization this can severely hamper new ideas, productivity, growth, and development. Avoidance and repression of differences are usually not viable solutions. When differences are present, they must be expressed and worked through. If not, conflict will result.

POSITIVE ASPECTS OF DIFFERENCES

1. Difference can be regarded as an opportunity. "Two heads are better than one" because they often represent a richer set of experiences and the variability of these combined may lead to a more creative approach than could be achieved independently.
2. Differences can be used to test the strength of a position. Have all the aspects been considered, all loops carefully closed? When developing policy or organizational processes, it is important to cover all the bases.

A healthy interaction among differences (gender, age, race, culture, styles of being, etc.) could answer these questions. Two factors influence the treatment of differences: first the needs, wants, and goals of the individual; and second, the value placed on the relationship. People are often motivated by the desire to meet their needs, satisfy wants and desires. The stronger the motivation the greater the likelihood of addressing differences. Furthermore, when the persons involved are important to each other or valued, the tendency to manage the difference increases to preserve the relationship. The reverse is likely when there is no value in the relationship. Once these factors have been assessed, it becomes necessary to recognize behavior and attitudes that will be helpful in managing the differences.

Differences are not problems to be solved; they are dilemmas to be managed. Successful managers of difference reduce their judgments and accept the differences as legitimate. Clear boundaries between self and others, a willingness and interest in being influenced, and an awareness of choice with the ability to make choices also help. Furthermore, using strong language such as must, should, will, ought, cannot, necessary, impossible, requirement, mandate, and so forth will diminish success.

Differences are experienced from interacting with others who are dissimilar. A range of experiences and success in interpersonal relationships supports the ability to deal with differences. Individuals who have traveled or have unusual experiences tend to develop an appreciation for differences. Managing differences is not

The Escalation of Differences into Conflict

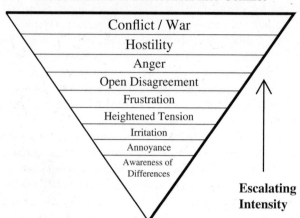

Figure 2.2

an individual process; it is interactive among individuals. When only one individual is attempting to deal with the difference, the result is coping behavior. Dealing with differences evokes emotion. A range of emotions for human interaction that lead to awareness of difference is necessary. These emotions can lead to conflict, but conflict **is not** a prerequisite to managing differences.

Differences evoke emotions at different levels, ranging from small or minor to large or major. An inverted triangle graphically shows the escalating intensity in each level as differences are heightened. See Figure 2.2.

The first level involves an awareness of the difference. Here the parties are exploring each other—what is similar, what is not. When the differences appear to be greater than the similarities, annoyance occurs. The parties are not able to appreciate how their differences may be beneficial to each other. Irritation, on the next level, may result from continued exploration, possibly through the dialectic process. Tension is heightened as more contact occurs, with an overlay of fear. The boundaries of self may be threatened (what will happen to me if I continue with this encounter?) and anger develops. After anger, open disagreements follow, and the dispute solidifies. Each party has developed a firm stance of his/her position. The final level is conflict or war, where each party works hard to repress or neutralize the other. In Figure 2.2, we suggest that an individual may, depending on the situation, traverse through each of these levels in addressing differences.

Conflict may result or emerge from differences. There are many publications defining conflict. For our purposes, conflict is briefly defined based on the experiences of participants in the Transcendus Exercise (found in Chapter Five of this text). From the moment Earthling groups come together to figure out how to explain conflict to their visitors, students often find themselves confronting substantial differences with respect to their ways of defining conflict and the positive and negative values attached to it. The following listed items are typical examples of definitions generated by Earthling groups about conflict:

1. Conflict exists when two or more parties want the same thing or their wants are incompatible in some way.
2. Conflict must involve emotionality; it is a disturbing emotion within ourselves and may involve feelings of anger and frustration.
3. The higher the stakes, the greater the conflict; one must care to have conflict.
4. Conflict can be within oneself, a group, and between groups. Conflict involves competition of wants and of viewpoints.
5. Conflict can be enjoyable.

It is important to distinguish conflict from difference. Difference is an important and necessary ingredient in human interaction and, if valued, can lead to opportunity, creativity, and appreciation. Difference is a component of diversity which is a constant in our environment. Managers and the workforce are beginning to grapple with this constant and are learning that appreciating or valuing differences opens the door to new and creative ways of addressing organizational challenges.

DISCUSSION QUESTIONS

1. How does conflict differ from difference?
2. What are some of the dangers of avoiding and repressing differences?
3. Think of an experience in an organizational or social setting that you have had involving the avoidance or repression of difference. What consequences has this led to?
4. What are some of the positive uses of difference?
5. Can you think of any examples of difference other than those already mentioned in the reading?
6. How can differences be managed while minimizing the risk of conflict?

An examination of affirmative action premises and programs underscoring the need to move beyond numbers recruiting into programs that better manage diversity of all types.

✗From Affirmative Action to Affirming Diversity

R. Roosevelt Thomas, Jr.

To compete globally, America needs to create workplaces that tap the full potential of every employee, says this author. Affirmative action programs, although appropriate, fail to deal with the root causes of prejudice and inequality and do little to develop people and strengthen organizations. In this reading, the author examines affirmative action programs and their shortcomings, contrasting them with more suitable contemporary approaches that affirm and make full use of an openly multicultural workplace.

Sooner or later, affirmative action will die a natural death. Its achievements have been stupendous, but if we look at the premises that underlie it, we find assumptions and priorities that look increasingly shopworn. Thirty years ago, affirmative action was invented on the basis of these five appropriate premises:

1. Adult, white males make up something called the U.S. business mainstream.
2. The U.S. economic edifice is a solid, unchanging institution with more than enough space for everyone.
3. Women, blacks, immigrants, and other minorities should be allowed in as a matter of public policy and common decency.
4. Widespread racial, ethnic, and sexual prejudice keeps them out.
5. Legal and social coercion are necessary to bring about the change.

Today all five of these premises need revising. Over the past six years, I have tried to help some 15 companies learn how to achieve and manage diversity, and I have seen that the realities facing us are no longer the realities affirmative action was designed to fix.

To begin with, more than half the U.S. work force now consists of minorities, immigrants, and women, so white, native-born males, though undoubtedly still dominant, are themselves a statistical minority. In addition, white males will make up only 15 percent of the increase in the work force over the next 10 years. The so-called mainstream is now almost as diverse as the society at large.

Second, while the edifice is still big enough for all, it no longer seems stable, massive, and invulnerable. In fact, American corporations are scrambling, doing their best to become more adaptable, to compete more successfully for markets and labor, foreign and domestic, and to attract all the talent they can find. (Exhibits 1 to 5 show what a number of U.S. companies are doing to manage diversity.)

Third, women and minorities no longer need a boarding pass, they need an upgrade. The problem is not getting them in at the entry level; the problem is making better use of their potential at every level, especially in middle-management and leadership positions. This is no longer simply a question of common decency, it is a questions of business survival.

Fourth, although prejudice is hardly dead, it has suffered some wounds that may eventually prove fatal. In the meantime, American businesses are now filled with progressive people—many of them minorities and women themselves—whose prejudices, where they still exist, are much too deeply suppressed to interfere with recruitment. The reason many companies are still wary of minorities and women has much more to do with education and perceived qualifications than with color or gender. Companies are worried about productivity and well aware that minorities and women represent a disproportionate share of the undertrained and undereducated.

Fifth, coercion is rarely needed at the recruitment stage. There are very few places in the United States today where you could dip a recruitment net and come up with nothing but white males. Getting hired is not the problem—women and blacks who are seen as having the necessary skills and energy can get into the work force relatively easily. It's later on that many of them plateau and lose their drive and quit or get fired. It's later on that their managers' inability to manage diversity hobbles them and the companies they work for.

In creating these changes, affirmative action had an essential role to play and played it very well. In many companies and communities it still plays that role. But affirmative action is an artificial, transitional intervention intended to give managers a chance to correct an imbalance, an injustice, a mistake. Once the numbers mistake has been corrected, I don't think affirmative action alone can cope with the remaining long-term task of creating a work setting geared to the upward mobility of *all* kinds of people, including white males. It is difficult for affirmative action to influence upward mobility even in the short run, primarily because it is perceived to conflict with the meritocracy we favor. For this reason, affirmative action is a red flag to every individual who feels unfairly passed over and a stigma for those who appear to be its beneficiaries.

Moreover, I doubt very much that individuals who reach top positions through affirmative action are effective models for younger members of their race or sex. What, after all, do they model? A black vice president who got her job through affirmative action is not necessarily a model of how to rise through the corporate meritocracy. She may be a model of how affirmative action can work for the people who find or put themselves in the right place at the right time.

If affirmative action in upward mobility meant that no person's competence and character would be overlooked or undervalued on account of race, sex, ethnicity, origins, or physical disability, then affirmative action would be the very thing we need to let every corporate talent find its niche. But what affirmative action means in practice is an unnatural focus on one group, and what it means too often to too many employees is that someone is playing fast and loose with standards in order to favor that group. Unless we are to compromise our standards, a thing no competitive company can even contemplate, upward mobility for minorities and women should always be a question of pure competence and character unmuddled by accidents of birth.

And that is precisely why we have to learn to manage diversity—to move beyond affirmative action, not to repudiate it. Some of what I have to say may strike some readers—mostly those with an ax to grind—as directed at the majority white males who hold most of the decision-making posts in our economy. But I am speaking to all managers, not just white males, and I certainly don't mean to suggest that white males somehow stand outside diversity. White males are as odd and as normal as anyone else.

THE AFFIRMATIVE ACTION CYCLE

If you are managing diverse employees, you should ask yourself this question: Am I fully tapping the potential capacities of everyone in my department? If the answer is no, you should ask yourself this follow-up: Is this failure hampering my ability to meet performance standards? The answer to this question undoubtedly will be yes.

Think of corporate management for a moment as an engine burning pure gasoline. What's now going into the tank is no longer just gas, it has an increasing percentage of, let's say, methanol. In the beginning, the engine will still work pretty well, but by and by it will start to sputter, and eventually it will stall. Unless we rebuild the engine, it will no longer burn the fuel we're feeding it. As the work force grows more and more diverse at the intake level, the talent pool we have to draw on for supervision and management will also grow increasingly diverse. So the question is: Can we burn this fuel? Can we get maximum corporate power from the diverse work force we're now drawing into the system?

Affirmative action gets blamed for failing to do things it never could do. Affirmative action gets the new fuel into the tank, the new people through the front door. Something else will have to get them into the driver's seat. That something else consists of enabling people, in this case minorities and women, to perform to their potential. This is what we now call managing diversity. Not appreciating or leveraging diversity, not even necessarily understanding it. Just managing diversity in such a way as to get from a heterogeneous work force the same productivity, commitment, quality, and profit that we got from the old homogeneous work force.

The correct question today is not, How are we doing on race relations? Or are we promoting enough minority people and women? but rather, given the diverse work force I've got, am I getting the productivity, does it work as smoothly, is morale as high, as if every person in the company was the same sex and race and nationality? Most answers will be, Well, no, of course not! But why shouldn't the answer be, You bet!?

EXHIBIT 1: Out of the Numbers Game and into Decision Making

Like many other companies, Avon practiced affirmative action in the 1970s and was not pleased with the results. The company worked with employment agencies that specialized in finding qualified minority hires, and it cultivated contacts with black and minority organizations on college campuses. Avon wanted to see its customer base reflected in its work force, especially at the decision-making level. But while women moved up the corporate ladder fairly briskly—not so surprising in a company whose work force is mostly female—minorities did not. So in 1984, the company began to change its policies and practices.

"We really wanted to get out of the numbers game," says Marcia Worthing, the corporate vice president for human resources. "We felt it was more important to have five minority people tied into the decision-making process than ten who were just heads to count."

First, Avon initiated awareness training at all levels.

"The key to recruiting, retaining, and promoting minorities is not the human resource department," says Worthing. "It's getting line management to buy into the idea. We had to do more than change behavior. We had to change attitudes."

Second, the company formed a Multicultural Participation Council that meets regularly to oversee the process of managing diversity. The group includes Avon's CEO and high-level employees from throughout the company.

Third, in conjunction with the American Institute for Managing Diversity, Avon developed a diversity-training program. For several years, the company has sent racially and ethnically diverse groups of 25 managers at a time to Institute headquarters at Morehouse College in Atlanta, where they spend three weeks confronting their differences and learning to hear and avail themselves of viewpoints they initially disagreed with. "We came away disciples of diversity," says one company executive.

Fourth, the company helped three minority groups—blacks, Hispanics, and Asians—form networks that crisscrossed the corporation in all 50 states. Each network elects its own leaders and has an adviser from senior management. In addition, the networks have representatives on the Multicultural Participation Council, where they serve as a conduit for employee views on diversity issues facing management.

When we ask how we're doing on race relations, we inadvertently put our finger on what's wrong with the question and with the attitude that underlies affirmative action. So long as racial and gender equality is something we grant to minorities and women, there will be no racial and gender equality. What we must do is create an environment where no one is advantaged or disadvantaged, an environment where "we" is everyone. What the traditional approach to diversity did was to create a cycle of crisis, action, relaxation, and disappointment that companies repeated over and over again without ever achieving more than the barest particle of what they were after.

Affirmative action pictures the work force as a pipeline and reasons as follows: If we can fill the pipeline with *qualified* minorities and women, we can solve our upward mobility problem. Once recruited, they will perform in accordance with our promotional criteria and move naturally up our regular developmental ladder. In the past, where minorities and women have failed to progress, they were simply unable to meet our performance standards. Recruiting qualified people will enable us to avoid special programs and reverse discrimination.

This pipeline perspective generates a self-perpetuating, self-defeating, recruitment-oriented cycle with six stages:

1. Problem Recognition   The first time through the cycle, the problem takes this form—We need more minorities and women in the pipeline. In later iterations, the problem is more likely to be defined as a need to retain and promote minorities and women.

2. Intervention   Management puts the company into what we may call an Affirmative Action Recruitment Mode. During the first cycle, the goal is to recruit minorities and women. Later, when the cycle is repeated a second or third time and the challenge has shifted to retention, development, and promotion, the goal is to recruit *qualified* minorities and women. Sometimes, managers indifferent or blind to possible accusations of reverse discrimination will institute special training, tracking, incentive, mentoring, or sponsoring programs for minorities and women.

3. Great Expectations   Large numbers of minorities and women have been recruited and a select group has been promoted or recruited at a higher level to serve as highly visible role models for the newly recruited masses. The stage seems set for the natural progression of minorities and women up through the pipeline. Management leans back to enjoy the fruits of its labor.

4. Frustration   The anticipated natural progression fails to occur. Minorities and women see themselves plateauing prematurely. Management is upset (and embarrassed) by the failure of its affirmative action initiative and begins to resent the impatience of the new recruits and their unwillingness to give the company credit for trying to do the right thing. Depending on how high in the hierarchy they have plateaued, alienated minorities and women either leave the company or stagnate.

5. Dormancy   All remaining participants conspire tacitly to present a silent front to the outside world. Executives say nothing because they have no solutions. As for those women and minorities who stayed on, calling attention to affirmative action's failures might raise doubts about their qualifications. Do they deserve their jobs, or did they just happen to be in the right place at the time of an affirmative action push? So no one complains, and if the company has a good public relations department, it may even wind up with a reputation as a good place for women and minorities to work.

If questioned publicly, management will say things like "Frankly, affirmative action is not currently an issue," or "Our numbers are okay," or "With respect to minority representation at the upper levels, management is aware of this remaining challenge."

In private and off the record, however, people say things like "premature plateauing is a problem, and we don't know what to do," and "Our top people don't seem interested in finding a solution," and "There's plenty of racism and sexism around this place—whatever you may hear."

6. Crisis   Dormancy can continue indefinitely, but usually it is broken by a crisis of competitive pressure, government intervention, external pressure from a special interest group, or internal unrest. One company found that its pursuit of a Total Quality program was hampered by the alienation of minorities and women. Senior management at another corporation saw the growing importance of minorities in their customer base and decided they need minority participation in their managerial ranks. In another case, growing expressions of discontent forced a break in the conspiracy of silence even after the company had received national recognition as a good place for minorities and women to work.

Whatever its cause, the crisis fosters a return to the Problem Recognition phase, and the cycle begins again. This time, management seeks to explain the shortcomings of the previous affirmative action push and usually concludes that the problem is recruitment.

EXHIBIT 2: "It Simply Makes Good Business Sense"

Corning characterizes its 1970s affirmative action program as a form of legal compliance. The law dictated affirmative action and morality required it, so the company did its best to hire minorities and women.

The ensuing cycle was classic: recruitment, confidence, disappointment, embarrassment, crisis, more recruitment. Talented women and blacks joined the company only to plateau or resign. Few reached upper-management levels, and no one could say exactly why.

Then James R. Houghton took over as CEO in 1983 and made the diverse work force one of Corning's three top priorities, alongside Total Quality and a higher return on equity. His logic was twofold:

First of all, the company had higher attrition rates for minorities and women than for white males, which meant that investments in training and development were being wasted. Second, he believed that the Corning work force should more closely mirror the Corning customer base.

In order to break the cycle of recruitment and subsequent frustration, the company established two quality-improvement teams headed by senior executives, one for black progress and one for women's progress. Mandatory awareness training was introduced for some 7,000 salaried employees—a day and a half for gender awareness, two-and-a-half days for racial awareness. One goal of the training is to identify unconscious company values that work against minorities and women. For example, a number of awareness groups reached the conclusion that working late had so much symbolic value that managers tended to look more at the quantity than at the quality of time spent on the job, with predictably negative effects on employees with dependent-care responsibilities.

The company also made an effort to improve communications by printing regular stories and articles about the diverse work force in its in-house newspaper and by publicizing employee success stories that emphasized diversity. It worked hard to identify and publicize promotion criteria. Career-planning systems were introduced for all employees.

With regard to recruitment, Corning set up a nationwide scholarship program that provides renewable grants of $5,000 per year for college in exchange for a summer of paid work at some Corning installation. A majority of program participants have come to work for Corning full-time after graduation, and very few have left the company so far, though the program has been in place only four years.

The company also expanded its summer intern program, with emphasis on minorities and women, and established formal recruiting contacts with campus groups such as the Society of Women Engineers and the National Black MBA Association.

Corning sees its efforts to manage diversity not only as a social and moral issue but also as a question of efficiency and competitiveness. In the words of Mr. Houghton, "It simply makes good business sense."

This assessment by a top executive is typical:

> The managers I know are decent people. While they give priority to performance, I do not believe any of them deliberately block minorities or women who are qualified for promotion. On the contrary, I suspect they bend over backward to promote women and minorities who give some indication of being qualified.
>
> However, they believe we simply do not have the necessary talent within those groups, but because of the constant complaints they have heard about their deficiencies in affirmative action, they feel they face a no-win situation. If they do not promote, they are obstructionists. But if they promote people who are unqualified, they hurt performance and deny promotion to other employees unfairly. They can't win. The answer, in my mind, must be an ambitious new recruitment effort to bring in quality people.

And so the cycle repeats. Once again blacks, Hispanics, women, and immigrants are dropped into a previously homogeneous, all-white all-Anglo, all-male, all native-born environment, and the burden of cultural change is placed on the newcomers. There will be new expectations and a new round of frustration, dormancy, crisis, and recruitment.

TEN GUIDELINES FOR LEARNING TO MANAGE DIVERSITY

The traditional American image of diversity has been assimilation: the melting pot, where ethnic and racial differences were standardized into a kind of American puree. Of course, the melting pot is only a metaphor. In real life, many ethnic and most racial groups retain their individuality and express it energetically. What we have is perhaps some kind of American mulligan stew; it is certainly no puree.

At the workplace, however, the melting pot has been more than a metaphor. Corporate success has demanded a good deal of conformity, and employees have voluntarily abandoned most of their ethnic distinctions at the company door.

Now those days are over. Today the melting pot is the wrong metaphor even in business, for three good reasons. First, if it ever was possible to melt down Scotsmen and Dutchmen and Frenchmen into an indistinguishable broth, you can't do the same with blacks, Asians, and women. Their differences don't melt so easily. Second, most people are no longer willing to be melted down, not even for eight hours a day—and it's a seller's market for skills. Third, the thrust of today's non-hierarchical, flexible, collaborative management requires a ten- or twentyfold increase in our tolerance for individuality.

So companies are faced with the problem of surviving in a fiercely competitive world with a work force that consists and will continue to consist of *unassimilated diversity*. And the engine will take a great deal of tinkering to burn that fuel.

What managers fear from diversity is a lowering of standards, a sense that anything goes. Of course, standards must not suffer. In fact, competence counts

EXHIBIT 3: Turning Social Pressures into Competitive Advantage

Like most other companies trying to respond to the federal legislation of the 1970s, Digital Equipment Corp. started off by focusing on numbers. By the early 1980s, however, company leaders could see it would take more than recruitment to make Digital the diverse workplace they wanted it to be. Equal Employment Opportunity (EEO) and affirmative action seemed too exclusive—too much "white males doing good deeds for minorities and women." The company wanted to move beyond these programs to the kind of environment where every employee could realize his or her potential, and Digital decided that meant an environment where individual differences were not tolerated but valued, even celebrated.

The resulting program and philosophy, called Valuing Differences, has two components:

First, the company helps people get in touch with their stereotypes and false assumptions through what Digital calls Core Groups. These voluntary groupings of 8 to 10 people work with company-trained facilitators whose job is to encourage discussion and self-development and, in the company's words, "to keep people safe" as they struggle with their prejudices. Digital also runs a voluntary two day training program called "Understanding the Dynamics of Diversity," which thousands of Digital employees have now taken.

Second, the company has named a number of senior managers to various Cultural Boards of Directors and Valuing Differences Boards of Directors. These bodies promote openness to individual differences, encourage younger managers committed to the goal of diversity, and sponsor frequent celebrations of racial, gender, and ethnic differences such as Hispanic Heritage Week and Black History Month.

In addition to the Valuing Differences program, the company preserved its EEO and affirmative action functions. Valuing Differences focuses on personal and group development, EEO on legal issues, and affirmative action on systematic change. According to Alan Zimmerle, head of the Valuing Differences program, EEO and Valuing Differences are like two circles that touch but don't overlap—the first representing the legal need for diversity, the second the corporate desire for diversity. Affirmative action is a third circle that overlaps the other two and holds them together with policies and procedures

Together, these three circles can transform legal and social pressures into the competitive advantage of a more effective work force, higher morale, and the reputation of being a better place to work. As Zimmerle puts it, "Digital wants to be the employer of choice. We want our pick of the talent that's out there."

more than ever. The goal is to manage diversity in such a way as to get from a diverse work force the same productivity we once got from a homogeneous work force, and to do it without artificial programs, standards, or barriers.

Managing diversity does not mean controlling or containing diversity, it means enabling every member of your work force to perform to his or her potential. It means getting from employees, first, everything we have a right to expect, and second—if we do it well—everything they have to give. If the old homogeneous work force performed dependably at 80 percent of its capacity, then the first result means getting 80 percent from the new heterogeneous work force too. But the second result, the icing on the cake, the unexpected upside that diversity can perhaps give as a bonus, means 85 percent to 90 percent from everyone in the organization.

For the moment, however, let's concentrate on the basics of how to get satisfactory performance from the new diverse work force. There are few adequate models. So far, no large company I know of has succeeded in managing diversity to its own satisfaction. But any number have begun to try.

On the basis of their experience, here are my 10 guidelines:

1. Clarify Your Motivation   A lot of executives are not sure why they should want to learn to manage diversity. Legal compliance seems like a good reason. So does community relations. Many executives believe they have a social and moral responsibility to employ minorities and women. Others want to placate an internal group or pacify an outside organization. None of these are bad reasons, but none of them are business reasons, and given the nature and scope of today's competitive challenges, I believe only business reasons will supply the necessary long-term motivation. In any case, it is the business reasons I want to focus on here.

In business terms, a diverse work force is not something your company ought to have; it's something your company does have, or soon will have. Learning to manage that diversity will make you more competitive.

2. Clarify Your Vision   When managers think about a diverse work force, what do they picture? Not publicly, but in the privacy of their minds?

One popular image is of minorities and women clustering on a relatively low plateau, with a few of them trickling up as they become assimilated into the prevailing culture. Of course, they enjoy good salaries and benefits, and most of them accept their status, appreciate the fact that they are doing better than they could do somewhere else, and are proud of the achievements of their race or sex. This is reactionary thinking, but it's a lot more common than you might suppose.

Another image is what we might call heightened sensitivity. Members of the majority culture are sensitive to the demands of minorities and women for upward mobility and recognize the advantages of fully utilizing them. Minorities and women work at all levels of the corporation, but they are the recipients of generosity and know it. A few years of this second-class status drives most of them away and compromises the effectiveness of those that remain. Turnover is high.

Then there is the coexistence-compromise image. In the interests of corporate viability, white males agree to recognize minorities and women as equals. They bargain and negotiate their differences. But the win-lose aspect of the relationship preserves tensions, and the compromises reached are not always to the company's competitive advantage.

Diversity and equal opportunity is a big step up. It presupposes that the white male culture has given way to one that respects difference and individuality. The problem is that minorities and women will accept it readily as their operating image, but many white males, consciously or unconsciously, are likely to cling to a vision that leaves them in the driver's seat. A vision gap of this kind can be a difficulty.

In my view, the vision to hold in your own imagination and to try to communicate to all your managers and employees is an image of fully tapping the human resource potential of every member of the work force. This vision sidesteps the question of equality, ignores the tensions of coexistence, plays down the uncomfortable realities of difference, and focuses instead on individual enablement. It doesn't say, "Let *us* give *them* a chance." It assumes a diverse work force that includes us and them. It says, "Let's create an environment where everyone will do their best work."

Several years ago, an industrial plant in Atlanta with a highly diverse work force was threatened with closing unless productivity improved. To save their jobs, everyone put their shoulders to the wheel and achieved the results they needed to stay open. The senior operating manager was amazed.

For years he had seen minorities and women plateauing disproportionately at the lower levels of the organization, and he explained that fact away with two rationalizations. "They haven't been here that long," he told himself. And "This is the price we pay for being in compliance with the law."

When the threat of closure energized this whole group of people into a level of performance he had not imagined possible, he got one fleeting glimpse of people working up to their capacity. Once the crisis was over, everyone went back to the earlier status quo—white males driving and everyone else sitting back, looking on—but now there was a difference. Now, as he put it himself, he had been to the mountaintop. He knew that what he was getting from minorities and women was nowhere near what they were capable of giving. And he wanted it, crisis or no crisis, all the time.

3. Expand Your Focus   Managers usually see affirmative action and equal employment opportunity as centering on minorities and women, with very little to offer white males. The diversity I'm talking about includes not only race, gender, creed, and ethnicity but also age, background, education, function, and personality differences. The objective is not to assimilate minorities and women into a dominant white male culture but to create a dominant heterogeneous culture.

The culture that dominates the United States socially and politically is heterogeneous, and it works by giving its citizens the liberty to achieve their potential. Channeling that potential, once achieved, is an individual right but still a national concern. Something similar applies in the workplace, where the keys to success are individual ability and a corporate destination. Managing disparate talents to achieve common goals is what companies learned to do when they set their sights on, say Total Quality. The secrets of managing diversity are much the same.

4. Audit Your Corporate Culture   If the goal is not to assimilate diversity into the dominant culture but rather to build a culture that can digest unassimilated diversity, then you had better start by figuring out what your present culture looks like. Because what we're talking about here is the body of unspoken and unexamined assumptions, values, and mythologies that make your world go round, this kind of cultural audit is impossible to conduct without outside help. It's a research activity, done mostly with in-depth interviews and a lot of listening at the water cooler.

The operative corporate assumptions you have to identify and deal with are often inherited from the company's founder. "If we treat everyone as a member of

---

EXHIBIT 4: Discovering Complexity and Value in P&G's Diversity

Because Procter & Gamble fills its upper-level management positions only from within the company, it places a premium on recruiting the best available entry-level employees. Campus recruiting is pursued nationwide and year-round by line managers from all levels of the company. Among other things, the company has made a concerted—and successful—effort to find and hire talented minorities and women.

Finding first-rate hires is only one piece of the effort, however. There is still the challenge of moving diversity upward. As one top executive put it, "We know that we can only succeed as a company if we have an environment that makes it easy for all of us, not just some of us, to work to our potential."

In May 1988, P&G formed a Corporate Diversity Strategy Task Force to clarify the concept of diversity, define its importance for the company, and identify strategies for making progress toward successfully managing a diverse work force.

The task force, composed of men and women from every corner of the company, made two discoveries: First, diversity at P&G was far more complex than most people had supposed. In addition to race and gender, it included factors such as cultural heritage, personal background, and functional experience. Second, the company needed to expand its view of the value of differences.

The task force helped the company to see that learning to manage diversity would be a long-term process of organizational change. For example, P&G has offered voluntary diversity training at all levels since the 1970s, but the program has gradually broadened its emphasis on race and gender awareness to include the value of self-realization in a diverse environment. As retiring board chairman John Smale put it, "If we can tap the total contribution that everybody in our company has to offer, we will be better and more competitive in everything we do."

P&G is now conducting a thorough, continuing evaluation of all management programs to be sure that systems are working well for everyone. It has also carried out a corporate survey to get a better picture of the problems facing P&G employees who are balancing work and family responsibilities and to improve company programs in such areas as dependent care.destination.

---

the family, we will be successful" is not uncommon. Nor is its corollary "Father Knows Best."

Another widespread assumption, probably absorbed from American culture in general, is that "cream will rise to the top." In most companies, what passes for cream rising to the top is actually cream being pulled or pushed to the top by an informal system of mentoring and sponsorship.

Corporate culture is a kind of tree. Its roots are assumptions about the company and about the world. Its branches, leaves, and seeds are behavior. You can't change the leaves without changing the roots, and you can't grow peaches on an oak. Or rather, with the proper grafting, you *can* grow peaches on an oak, but they come out an awful lot like acorns—small and hard and not much fun to eat. So if you want to grow peaches, you have to make sure the tree's roots are peach friendly.

5. Modify Your Assumptions   The real problem with this corporate culture tree is that every time you go to make changes in the roots, you run into terrible opposition. Every culture, including corporate culture, has root guards that turn out in force every time you threaten a basic assumption.

Take the family assumption as an example. Viewing the corporation as a family suggests not only that father knows best; it also suggests that sons will inherit the business, that daughters should stick to doing the company dishes, and that if Uncle Deadwood doesn't perform, we'll put him in the chimney corner and feed him for another 30 years regardless. Each assumption has its constituency and its defenders. If we say to Uncle Deadwood, "Yes, you did good work for 10 years, but years 11 and 12 look pretty bleak; we think it's time we helped you find another chimney," shock waves will travel through the company as every family-oriented employee draws a sword to defend the sacred concept of guaranteed jobs.

But you have to try. A corporation that wants to create an environment with no advantages or disadvantages for any group cannot allow the family assumption to remain in place. It must be labeled dishonest mythology.

Sometimes the dishonesties are more blatant. When I asked a white male middle manager how promotions were handled in his company, he said, "You need leadership capability, bottom-line results, the ability to work with people, and compassion." Then he paused and smiled, "That's what they say. But down the hall there's a guy we call Captain Kickass. He's ruthless, mean-spirited, and he steps on people. That's the behavior they really value. Forget what they say."

In addition to the obvious issue of hypocrisy, this example also raises a question of equal opportunity. When I asked this young middle manager if he thought minorities and women could meet the Captain Kickass standard, he said he thought they probably could. But the opposite argument can certainly be made. Whether we're talking about blacks in an environment that is predominantly white, whites in one predominantly black, or women in one predominantly male, the majority culture will not readily condone such tactics from a member of a minority. So the corporation with the unspoken kickass performance standard has at least one criterion that will hamper the upward mobility of minorities and women.

Another destructive assumption is the melting pot I referred to earlier. The organization I'm arguing for respects differences rather than seeking to smooth them out. It is multicultural rather than culture blind, which has an important consequence. When we no longer force people to "belong" to a common ethnicity or culture, then the organization's leaders must work all the harder to define belonging in terms of a set of values and a sense of purpose that transcend the interests, desires, and preferences of any one group.

6. Modify Your Systems   The first purpose of examining and modifying assumptions is to modify systems. Promotion, mentoring, and sponsorship comprise one such system, and the unexamined cream-to-the-top assumption I mentioned earlier can tend to keep minorities and women from climbing the corporate ladder. After all, in many companies it is difficult to secure a promotion above a certain level without a personal advocate or sponsor. In the context of managing diversity, the

EXHIBIT 5: The Daily Experience of Genuine Workplace Diversity

Chairman David T. Kearns believes that a firm and resolute commitment to affirmative action is the first and most important step to work-force diversity. "Xerox is committed to affirmative action," he says. "It is a corporate value, a management priority, and a formal business objective."

Xerox began recruiting minorities and women systematically as far back as the mid-1960s, and it pioneered such concepts as pivotal jobs (described later). The company's approach emphasizes behavior expectations as opposed to formal consciousness-raising programs because, as one Xerox executive put it, "It's just not realistic to think that a day-and-a-half of training will change a person's thinking after 30 or 40 years."

On the assumption that attitude changes will grow from the daily experience of genuine workplace diversity, the Xerox Balanced Work Force Strategy sets goals for the number of minorities and women in each division and at every level. (For example, the goal for the top 300 executive-level jobs in one large division is 35% women by 1995, compared with 15% today.) "You *must* have a laboratory to work in," says Ted Payne, head of Xerox's Office of Affirmative Action and Equal Opportunity.

Minority and women's employee support groups have grown up in more than a dozen locations with the company's encouragement. But Xerox depends mainly on the three pieces of its balanced strategy to make diversity work.

First are the goals. Xerox sets recruitment and representation goals in accordance with federal guidelines and reviews them constantly to make sure they reflect work-force demographics. Any company with a federal contract is required to make this effort. But Xerox then extends the guidelines by setting diversity goals for its upper-level jobs and holding division and group managers accountable for reaching them.

The second piece is a focus on pivotal jobs, a policy Xerox adopted in the 1970s when it first noticed that minorities and women did not have the upward mobility the company wanted to see. By examining the backgrounds of top executives, Xerox was able to identify the key positions that all successful managers had held at lower levels and to set goals for getting minorities and women assigned to such jobs.

The third piece is an effort to concentrate managerial training not so much on managing diversity as on just plain managing people. What the company discovered when it began looking at managerial behavior toward minorities and women was that all too many managers didn't know enough about how to manage anyone, let alone people quite different from themselves.

question is not whether this system is maximally efficient but whether it works for all employees. Executives who only sponsor people like themselves are not making much of a contribution to the cause of getting the best from every employee.

Performance appraisal is another system where unexamined practices and patterns can have pernicious effects. For example, there are companies where official performance appraisals differ substantially from what is said informally, with the result that employees get their most accurate performance feedback through the grapevine. So if the grapevine is closed to minorities and women, they are left at a severe disadvantage. As one white manager observed, "If the blacks around here knew how they were really perceived, there would be a revolt." Maybe so. More important to your business, however, is the fact that without an accurate appraisal of performance, minority and women employees will find it difficult to correct or defend their alleged shortcomings.

7. Modify Your Models   The second purpose of modifying assumptions is to modify models of managerial and employee behavior. My own personal hobgoblin is one I call the Doer Model, often an outgrowth of the family assumption and of unchallenged paternalism. I have found the Doer Model alive and thriving in a dozen companies. It works like this:

Because father knows best, managers seek subordinates who will follow their lead and do as they do. If they can't find people exactly like themselves, they try to find people who aspire to be exactly like themselves. The goal is predictability and immediate responsiveness because the doer manager is not there to manage people but to do the business. In accounting departments, for example, doer managers do accounting, and subordinates are simply extensions of their hands and minds, sensitive to every signal and suggestion of managerial intent.

Doer managers take pride in this identity of purpose. "I wouldn't ask my people to do anything I wouldn't do myself," they say. "I roll up my sleeves and get in the trenches." Doer managers love to be in the trenches. It keeps them out of the line of fire.

But managers aren't supposed to be in the trenches, and accounting managers aren't supposed to do accounting. What they are supposed to do is create systems and a climate that allow accountants to do accounting, a climate that enables people to do what they've been charged to do. The right goal is doer subordinates, supported and empowered by managers who manage.

8. Help Your People Pioneer   Learning to manage diversity is a change process, and the managers involved are change agents. There is no single tried-and-tested "solution" to diversity and no fixed right way to manage it. Assuming the existence of a single or even dominant barrier under values the importance of all the other barriers that face any company, including, potentially, prejudice, personality, community dynamics, culture, and the ups and downs of business itself.

While top executives articulate the new company policy and their commitment to it, middle managers—most or all of them still white males, remember—are placed in the tough position of having to cope with a forest of problems and simultaneously develop the minorities and women who represent their own competition for an increasingly limited number of promotions. What's more, every time they stumble they will themselves be labeled the major barriers to progress. These managers need help, they need a certain amount of sympathy, and most of all, perhaps, they need to be told that they are pioneers and judged accordingly.

In one case, an ambitious young black woman was assigned to a white male manager, at his request, on the basis of her excellent company record. They looked forward to working together, and for the first three months, everything went well.

But then their relationship began to deteriorate, and the harder they worked at patching it up, the worse it got. Both of them, along with their superiors, were surprised by the conflict and seemed puzzled as to its causes. Eventually, the black woman requested and obtained reassignment. But even though they escaped each other, both suffered a sense of failure severe enough to threaten their careers.

What could have been done to assist them? Well, empathy would not have hurt. But perspective would have been better yet. In their particular company and situation, these two people had placed themselves at the cutting edge of race and gender relations. They needed to know that mistakes at the cutting edge are different—and potentially more valuable—than mistakes elsewhere. Maybe they needed some kind of pioneer training. But at the very least they needed to be told that they were pioneers, that conflicts and failures came with the territory, and that they would be judged accordingly.

9. Apply the Special Consideration Test   I said earlier that affirmative action was an artificial, transitional, but necessary stage on the road to a truly diverse work force. Because of its artificial nature, affirmative action requires constant attention and drive to make it work. The point of learning once and for all how to manage diversity is that all that energy can be focused somewhere else.

There is a simple test to help you spot the diversity programs that are going to eat up enormous quantities of time and effort. Surprisingly, perhaps, it is the same test you might use to identify the programs and policies that created your problems in the first place. The test consists of one question: Does this program, policy, or principle give special consideration to one group? Will it contribute to everyone's success, or will it only produce an advantage for blacks or whites or women or men? Is it designed for *them* as opposed to *us*? Whenever the answer is yes, you're not yet on the road to managing diversity.

This does not rule out the possibility of addressing issues that relate to a single group. It only underlies the importance of determining that the issue you're addressing does not relate to other groups as well. For example, management in one company noticed that blacks were not moving up in the organization. Before instituting a special program to bring them along, managers conducted interviews to see if they could find the reason for the impasse. What blacks themselves reported was a problem with the quality of supervision. Further interviews showed that other employees too—including white males—were concerned about the quality of supervision and felt that little was being done to foster professional development. Correcting the situation eliminated a problem that affected everyone. In this case, a solution that focused only on blacks would have been out of place.

Had the problem consisted of prejudice, on the other hand, or some other barrier to blacks or minorities alone, a solution based on affirmative action would have been perfectly appropriate.

10. Continue Affirmative Action   Let me come full circle. The ability to manage diversity is the ability to manage your company without unnatural advantage or disadvantage for any member of your diverse work force. The fact remains that first you must have a work force that is diverse at every level, and if you don't, you're going to need affirmative action to get from here to there.

The reason you then want to move beyond affirmative action to managing diversity is because affirmative action fails to deal with the root causes of prejudice and inequality and does little to develop the full potential of every man and woman in the company. In a country seeking competitive advantage in a global economy, the goal of managing diversity is to develop our capacity to accept, incorporate, and empower the diverse human talents of the most diverse nation on earth. It's our reality. We need to make it our strength.

DISCUSSION QUESTIONS

1. According to Thomas, what is the primary value of Affirmative Action programs?
2. Assess one of your current/past employers, or this college, in terms of Thomas' six-step cycle. Where are these organizations in terms of managing diversity? What changes have you observed as a result of their successes or failures in this process?
3. Thomas writes that the "melting pot" metaphor is really a myth. Do you agree or disagree with his views? Why?
4. The Avon, Procter & Gamble, Digital, Corning, and Xerox examples indicate that organizations can approach the challenge of managing diversity from different perspectives. Which of these seems the most directed toward improving customer service, which toward understanding its customers better, and which toward promoting productivity?
5. How can an organization work toward "managing diversity" when resources are restricted due to economic downturns?
6. What are some of the advantages for white males in a company that has managing diversity as a strategic imperative?

A review of the "arguments and research data on how managing diversity can create a competitive advantage." Cox and Blake

Managing Cultural Diversity: Implications for Organizational Competitiveness

Taylor H. Cox
Stacy Blake
Both of University of Michigan

OVERVIEW

The recent business trends of globalization and increasing ethnic and gender diversity are turning managers' attention to the management of cultural differences. The management literature has suggested that organizations should value diversity to enhance organizational effectiveness. However, the specific link between managing diversity and organizational competitiveness is rarely made explicit and no article has reviewed actual research data supporting such a link.

This article reviews arguments and research data on how managing diversity can create a competitive advantage. We address cost, attraction of human resources, marketing success, creativity and innovation, problem-solving quality, and organizational flexibility as six dimensions of business performance directly impacted by the management of cultural diversity. We then offer suggestions for improving organizational capability to manage this diversity

Workforce demographics for the United States and many other nations of the world indicate that managing diversity will be on the agendas of organizational leaders throughout the 90s. For example, a recent report of the workforces of 21 nations shows that nearly all of the growth in the labor force between now and 2000 will occur in nations with predominately non-Caucasian populations. Behind these statistics are vastly different age and fertility rates for people of different racioethnic groups. In the United States for example, the average white female is 33 years old and has (or will have) 1.7 children. Corresponding figures for blacks are 28 and 2.4, and for Mexican-Americans, 26 and 2.9.[1]

Leading consultants, academics and business leaders have advocated that organizations respond to these trends with a "valuing diversity" approach. They point out that a well managed, diverse workforce holds potential competitive advantages for organizations.[2] However, the logic of the valuing diversity argument is rarely made explicit, and we are aware of no article that reviews actual data supporting the

Reprinted with permission of Academy of Management from *Academy of Management Executive* (1991, vol. 5, no. 3).

linkage of managing diversity and organizational competitiveness. This article reviews the arguments and research data on this link, and offers suggestions on improving organizational capability for managing cultural diversity. As shown in Exhibit 1, the term managing diversity refers to a variety of management issues and activities related to hiring and effective utilization of personnel from different cultural backgrounds.

DIVERSITY AS A COMPETITIVE ADVANTAGE

Social responsibility goals of organizations is only one area that benefits from the management of diversity. We will focus on six other areas where sound management can create a competitive advantage: (1) cost, (2) resource acquisition, (3) marketing, (4) creativity, (5) problem-solving, (6) organizational flexibility.[3] Exhibit 2 briefly explains their relationship to diversity management.

The first two items of the exhibit, the cost and resource acquisition arguments, are what we call the "inevitability-of-diversity" issues. Competitiveness is affected by the need (because of national and cross-national workforce demographic trends) to hire more women, minorities, and foreign nationals. The marketing, creativity, problem-solving, and system flexibility argument, are derived from what we call the value-in-diversity hypothesis—that diversity brings net-added value to organization processes.

Cost

Organizations have not been as successful in managing women and racioethnic minorities (racially and/or ethnically different from the white/Anglo majority) as white males. Data show that turnover and absenteeism are often higher among women and racioethnic minorities than for white males. For example, one study reported that the overall turnover rate for blacks in the United States workforce is forty percent higher than for whites. Also, Corning Glass recently reported that between 1980-87, turnover among women in professional jobs was double that of men, and the rates for blacks were 2.5 times those of whites. A two-to-one ratio for women/men turnover was also cited by Felice Schwartz in her article on multiple career tracks for women in management.[4]

Job satisfaction levels are also often lower for minorities. A recent study that measured job satisfaction among black and white MBAs revealed that blacks were significantly less satisfied with their overall careers and advancement than whites.[5]

Frustration over career growth and cultural conflict with the dominant, white-male culture may be the major factor behind the different satisfaction levels. Two recent surveys of male and female managers in large American companies found that although women expressed a much higher probability of leaving their current employer than men, and had higher actual turnover rates, their primary reasons for quitting were lack of career growth opportunity or dissatisfaction with rates of

EXHIBIT 1: Spheres of Activity in the Management of Cultural Diversity

Organization Culture
- valuing differences
- prevailing value system
- cultural inclusion

HR Management Systems (Bias Free)
- recruitment
- training and development
- performance appraisal
- compensation and benefits
- promotion

Higher Career Involvement of Women
- dual-career couples
- sexes and sexual harassment
- work-family conflict

Heterogeneity in Race/Ethnicity/Nationality
- effect on cohesiveness, communication, conflict, morale
- effects of group identity on interactions (e.g., stereotyping)
- prejudice (racism, ethnocentrism)

Management of Cultural Diversity

Mind-Sets about Diversity
- problem or opportunity?
- challenge met or barely addressed?
- level of majority-culture buy-in (resistance or support)

Cultural Differences
- promoting knowledge and acceptance
- taking advantage of the opportunities that diversity provides

Education Programs
- improve public schools
- educate management on valuing differences

66

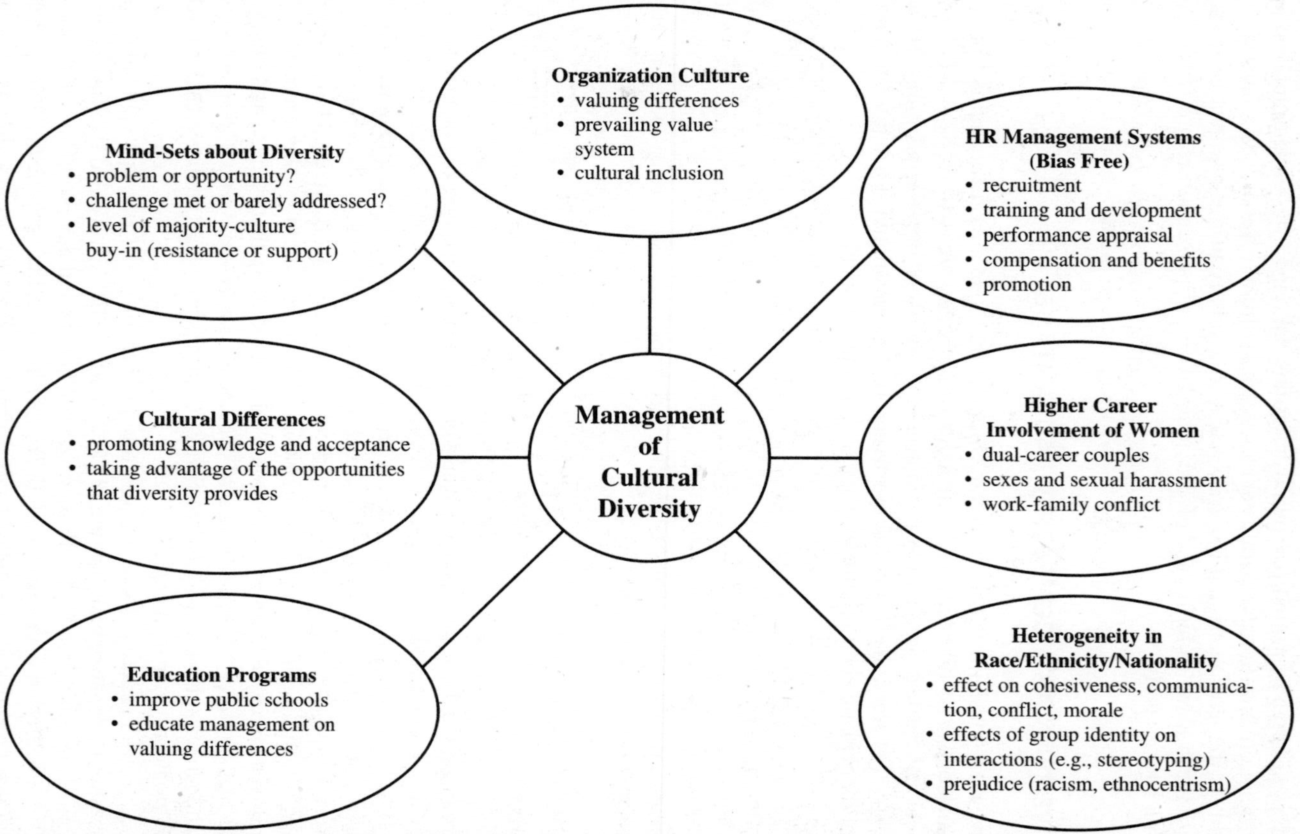

EXHIBIT 2: Managing Cultural Diversity Can Provide Competitive Advantage

1. Cost Argument	As organizations become more diverse, the cost of a poor job in integrating workers will increase. Those who handle this well will thus create cost advantages over those who don't.
2. Resource-acquisition Argument	Companies develop reputations on favorability as prospective employers of women and ethnic minorities. Those with the best reputations for managing diversity will win the competition for the best personnel. As the labor pool shrinks and changes composition, this edge will become increasingly important.
3. Marketing Argument	For multinational organizations, the insight and cultural sensitivity that members with roots in other countries bring to the marketing effort should improve these efforts in important ways. The same rationale applies to marketing to subpopulations within domestic operations.
4. Creativity Argument	Diversity of perspectives and less emphasis on conformity to norms of the past (which characterize the modern approach to management of diversity) should improve the level of creativity.
5. Problem-solving Argument	Heterogeneity in decision and problem solving groups potentially produces better decisions through a wider range of perspectives and more thorough critical analysis of issues.
6. System Flexibility Argument	An implication of the multicultural model for managing diversity is that the system will become less determinant, less standardized, and therefore more fluid. The increased fluidity should create greater flexibility to react to environmental changes (i.e., reactions should be faster and at less cost).

progress. One of the surveys also discovered that women have higher actual turnover rates at all ages, and not just during the child-bearing and child-rearing years.[6]

Organizations that fail to make appropriate changes to more successfully use and keep employees from different backgrounds can expect to suffer a significant competitive disadvantage compared to those that do. Alternatively, organizations quick to create an environment where all personnel can thrive should gain a competitive cost advantage over nonresponsive or slowly responding companies.

Cost implications in managing diversity also occur in benefits and work schedules. In one study, companies were assigned an "accommodation score" based on the adoption of four benefit-liberalization changes associated with pregnant workers. Analysis revealed that the higher the company's accommodation score, the lower the number of sick days taken by pregnant workers and the more willing they were to work overtime during pregnancy.[7]

Two other studies investigated the effect of company investment in day care on human resource cost variables. In one study, turnover and absenteeism rates for working mothers using a company-sponsored child development center were compared to those who either had no children or had no company assistance. Absenteeism for the day care users versus the other groups was thirty-eight percent lower and the turnover rate was less than two percent compared to more than six percent for the nonbenefit groups. The second study showed that in a company that initiated an in-house child care facility, worker attitudes improved on six measures including organizational commitment and job satisfaction. In addition, turnover declined by sixty-three percent.[8]

Greater use of flextime work scheduling is another type of organizational accommodation to diversity. A recent field experiment assessing the impact of flextime use on absenteeism and worker performance found that both short- and long-term absence declined significantly. Three out of four worker efficiency measures also increased significantly.[9]

Cost savings of organizational changes must be judged against the investment. Nevertheless, the data strongly suggest that managing diversity efforts have reduced absenteeism and turnover costs, as cited earlier.

Research evidence relevant to cost implications of managing diversity on some dimensions other than benefit and work-schedule changes comes from a UCLA study of the productivity of culturally heterogeneous and culturally homogeneous work teams. Among the heterogeneous teams, some were more and some were less productive than the homogeneous teams.[10] This research suggests that if work teams "manage" the diversity well, they can make diversity an asset to performance. For example, all members should have ample opportunity to contribute and potential communications, group cohesiveness, and interpersonal conflict issues need to be successfully addressed. Alternatively, if diversity is ignored or mishandled, it may detract from performance.

Actual cost savings from improving the management of diversity are difficult to determine. It is, however, possible to estimate those related to turnover. For example, let us assume an organization has 10,000 employees in which 35 percent of personnel are either women or racio-ethnic minorities. Let us also assume a white male turnover rate of ten percent. Using the previous data on differential turnover rates for women and racioethnic minorities of roughly double the rate for white males, we can estimate a loss of 350 additional employees from the former groups. If we further assume that half of the turnover rate difference can be eliminated with better management, and that total turnover cost averages $20,000 per employee, the potential annual cost savings is $3.5 million. This example only addresses turnover, and additional savings may be realized from other changes such as higher productivity levels.

Although accurate dollar cost savings figures from managing diversity initiatives of specific companies are rarely published, Ortho Pharmaceuticals has calculated its savings to date at $500,000, mainly from lower turnover among women and ethnic minorities.[11]

Resource Acquisition

Attracting and retaining excellent employees from different demographic groups is the second "inevitability"-related competitiveness issue. As women and racioethnic minorities increase in proportional representation in the labor pool, organizations must compete to hire and retain workers from these groups. Recently published accounts of the "best companies" for women and for blacks have made public and highlighted organizations which are leaders in organizational change efforts to effectively manage diversity.[12] In addition to listing the best companies, the publications also discuss why certain companies were excluded from the list.

The impact of these publications on recruitment of quality personnel has already begun to surface. Merck, Xerox, Syntex, Hoffman-La Roche, and Hewlett-Packard have been aggressively using favorable publicity to recruit women and racioethnic minorities. According to company representatives, the recognitions are, in fact, boosting recruiting efforts. For example, Merck cites its identification as one of the ten best companies for working mothers as instrumental in recent increases in applications.[13]

As these reputations grow, and the supply of white males in the labor market shrinks, the significance of the resource acquisition issue for organizational competitiveness will be magnified.

Marketing

Markets are becoming as diverse as the workforce. Selling goods and services is facilitated by a representational workforce in several ways. First, companies with good reputations have correspondingly favorable public relations. Just as people, especially women and racioethnic minorities, may prefer to work for an employer who values diversity, they may also prefer to buy from such organizations.

Second, there is evidence that culture has a significant effect on consumer behavior. For example, in the Chinese culture, values such as a tradition of thrift, and teenagers' deference to their parent's wishes in making purchases, have been identified as affecting consumer behavior.[14] While much of the research on cross-cultural differences in consumer behavior has focused on cross-national comparisons, this research is also relevant to intra-country ethnic group differences.

Immigration from Latin American and Asia will continue to be high in the 90's. This represents a large influx of first-generation Americans having strong ties to their root cultures. Acculturation patterns among Asian and Hispanic Americans indicates that substantial identity with the root cultures remain even after three or more generations of United States citizenship. This implies that firms may gain competitive advantage by using employee insight to understand culture effects on buying decisions and map strategies to respond to them.

USA Today provides a good example. Nancy Woodhull, president of Gannett News Media, maintains that the newspaper's marketing success is largely attributable to the presence of people from a wide variety of cultural backgrounds in daily news meetings. Group diversity was planned and led to a representation of different viewpoints because people of different genders and racioethnic backgrounds have different experiences shaped by group identities.

Avon Corporation used cultural diversity to turn around low profitability in its inner-city markets. Avon made personnel changes to give black and Hispanic managers substantial authority over these markets. These formerly unprofitable sectors improved to the point where they are now among Avon's most productive U.S. markets. Avon President Jim Preston commented that members of a given cultural group are uniquely qualified to understand certain aspects of the world view of persons from that group.

In some cases, people from a minority culture are more likely to give patronage to a representative of their own group. For at least some products and services, a multicultural salesforce may facilitate sales to members of minority culture groups.

Cultural diversification of markets is not limited to U.S. companies. Globalization is forcing major companies from many nations to address cultural difference effects among consumers. The fact that the U.S. contains one of the most culturally heterogeneous populations in the world represents a possible advantage in "national" competitiveness. Just having diversity, however, is not sufficient to produce benefits. We must also manage it.

Creativity

Advocates of the value-in-diversity hypothesis suggest that work team heterogeneity promotes creativity and innovation (see endnote 1). Research tends to support this relationship. Kanger's study of innovation in organizations revealed that the most innovative companies deliberately establish heterogeneous teams to "create a marketplace of ideas, recognizing that a multiplicity of points of view need to be brought to bear on a problem" (p. 167). Kanter also specifically noted that companies high on innovation had done a better job than most on eradicating racism, sexism, and classism and, tended to employ more women and racioethnic minorities than less innovative companies.[15]

Research by Charlene Nemeth found that minority views can stimulate consideration of non-obvious alternatives in task groups. In a series of experiments, participants were asked to form as many words as possible from a string of 10 letters. Individual approaches to the task were determined and then groups formed that were either majority (all members subscribed to the strategy for forming letters advocated by the majority of participants) and minority (non-majority individuals were present in the groups). Nemeth found that the "minority" groups adopted multiple strategies and identified more solutions than the "majority" groups. She concluded that the groups exposed to minority views were more creative than the more homogeneous, majority groups. She further concluded that persistent exposure to minority viewpoints stimulates creative thought processes.

Another experiment compared the creativity of teams that were homogeneous on a series of attitude measures against teams with heterogeneous attitudes. Problem solution creativity was judged on originality and practicality. Results indicated that as long as the team members had similar ability levels, the heterogeneous teams were more creative than the homogeneous ones.[16] If people from different gender, nationality, and racioethnic groups hold different attitudes and perspectives on issues, then cultural diversity should increase team creativity and innovation.

> *Attitudes, cognitive functioning, and beliefs are not randomly distributed in the population but tend to vary systematically with demographic variables such as age, race, and gender.[17] Thus, an expected consequence of increased cultural diversity in organizations is the presence of different perspectives for problem solving, decision making, and creative tasks.*

Specific steps must be taken, however, to realize this benefit. The research shows that in order to obtain the performance benefits, it was necessary for heterogeneous team members to have awareness of the attitudinal differences of other members. Similarly, diversity needs to be managed in part, by informing workgroup members of their cultural differences. In recognition of this, cultural awareness training has become a standard element of organization change projects focusing on managing diversity.

Problem Solving

Diverse groups have a broader and richer base of experience from which to approach a problem. Thus, managing diversity also has the potential to improve problem solving and decision making.

In the 1960s, several University of Michigan studies discovered that heterogeneous groups produced better quality solutions to assigned problems that homogeneous groups. Dimensions of group diversity included personality measures and gender. In one study, sixty-five percent of heterogeneous groups produced high quality solutions (solutions that provided either new, modified, or integrative approaches to the problem) compared to only twenty-one percent of the homogeneous groups. This difference was statistically significant. The researchers noted that "mixing sexes and personalities appears to have freed these groups from the restraints of the solutions given in the problem."[18]

Later studies also confirmed the effects of heterogeneity on group decision quality. The same conclusion is indirectly indicated by research on the "groupthink" phenomenon—the absence of critical thinking in groups caused partly by excessive preoccupation with maintaining cohesiveness. Most of the examples of groupthink cited in the literature, such as the decision of the Kennedy administration to invade Cuba in 1961, portray decision processes as producing disastrous results. Because group cohesiveness is directly related to degrees of homogeneity, and groupthink only occurs in highly cohesive groups, the presence of cultural diversity in groups should reduce its probability.[19]

Decision quality is best when neither excessive diversity nor excessive homogeneity are present. This point has been well summarized by Sheppard: "Similarity is an aid to developing cohesion; cohesion in turn, is related to the success of a group. Homogeneity, however, can be detrimental if it results in the absence of stimulation. If all members are alike, they may have little to talk about, they may compete with each other, or they may all commit the same mistake. Variety is the spice of life in a group, so long as there is a basic core of similarity."[20]

A core of similarity among group members is desirable. This theme is similar to the "core value" concept advocated in the organization culture literature.[21] Our interpretation is that all members must share some common values and norms to promote coherent actions on organizational goals. The need for heterogeneity, to promote problem solving and innovation, must be balanced with the need for organizational coherence and unity of action.

Additional support for the superior problem solving of diverse workgroups comes from the work of Nemeth cited earlier. In a series of studies, she found that the level of critical analysis of decision issues and alternatives was higher in groups subjected to minority views than in those which were not. The presence of minority views improved the quality of the decision process regardless of whether or not the minority view ultimately prevailed. A larger number of alternatives were considered and there was a more thorough examination of assumptions and implications of alternative scenarios.[22]

In sum, culturally diverse workforces create competitive advantage through better decisions. A variety of perspectives brought to the issue, higher levels of critical analysis of alternatives through minority-influence effects, and lower probability of groupthink all contribute.

System Flexibility

Managing diversity enhances organizational flexibility. There are two primary bases for this assertion. First, there is some evidence that women and racioethnic minorities tend to have especially flexible cognitive structures. For example, research has shown that women tend to have a higher tolerance for ambiguity than men. Tolerance for ambiguity, in turn, has been linked to a number of factors related to flexibility such as cognitive complexity, and the ability to excel in performing ambiguous tasks.[23]

Studies on bilingual versus monolingual sub-populations from several nations show that compared to monolinguals, bilinguals have higher levels of divergent thinking and of cognitive flexibility.[24] Since the incidence of bilingualism is much greater among minority culture groups (especially Hispanics and Asians) than the majority-white Anglo group, this research strongly supports the notion that cognitive flexibility is enhanced by the inclusion of these groups in predominantly Anglo workforces.

The second way that managing cultural diversity may enhance organizational flexibility is that as policies and procedures are broadened and operating methods become less standardized, the organization becomes more fluid and adaptable. The tolerance for different cultural viewpoints should lead to greater openness to new ideas in general. Most important of all, if organizations are successful in overcoming resistance to change in the difficult area of accepting diversity, it should be well positioned to handle resistance to other types of change.

SUGGESTIONS FOR ORGANIZATION CHANGE

We have reviewed six ways in which the presence of cultural diversity and its effective management can yield a competitive advantage. Organizations wishing to maximize the benefits and minimize the drawbacks of diversity, in terms of work-group cohesiveness, interpersonal conflict, turnover, and coherent action on major organizational goals, must create "multicultural" organizations. The typical organization of the past has been either monolithic (homogeneous membership with a culture dominated by one cultural group) or plural (ostensibly diverse membership but still culturally monolithic and without valuing and using differences to benefit the organization). By contrast, the multicultural organization is one where members of nontraditional backgrounds can contribute and achieve to their fullest potential.

The multicultural organization's specific features are as follows: (1) Pluralism: reciprocal acculturation where all cultural groups respect, value, and learn from one another; (2) full structural integration of all cultural groups so that they are well represented at all levels of the organization; (3) full integration of minority culture-group members in the informal networks of the organization; (4) an absence of prejudice and discrimination; (5) equal identification of minority- and majority-group members with the goals of the organization, and with opportunity for alignment of organizational and personal career goal achievement; (6) a minimum of inter-group conflict which is based on race, gender, nationality, and other identity groups of organization members.[25]

Five key components are needed to transform traditional organizations into multicultural ones.

1. Leadership
2. Training
3. Research
4. Analysis and change of culture and human resource management systems
5. Follow up

Each of these are briefly discussed.

Leadership

Top management's support and genuine commitment to cultural diversity is crucial. Champions for diversity are needed—people who will take strong personal stands on the need for change, role model the behaviors required for change, and assist with the work of moving the organization forward. Commitment must go beyond sloganism. For example, are human, financial, and technical resources being provided? Is this item prominently featured in the corporate strategy and consistently made a part of senior level staff meetings? Is there a willingness to change human resource management systems such as performance appraisal and executive bonuses? Is there a willingness to keep mental energy and financial support focused on this for a period of years, not months or weeks? If the answer to all of these questions is yes, the organization has genuine commitment, if not, then a potential problem with leadership is indicated.

Top management commitment is crucial but not sufficient. Champions are also needed at lower organizational levels, especially key line managers. Many organizations are addressing the leadership requirement by the formation of task forces or advisory committees on diversity, often headed by a senior manager. Some companies also have a designated manager for diversity who oversees the work company-wide (examples include Corning Inc. and Allstate Insurance). We advise using the manager of diversity in addition to, rather than as a substitute for, a broader involvement team such as a diversity task force. This is especially important in the early stages of the work.

Training

Managing and valuing diversity (MVD) training is the most prevalent starting point for managing diversity. Two types of training are popular: awareness training and skill-building training. Awareness training focuses on creating an understanding of the need for, and meaning of, managing and valuing diversity. It is also meant to increase participants self awareness on diversity related issues such as stereotyping and cross-cultural differences and how to respond to differences in the workplace. Often the two types are combined. Avon, Ortho Pharmaceuticals, Procter and Gamble, and Hewlett-Packard are examples of companies with extensive experience with training programs.

Training is a crucial first step. However, it has limitations as an organization change tool and should not be used in isolation. It is also important to treat training as an on-going education process rather than a one-shot seminar.

Research

Collection of information about diversity-related issues is the third key component. Many types of data are needed including traditional equal-opportunity profile data, analysis of attitudes and perceptions of employees, and data which highlights the career experiences of different cultural groups (e.g., are mentors equally accessible to all members).

Research has several important uses. First, it is often helpful for identifying issues to be addressed in the education process. For example, data indicating differences of opinion about the value in diversity based on culture group can be used as a launching point for mixed-culture discussion groups in training sessions. Second, research helps identify areas where changes are needed and provides clues about how to make them. Third, research is necessary to evaluate the change effort. Baseline data on key indicators of the valuing diversity environment needs to be gathered and periodically updated to assess progress.

Culture and Management Systems Audit

A comprehensive analysis of the organization culture and human resource systems such as recruitment, performance appraisal, potential assessment and promotion, and compensation should be undertaken. The primary objectives of this audit are: (1) to uncover sources of potential bias unfavorable to members of certain cultural groups, and (2) to identify ways that corporate culture may inadvertently put some members at a disadvantage.

It is important to look beyond surface data in auditing systems. For example, research that we reviewed or conducted indicated that even when average performance ratings for majority versus minority culture members are essentially the same, there may be differences in the relative priority placed on individual performance criteria, the distribution of the highest ratings, or the relationship between performance ratings and promotion.[26] The audit must be an in-depth analysis, and the assistance of an external cultural diversity expert is strongly advised.

> To identify ways that corporate culture may put some members at a disadvantage, consider a scenario where a prominent value in the organization culture is "aggressiveness." Such a value may place certain groups at a disadvantage if the norms of their secondary or alternative culture discouraged this behavior. This is indeed the case for many Asians and for women in many countries including the United States. While it is conceivable that the preservation of this value may be central to organizational effectiveness (in which case the solution may be to acknowledge the differential burden of conformity that some members must bear and to give assistance to them in learning the required behaviors), it may also be that the organizational values need to change so that other styles of accomplishing work are acceptable and perhaps even preferred. The point is that the prevailing values and norms must be identified and then examined critically in light of the diversity of the workforce.

Follow-up

The final component, follow-up, consists of monitoring change, evaluating the results, and ultimately institutionalizing the changes as part of the organization's regular on-going processes. Like other management efforts, there is a need for account-ability and control for work on diversity. Accountability for overseeing the change process might initially be assigned to the diversity task force, or if available, man-ager of diversity. Ultimately, however, accountability for preserving the changes must be established with every manager. Changes in the performance appraisal and reward processes are often needed to accomplish this.

Follow-up activities should include additional training, repetition of the sys-tems audit, and use of focus groups for on-going discussions about diversity is-sues.[27]

> *The results of the audit must be translated into an agenda for specific changes in the organization culture and systems which management must then work to implement.*

CONCLUSION

Organizations' ability to attract, retain, and motivate people from diverse cultural backgrounds may lead to competitive advantages in cost structures and through maintaining the highest quality human resources. Further capitalizing on the poten-tial benefits of cultural diversity in work groups, organizations may gain a competi-tive advantage in creativity, problem solving, and flexible adaptation to change. We have identified steps that organizations can take toward accomplishing this.

While this article has reviewed a significant amount of relevant research, ad-ditional work clearly needs to be done, especially on the "value-in-diversity" issues. Nevertheless the arguments, data, and suggestions presented here should be useful to organizations to build commitment and promote action for managing diversity ef-forts in the 1990s and beyond.

NOTES

1. See William B. Johnston, Global Work Force 2000. *Harvard Business Review.* March/April 1991, and "Middle-age at 26," *Wall Street Journal*, April 10, 1990.
2. For examples of the competitive advantage argument, see R. Roosevelt Thomas, Jr., "From Affirmative Action to Affirming Diversity," *Harvard Business Re-view*, 2, March/April 1990, 107–117; Lennie Copeland, "Learning to Manage a Multicultural Workforce," *Training*, May 1988, 48–56; Barbara Mandrell and Susan Kohler-Gray, "Management Development that Values Diversity," *Per-sonnel*, 67, March 1990, 41–47; Katherine Etsy, "Diversity Is Good for Busi-ness," *Executive Excellence*, 5, 1988, 5–6; and A.G. Sodano and S.G. Baler, "Accommodation to Contrast: Being Different in the Organization," *New Direc-tions in Mental Health*, 20, 1983, 25–36.
3. This focus is not intended to undermine the importance of social, moral, and le-gal reasons for attention to diversity. We have chosen to address its relevance for other types of goals, such as worker productivity and quality of decision

making, because the impact of diversity in these areas has received relatively little attention in the past compared to the equal-opportunity related goals.

4. See the following sources for details on the turnover data: B.R. Bergmann and W.R. Krause, "Evaluating and Forecasting Progress in Racial Integration of Employment," *Industrial and Labor Relations Review*, 1968, 399–409; Carol Hymowitz, "One Firm's Bid to Keep Blacks, Women," *Wall Street Journal*, February 16, 1989, Sec. B, 1; Felice Schwartz, "Management Women and the New Facts of Life," *Harvard Business Review*, January/February 1989, 65–76.

5. Taylor Cox, Jr., and Stella Nkomo, "A Race and Gender Group Analysis of the Early Career Experience of MBA," *Work and Occupations*, 1991.

6. These surveys were reviewed by Cathy Trost, "Women Managers Quit Not for Family But to Advance Their Corporate Climb," *Wall Street Journal*, May 2, 1990. For additional evidence on this point, including discussions of the cultural-conflict issue, see Schwartz, Endnote 3; A.M. Morrison, R.P. White and E. Van Velsor, "Executive Women: Substance Plus Style," *Psychology Today*, August 1987, 18–25; and Gail DeGeorge, "Corporate Women: They're About to Break Through to the Top," *Business Week*, June 22, 1987, 72–77.

7. "Helping Pregnant Workers Pays Off," *USA Today*, December 2, 1987.

8. Stewart A. Youngblood and Kimberly Chambers-Cook, "Child Care Assistance Can Improve Employee Attitudes and Behavior," *Personnel Administrator*, February 1984, 93–95 +.

9. Jay S. Kim and Anthony F. Campagna, "Effects of Flextime on Employee Attendance and Performance: A Field Experiment," *Academy of Management Journal*, December 14, 1981, 729–741.

10. Reported in Nancy Adler, *International Dimensions of Organizational Behavior* (Boston: Kent Publishing Co., 1986), 111.

11. The figure of $20,000 is based on computations of Michael Mercer for turnover costs of a computer programmer. Readers may wish to consult one of the following Sources for turnover cost formulas and then use their own job structure to determine cost factors for the actual turnover costs: Michael Mercer, "Turnover: Reducing the Costs," *Personnel,* Vol. 5, 1988, 36–42; Rene Darmon, "Identifying Sources of Turnover Costs," *Journal of Marketing*, 1990, Vol. 54, 46–56. The data on Ortho is provided in Juliane Bailey, "How to be Different but Equal," *Savvy Woman*, November, 1989, 47 +.

12. Examples of these publications include Baila Zeitz and Lorraine Dusky. *Best Companies for Women* (New York: Simon and Schuster, 1988); and "The 50 Best Places for Blacks to Work," *Black Enterprise*, February 1989, 73–91.

13. Selwyn Feinstein, "Being the Best on Somebody's List Does Attract Talent," *Wall Street Journal*, October 10, 1989. For other examples supporting the resource acquisition argument, see Joel Dreyfuss, "Get Ready for the New Work Force," *Fortune*, April 23, 1990, 165–181.

14. S.G. Redding, "Cultural Effects on the Marketing Process in Southeast Asia," *Journal of Market Research Society*, Vol. 24, 19, 98–114.

15. Rosabeth Moss Kanter, *The Change Masters*, (New York: Simon and Schuster, 1983).

16. For details on the research in this section, readers should see: Charlan Jeanne Nemeth, "Differential Contributions of Majority and Minority Influence," *Psychological Review*, 93, 1986, 23–32 and H.C. Triandis, E.R. Hall, and R.B. Ewen, "Member Homogeneity and Dyadic Creativity," *Human Relations*, 19, 1965, 33–54.

17. Susan E. Jackson, "Team Composition in Organizational Settings: Issues in Managing a Diverse Workforce," in *Group Process & Productivity*, J. Simpson, S. Warchel and W. Woods (eds.) (Beverly Hills, CA: Sage Publications, 1989).

18. L. Richard Hoffman and Norman R.F. Maier, "Quality and Acceptance of Problem Solving by Members of Homogeneous and Heterogeneous Groups," *Journal of Abnormal and Social Psychology*, 62, 1961, 401–407. The quote in the text is from page 404.

19. For reviews of research on the effect of group heterogeneity on problem solving, see M.E. Shaw, *Group Dynamics: The Psychology of Small Group Behavior*, (New York: McGraw Hill, 1981); J.E. McGrath, *Groups: Interaction and Performance*, (Englewood Cliffs, N.J.: Prentice-Hall, 1984); and Irving Janis, *Victims of Groupthink*, (Boston: Houghton Mifflin Co., 1972).

20. C.R. Shepard, *Small Groups*, (San Francisco: Chandler Publishing Co., 1964), 118.

21. See Ed Schein, "Organizational Socialization and the Profession of Management," in D.A. Kolb, I.M. Rubin, and J.M. McIntyre (eds.), *Organizational Psychology*, Englewood Cliffs: Prentice-Hall, 1984, 7–21; and Y. Weiner, "Forms of Value Systems: A Focus on Organizational Effectiveness and Cultural Change and Maintenance," *Academy of Management Review*, 13, 1988, 534–545.

22. See Charlan Jeanne Nemeth, "Dissent, Group Process, and Creativity," *Advances in Group Processes,* 2, 1985, 57–75; and Charlan Jeanne Nemeth and Joel Wachter, "Creative Problem Solving as a Result of Majority versus Minority Influence," *European Journal of Social Psychology*, 13, 1983, 45–55.

23. See Naomi G. Rotter and Agnes N. O'Connell, "The Relationships Among Sex-Role Orientation, Cognitive Complexity, and Tolerance for Ambiguity," *Sex Roles*, 8(12), 1982, 1209–1220; and David R. Shaffer et al., "Interactive Effects of Ambiguity Tolerance and Task Effort on Dissonance Reduction," *Journal of Personality*, 41(2), June, 1973, 224–233.

24. These research studies are reviewed by Wallace Lambert, "The Effects of Bilingualism on the Individual: Cognitive and Sociocultural Consequences," in Peter A. Hurnbey (ed.), *Bilingualism: Psychological, Social, and Educational Implications*, New York: Academic Press, 1977, 15–27.

25. This discussion of traditional versus multicultural organizations is based on Taylor Cox's article, "The Multicultural Organization" which appeared in the May 1991 issue of *The Executive*.

26. For a specific example of race differences in priorities of performance rating criteria, see Taylor Cox and Stella Nkomo, "Differential Performance Appraisal Criteria," *Group and Organization Studies*, 11, 1986, 101–119. For an example of subtle bias in performance rating distributions see Asya Pazy's article: "The

Persistence of Pro-Male Bias," *Organization Behavior and Human Decision Processes*, 38, 1986, 366–377.

27. For additional discussion of organization change processes to manage diversity including specific examples of what pioneering companies are doing in this area, please see Taylor Cox's article, "The Multicultural Organization" (Endnote 24).

DISCUSSION QUESTIONS

1. This article discusses the benefits of worker diversity in terms of gender and race/ethnicity. Do you think the same benefits can occur with diversity of physical disability? Age? Sexual orientation? Explain why or why not.

2. Why is excessive heterogeneity (diversity) not recommended in the article? How do you avoid this?

3. List some of the possible reasons that women and minorities are often less satisfied with their jobs than are white men.

4. How does an organization's failure to manage women and minorities effectively translate into unnecessary costs? How can more effective management of these groups lead to competitive advantages?

5. If some managers do not seem to be handling the diversity of their personnel well, how might the performance appraisal and reward process be used to encourage them to improve?

A presentation of the arguments for and against affirmative actions programs lead-ing to the conclusion that these preferential treatment policies do not violate the principle of equal justice for all and, therefore, should be continued.

Moving Forward on Reverse Discrimination

Nancy Kubasek
Andrea M. Giapetro

During 1986, the U.S. Supreme Court finally agreed to consider the legality of affir-mative action plans. In seventeen separate opinions handed down in four cases, this country's highest court concluded that race-conscious remedies granted to those who have not proven that they were the victims of specific acts of racial discrimina-tion are not unconstitutional.

An end to the debate over the legality of a remedy, however, does not neces-sarily signify the end of the debate over the desirability of the remedy. Although the Supreme Court's decision may silence some who oppose affirmative action and may change the behavior of others, the debates over affirmative action will not cease; rather, their focus will change. Those who are opposed to the use of nonvictim-spe-cific race-conscious remedies will still continue to oppose their use. But the oppo-nents of affirmative action will now focus their efforts on raising philosophical ob-jections to affirmative action. They will no longer try to use legal precedents to argue that such programs are unlawful; instead, they will question the fairness or justice of using such legally available remedies.

What are these philosophical objections to affirmative action? How should the proponents of affirmative action respond to these objections? Are affirmative action programs philosophically unjustifiable?

OPPONENTS' ARGUMENTS

Many of those who are philosophically opposed to affirmative action do not see any distinction between discrimination against minorities and discrimination in favor of minorities. They call the latter reverse discrimination, claiming that discrimination has been reversed and is now being used to prevent qualified whites from getting the jobs to which they are entitled, just as discrimination used to prevent blacks from obtaining the jobs to which they were entitled. To evaluate this reverse discrimina-tion objection fairly, we must state it in its strongest form. The reverse discrimina-tion argument is that since the time of Aristotle, the concept of distributive justice has required that equals be treated unequally. This means that individuals are not to be denied benefits or forced to bear burdens based on irrelevant characteristics. Such

"Moving Forward on Reverse Discrimination," Reprinted from *Business and Society Review*, (Winter, 1987, no. 60), Management Reports, 25–13 Old Kings Highway North, Suite 107, Darien, CT.

actions would be arbitrary discrimination, which violates the concept of distributive justice.

It is now generally agreed that race is an irrelevant characteristic for purposes of distributing the benefits of education and employment. Therefore, affirmative action in the form of preferential treatment or reverse discrimination is violative of the principle of distributive justice because it distributes benefits and burdens on the basis of an irrelevant characteristic: race. Discrimination in employment or education based on race is arbitrary discrimination regardless of which race is being singled out.

Further, the ideal of equality is that all share the benefits and burdens of citizenship. The law governs all citizens equally, with all citizens regarding all others as having the same rights and protections. No inequalities not absolutely necessary for the functioning of society and the benefit of all are tolerable. Justice is equal treatment under the law for all citizens. Injustice occurs when all are not treated equally under the law. Reverse discrimination, or preferential treatment, violates equality because it treats one group of citizens differently; it destroys the protections of the law for one group of citizens. The very fact that we can talk about preferential treatment implies that before such treatment there was equality.

COMPENSATORY JUSTICE

Reverse discrimination also violates the principle of compensatory justice. Compensatory justice requires that when one is unjustly deprived of something that he rightfully possesses, he is entitled to compensation for his loss from the one who harmed him. This principle does not allow one to randomly seek compensation from those who did not harm him; they are as innocent as the one originally harmed. Preferential treatment policies, which require a minority to be hired, promoted, or admitted to a program instead of a more qualified nonminority, provide compensation for the allegedly wronged minority at the expense of the rejected innocent nonminority.

One approach to the foregoing philosophical objection to reverse discrimination is to point out that when so-called reverse discrimination occurs and blacks are given preferential treatment, the relevant basis for the discrimination is not race, which is arguably an arbitrary characteristic. Rather, it is the wrongs and losses blacks have suffered and the special needs they have that now form the relevant characteristics on which the discrimination is based. In other words, the reason for preferring blacks is not that they are black, which is why they have been denied housing and employment in the past. Instead, blacks are being treated differently because they have been victimized by a history of slavery and discrimination. We are preferring people with a history of suffering that makes them different from others, and different in a manner relevant to the preference they are now receiving. Therefore, the discrimination is not arbitrary. Race, when explicitly used as a classification, is being used for administrative convenience. Because there is a high correlation between being black and being a victim of invidious discrimination, race is a valid administrative tool for discerning who has suffered a history of slavery and discrimination.

One may, however, accept race as the relevant characteristic yet still find the reverse discrimination objection untenable. To accept the reverse discrimination objection, one must see blacks and nonminorities as equal in all relevant respects—including having the equal opportunity to compete for positions of power and prestige in our society.

Thus, in order to accept the reverse discrimination objection, one must define equality as meaning simply the absence of overt bars to quality education, housing, and employment. If one accepts this definition, one can then point to the civil rights laws prohibiting discrimination and say that these laws now ensure equal opportunity for all. Blacks and whites are therefore equals and must be treated equally.

Supporters of affirmative action, however, subscribe to a different definition of equality. As Justice Blackmun pointed out in *Bakke*: "In order to get past racism, we must take into account race. There is no other way. In order to treat people equally, we must treat them differently."

There is a plethora of evidence to support the proposition that when we are talking about competition in America among members of different races, equality, or equality of opportunity, means more than the elimination of overt barriers. As Lyndon Johnson said in a 1965 commencement address at Howard University, "You do not take a person who for years has been hobbled by chains and liberate him, bring him up to the starting line of a race, and then say, 'You are free to compete against all the others', and still justly believe that you have been completely fair."

SEGREGATION FACTOR

A major factor affecting blacks' access to training, education, health care, and employment opportunities is the pattern of housing that exists and has existed in this country. In today's society, housing not only provides needed shelter from the elements but also significantly influences one's ability to get a decent education and a prestigious job. It affects one's self-concept, which in turn further affects one's ability to compete for the economic goods available in our society.

We have a situation today in which the older inner cities are populated by poorly educated and economically disadvantaged persons, a large proportion of whom are minority families. The suburbs are primarily populated by whites who are looking for better health care, quality education, and personal safety. Increasingly, industrial parks are also moving out to the more attractive suburbs. There is little affordable housing accessible to minorities near these suburban industrial centers.

When there is a concentration of minority families in the inner cities and a loss of taxpaying families and industries to the suburbs, the tax base in the city becomes eroded. This makes it difficult for the government to meet the physical and social needs of the remaining residents, thus worsening the conditions under which they live and lessening their "equal opportunities" to develop themselves so they can realistically become competitive with nonminorities.

SCHOOL SEGREGATION

An additional problem caused by segregated housing is that it tends to result in a large number of schools being primarily minority or nonminority, despite the fact that intentional school segregation in most states is still unlawful. While school districts cannot be drawn so as to segregate the races, there are many instances where any way the districts are drawn, schools will be predominantly black or white due to segregated housing patterns. Most of the schools that are primarily black are located in lower-income areas of the inner cities. In such lower-income schools with their large classes, it is not uncommon for the teachers to contribute to the low student achievement levels by having low expectations. When teachers expect little from their students, a self-fulfilling prophecy may be put into effect. Thus, lower-income black competitors will be competing with an academic disadvantage as a result of their having attended segregated schools in economically depressed neighborhoods.

Even many blacks who have been relatively successful in the economic competition feel that after a certain level of success, their chances for continued progress are slim, to a large extent because top-level white management people do not feel comfortable working with blacks. This discomfort arises to a great extent from a lack of early experiences in interacting with blacks on any sort of equal basis.

These lower-level minority managers believe that the general cultural and social separation of the races has a significant impact on such conditions as the existence of only four black senior executives in the largest thousand United States corporations in 1985. As one black female executive explained, "People in the senior ranks might have gone to the same prep schools, fraternity, and church. Put yourself in corporate America's shoes—you hire those who you feel comfortable with." Institutions tend to perpetuate themselves unless something interferes with the process. Thus, the all-white executive suites will tend to stay that way unless forced to change.

The impact of not growing up in an interactive environment with members of the white community will often preclude blacks from even getting inside the corporate door, because potential minority candidates often do not know that many contests exist. This is because many jobs are filled through informal social contacts. A job opening occurs and the person responsible for filling the position asks a few of his colleagues if they know of anyone who might be good for the job. These white males will usually respond with recommendations for people like themselves, other white males with whom they socialize. Those people will be contacted and one of them hired. Even if the job is minimally advertised to meet EEOC regulations, the hiring decision has, in effect, already been made. Whites are generally the ones in powerful positions who can affect who is hired. If blacks do not have white friends, they will never find out about a large number of job opportunities and may never really be considered for many jobs for which they apply.

UNEQUALS TREATED UNEQUALLY

It is apparent that blacks do not have the equal opportunity to compete for the desirable economic goods that one gets by acquiring a position of power and prestige. As several commentators have correctly pointed out, whites could never be kicked around in the way blacks have. Whites today who complain about reverse discrimination have not been "beaten, lynched, denied the right to use a bathroom, a place to sleep or eat, forced to take the dirtiest jobs or denied work at all, forced to attend dilapidated and mind-killing schools, subjected to brutal unequal justice or stigmatized as an inferior being."

Since blacks are so clearly not the equals of whites in terms of their opportunities and treatment, preferential treatment of blacks is not a violation of distributive justice because equals are not being treated unequally. Unequals are being treated unequally, which is what distributive justice requires. Thus the argument that preferential treatment policies violate the principles of distributive justice cannot withstand careful examination and must be rejected.

Reverse discrimination does not violate the principle of compensatory justice either. While it is true that whites who may never have directly discriminated against the blacks receiving preferential treatment will be denied jobs or admission to programs that they would have received in the absence of preferential treatment policies, whites are not necessarily being unjustly forced to compensate the policies' beneficiaries. All that these white "victims" really lose is the expectation that they maintain the same positions that societal discrimination has helped them to acquire. The reverse discrimination that nonminorities suffer only partially offsets the advantages they have received for years.

This point becomes more clear when we examine the case of a typical reverse discrimination claim. When a nonminority applicant is not admitted to a professional school because preferential policies require admission of a minority, it is not the most qualified white who is being denied admission. It is the white who was barely qualified to meet the admissions standards. Chances are good, therefore, that this complaining applicant is able to meet the standards only because initial conditions were unfair. Were it not for the educational and housing advantages that this white applicant received, at the expense of minorities, he would not have met the standards for admission in the first place. While this is not necessarily true to every instance, when it is true it provides added support for the argument that "innocent" whites are not being forced to compensate minorities.

Thus, because the preferred treatment of minorities does not require compensation from those who are denied positions given to minorities, "reverse discrimination" does not violate the principle of compensatory justice either.

Many of those who are philosophically opposed to affirmative action believe that we should base employment and admission decisions solely on merit. Obviously, affirmative action is to some extent inconsistent with the merit system. And this merit system is deeply embedded into our culture. Most of us accept unquestionably the idea that no matter how oppressed our backgrounds, we can attain any position if we develop our talents and work hard. Affirmative action, however, gives some people a head start. These people may subsequently attain positions ahead of individuals who are more qualified.

Let us consider an example of the merit objection, if for no other reason than to entertain the reader who values highly logical reasoning. Clarence Pendleton, Jr., of the U.S. Commission on Civil Rights, relies on a merit objection when he speaks against affirmative action. He says "I think [the fact that over 60 percent of most professional football teams and about 80 percent of basketball teams are black] deals with market forces. I think people have ability and you put down your money and take your pick." Apparently, in Pendleton's eyes, blacks have merit at sports so teams pick them. It follows, then, that blacks do not have merit regarding other types of employment, so employers do not pick them. Is that what he has in mind? His analysis is unclear but still illustrative of the merit objection.

What is wrong with the merit objection? One major problem with the merit objection is that when we befriend merit, we inaccurately assume that a merit system has always existed; merit accepts the status quo. But a true merit system has not, does not, and will never prevail. Many jobs simply required "knowing somebody." The saying "It's not what you know, it's who you know" is not just a trite, old statement. Since human beings make employment decisions, it is impossible to prevent human bias from being a factor. Blacks have been ostracized from the buddy system. The merit objection fails to recognize this fact.

Even if the "old-boy network" did not exist, can we really measure merit for most jobs? To go back to Clarence Pendleton's example, we do have a pretty good way to measure the merit of a baseball player. We can look at his batting average. What comparable statistics do we have to measure someone's abilities as a manager? Or a chief executive officer? For most of the more prestigious positions in our society, there is no objective way to measure merit.

Another inadequacy of the merit objection is that it ignores the possibility that our need to compensate blacks for past unequal treatment is greater than our need to consider merit. A closely related consequentialist response is that while it may be unjust to the more meritorious individual who was denied a job or admission to a professional program, this temporary injustice will provide the best overall consequences for society and this outweighs the injustice to the individuals.

Finally, some argue that the merit objection is inadequate because race and merit are not mutually exclusive. Some writers define merit in such a way that race is an element of merit. If we value the goal of having blacks contribute to society, race becomes a "plus" or meritorious factor in employment and admissions decisions. Did the fact that Sandra Day O'Connor was a woman and Thurgood Marshall was a black contribute to their being named to the Supreme Court? Should it have? Probably, if we believe that it is important that society's institutions, including its workplaces, reflect society, the minority status of candidates in these and many other situations is indeed important. For example, when establishing standards for admission to professional programs, a diverse student body may be desirable, and thus race will become a meritorious condition when someone is of a race not highly represented in the program.

In some cases, when one examines the job description, race may be directly implicated as a meritorious characteristic. Police work provides such an example. Black policemen are much more likely to obtain needed information from inner-city residents than are white policemen. This is especially true where there have been racial conflicts in a particular community. Thus, if we had a predominantly white police force in an area with a large black population, being black would be a characteristic to search for in new recruits.

It is interesting to note that affirmative action programs are more abhorrent to some people than programs like welfare, which require the outright giving of money to individuals, not simply the giving of opportunities. In fact, some who raise the merit objection propose to replace them [affirmative action programs] with monetary compensation for proven victims of racial discrimination. The reason for this apparent inconsistency is rooted in our attitudes toward merit and charity. Americans, as a group, are highly individualistic and believe that it is of utmost importance to reward merit. However, we also have some sympathy for those who have met with misfortune and are willing to accept our generosity.

Welfare is, to some people, charity. The reason welfare is more acceptable than affirmative action is that welfare recipients do not participate in society the way we do; they are accepting our help because they have failed and we are generous enough to give them some aid so that they can survive. Our generosity, however, is not cost-free.

Society typically scorns welfare recipients, and they know it. The same is not as true for those who benefit from affirmative action programs, because the benefits are not as tangible as, for instance, food stamps. Hence, they are not visible. With affirmative actions, we give opportunity and mobility, not "charity." We allow "less deserving" people to participate in society in the same way we do. What is even worse to some opponents of affirmative action is that not only do some minorities participate, but they may actually be successful. And such participation and success is something they do not deserve.

While there may be practical problems in the implementation of certain affirmative action programs, and these should be addressed, we should recognize that from a philosophical perspective, such programs are not objectionable. Thus preferential treatment policies should not be abandoned. Perhaps with the use of affirmative action, it may one day no longer be true that blacks are unequal to whites and therefore do not need such programs to compete in the economic game.

DISCUSSION QUESTIONS

1. In this article the authors argue the merits of affirmative action from several viewpoints. Which of their arguments makes the most sense to you and which the least? Why?
2. How can managers and organizations overcome the negative backlash associated with quotas?
3. If you are Caucasian, assume for a moment that you are a member of a racial minority group. What problems might you experience when applying for a job for which you are qualified, that as a white person you have not experienced?

or

If you are a racial minority, assume for a moment that you are Caucasian. How would applying for a job, for which you are qualified, be different from what you have experienced in your own job searches?

4. As a class, discuss why the answers to question 3 were different for the two groups.
5. By demographics we know that the workforce is becoming increasingly non-white. Assume for a moment that the government has eliminated all affirmative action programs. In the next ten years would nonwhites and women be represented in proportion to their numbers in the workforce and/or in higher manage-

An illustration with specific examples showing that affirmative action has draw-backs as well as advantages for minorities and reporting that even its beneficiaries have ambivalent feelings about it.

ˣ Many Minorities Feel Torn by Experience of Affirmative Action

Sonia L. Nazario

At first, Roland Lee was thrilled to be the newest lieutenant in the San Francisco Fire Department. Then he learned he had beaten out a close friend in the department for the promotion. Then he discovered that his friend had scored higher on the qualifying exam. Then his friend quit.

The son of Chinese immigrants, Mr. Lee welcomed being hired and promoted under affirmative action quotas at the department. Without them, he believes, minorities would have been barred from the fire station's doors. But he also says he is "disgusted" that race denied his white friend the promotion.

Mr. Lee is plagued by the stigma he feels is attached to affirmative action: white co-workers questioning his abilities and assuming he's not as qualified as they. He says that this has forced him "to work twice as hard" to prove others wrong, and that at times, his own self-esteem has been battered. "If I had to do it over again," he says with regret, "I would get my promotion" without using affirmative action preferences. "That would give me back my credibility."

AMBIVALENT BENEFICIARIES

Such an overt rejection of affirmative action by one of its beneficiaries is uncommon. But as minorities look at the effects of affirmative action nearly a quarter-century after its inception, many feel torn by the policy's outcome.

Minorities say it has opened doors that would have remained shut, forced companies to look to employment groups they had ignored, and decreased racism by prodding workplace integration. But it has also brought unwelcome baggage: assumptions that minorities were hired only because of race, and what may be unwarranted skepticism about their abilities. This makes some minorities fear that even promotions and accomplishments they earn by working harder than their peers won't be respected.

Some minority employees believe racism—on the part of co-workers or employers—has a lot to do with their ambivalence. Others believe companies and government agencies approach affirmative action too much as a burden to be met as painlessly as possible rather than as something that can truly benefit the workplace. Still others, like Mr. Lee, believe the problem is inherent in affirmative action, part and parcel of a process that gives preference to people for reasons other than strictly merit.

"I don't know if promoting someone because they are Chinese is the way to do it," he says.

"Stigma of incompetance"

THE HIGH COURT

Several recent Supreme Court decisions have sparked a renewed debate over the legitimacy of affirmative action. Many now see an increasingly conservative court turning against the concept of setting quotas for hiring minorities.

First, the high court in January toughened the criteria under which a court could impose an affirmative action program on a business or municipality. Then earlier this month, the court made it easier for white workers to challenge affirmative action plans in court, and it also raised the difficulty for a plaintiff alleging racial discrimination in hiring.

Buoyed by the high court's recent decisions, conservatives are hoping they soon will be able to lessen what they see as "reverse" discrimination, while civil-rights activists are appalled at what they see as a chilling threat to years of progress in integrating the workplace.

Rarely heard in the debate, however, are the voices of those who actually have been hired or promoted under an affirmative action plan. In the workplace itself, lines that divide liberals and conservatives are blurred by the intrusion of a more complex reality. "I'm reluctantly appreciative of the affirmative action jobs I've had," says Migdia Chinea-Varela, a Hispanic Hollywood scriptwriter. "But at the same time, they made me really depressed."

EMPLOYEES ARE HEARD

The personal responses to affirmative action are diverse, as are the difficulties minorities have experienced using such programs. Mary Whitmore, a carpenter in Los Angeles who pried her way into the male-dominated construction business with the help of affirmative action, says her experience has been a wholly positive one. Co-workers "treat me equal. They let me use the saw. They give me the nails. They let me work."

Many minorities agree with William Mays, a black who now owns his own Indianapolis-based chemical-distribution company, and who got a graduate fellowship and several jobs through affirmative action. "I had to deal with the grief [affirmative action] brought," he says, "but it was well worth it."

Others argue that the emphasis of government-sponsored integration plans must change toward encouraging equal educational and hiring opportunities rather than setting numerical goals and timetables. And a small number believe affirmative action should be abolished. "Affirmative action robs us of our dignity. It says that somehow color, not our hard work, can bring us advancements," says Shelby Steele, a black associate professor of English at San Jose State University who says he no longer applies for affirmative-action-related research grants so he can shake the stigma that he somehow isn't as talented as a white professor.

All employers must by law provide equal hiring opportunities to people of all races, but affirmative action requires much more: specific goals and timetables for hiring and promoting underepresented women and minorities. Since a 1965 executive order by President Johnson, all companies that do more than $50,000 in annual business with the federal government and have more than 50 employees have been required to institute affirmative action plans. Companies and government agencies are bound to more rigid quotas when they are sued for discrimination under the 1964 Civil Rights Act and either agree to or are ordered by the court to remedy it through hiring and promotions.

THE NEED FOR ACTION

Interviews with scores of affirmative action employees reveal that despite their individual impressions of specific programs, all cite a strong need for some effort to combat racism and purposefully open jobs to minorities that they might have held, absent past discriminations. Louis Winston, a black who is the affirmative action officer for Stockham Valves & Fittings Inc. in Birmingham, Ala., recalls the days when that company had two entry gates—one for whites, one for blacks—and a divided cafeteria. When he began in the 1960s, blacks were forced to work in the sweltering heat of the foundry, while only whites could qualify for training programs to become machinists or electricians.

In part because of a 1969 lawsuit he helped initiate that then led to an affirmative action plan, he became the first black electrician trained at Stockham in 1975; now there are many, and blacks hold 60 percent of Stockham's jobs. Affirmative action, he says has "put some blacks in higher jobs, and shown the company that we aren't ignorant. We can do the job, if given the chance."

It has also helped reduce racial tensions by forcing blacks and whites to work together, he says. "Without affirmative action, Stockham may have come around, but I wouldn't swear on it," he says. More important, he says, there are still no blacks among the company's 35 managers.

BREAKING THE RANKS

Diane Joyce believes that without affirmative action, she couldn't have advanced in the male-dominated Santa Clara County, Calif., road-maintenance department. A road worker for six years, she took an oral test to become a dispatcher in 1980 and was ranked fourth of those who took the test.

County rules allowed the supervisors to give the job to any one of the seven highest-scoring candidates, and she knew that one wouldn't be her; she claims the men who administered her test told her they didn't like her. So she phoned the county affirmative action officer, and got the job. A man who scored second on the test and was about to get the job sued the county in a case that went all the way to the Supreme Court. He lost.

Three years later, Ms. Joyce scored first in a written and oral test to become a road foreman. A man who ranked fifth got the job. This time, she didn't challenge it, even though she again felt unfairly treated. "I'm tired of fighting," she says.

One reason she and some others weary of the fight is the way their accelerated promotions or even their hiring are received by co-workers. Take for example, the Birmingham, Ala., fire department.

PROBLEMS IN BIRMINGHAM

When Carl Cook applied to be a firefighter in 1964, a city clerk took one look at his face and refused to even hand over an application to the young black man, he says. In 1976, two years after Mr. Cook finally was hired, only 1.4 percent of firefighters were black. Attorney Susan Reeves, who helped file a suit for blacks against the city, says a Birmingham official once explained that "blacks congenitally don't like to fight fires."

Now the department is divided by a court-imposed affirmative action plan: Some white and black firefighters don't even speak to each other. Some whites refer to promoted minorities as "welfare captains." In a highly publicized case, the Supreme Court last month gave Birmingham's white firefighters the right to challenge the affirmative action plan initiated by the lower court.

Mr. Cook, who was both hired and promoted under affirmative action, says, "I feel I am under a microscope." He won't ask white supervisors for advice or information for fear that they are looking for an excuse to label him incompetent, he says. Battalion chief Tony Jackson, the city's highest-ranking black firefighter, says a white colleague once approached him and said, "Well, it sure is nice to be black. If I were black, I could have been promoted."

A white firefighter in Birmingham, David Morton, believes such suspicions will continue as long as some minorities are given special treatment—promoted over whites who rank higher in test scores and experience. "If you take an airplane, do you want a pilot who was ranked No. 1 or one who is ranked No. 50 but is black?" he asks.

A WRITER'S STORY

Ms. Chinea-Varela, the scriptwriter, says he has participated in four programs to encourage ethnic writers at four different production companies. No show she worked on was ever produced, she says. In one of the programs, sponsored by CBS Inc., a secretary explained to Ms. Chinea-Varela that she was just part of the network's minority headcount, the scriptwriter says.

As part of the CBS program, Ms. Chinea-Varela says she developed a situation comedy involving a young Hispanic woman who, trying to make ends meet after the death of her husband, takes in a white male boarder. "Because I came through the affirmative action door," she says, "there was no seriousness to the project."

A CBS spokeswoman says that this specific minority program no longer exists, and that the company has a strong commitment to affirmative action.

Regardless of the reaction of employers and co-workers, the mere fact that affirmative action involves special treatment has the potential to damage one's self-confidence, some minorities say. "Sometimes I wonder: Did I get this job because of my abilities, or because they needed to fill a quota?" says Caridad Dominguez, a Hispanic who is director of special studies for Bank of America, and who nonetheless says her own self-esteem carries her through such situations. "I consider myself a good contributor," she says.

QUESTIONING QUOTAS

The perception that affirmative-action hires sometimes aren't as good as other workers is perpetuated in some respects by employers so bound by court-ordered quotas that the measurable qualifications of minorities hired fall far below white counterparts. "We hire 60 percent Hispanics here, regardless of qualifications," says Freddie Hernandez, a Hispanic lieutenant in the Miami Fire department. "The fire department doesn't go to schools in other cities to recruit for minorities. They just have people take a test, and they pick minorities [even] from the bottom of the list." Fire Chief C.H. Duke says that a city ordinance requires his hires to be 80 percent women and minorities, and that this does require passing up whites with higher test scores for minorities, although anyone considered must pass the test.

Theodore Edwards, a black division manager at Ameritech Corp.'s Illinois Bell Telephone and an affirmative-action hire, says, "I think affirmative action is necessary, but I don't think it should be administered so that we say we have to have X number of minorities regardless of qualifications." He sees a need for more active recruiting so that firms can find minorities who are as qualified as other workers.

Whether they blame bosses, co-workers or simply human nature for their dissatisfaction with affirmative action, some minorities have been led by years of experience to call for major changes in government's approach to integrating the workplace.

The scriptwriter, Ms. Chinea-Varela, argues that hiring based on quotas should be done only in entry-level jobs, and that thereafter, a pure merit system should be used. She and others note that any hiring may at times be based less on merit than such factors as whom you know, ties to the appropriate Ivy League college, or nepotism. Still, she says that "there's a point where affirmative action should stop: I'd like to by now be considered on my own merits," having been in the business 10 years.

A Hispanic scriptwriter friend of hers, Julio Vera, is opposed to affirmative action altogether and will no longer apply for minority writing programs. "Martin Luther King's dream was to erase color lines; affirmative action hasn't done that," he says. Mr. Vera advocates spending more to redress the legacy of unequal education for minorities so they have a better chance of being equally qualified when they apply for a job. Affirmative action, he says, "is a handout."

Mr. Hernandez, the 34 year-old Hispanic firefighter from Miami, agrees. He turned down an affirmative-action promotion to lieutenant six years ago, waiting three years until he had the seniority and test scores to qualify for the promotion under normal procedures.

By doing so, he passed up $4,500 a year in extra pay and had to undergo 900 hours of extra study time. But "it was a self-pride thing," he says. "I knew I could make it on my own." Mr. Hernandez plans to take the exam for fire chief soon, but says he'll accept the job only if he wins it on paper. "I will stick to merit," he says.

DISCUSSION QUESTIONS

1. If you were a manager in the Birmingham, Alabama, Fire Department, what would you do to improve racial harmony?
2. What kinds of things might organizations of all kinds (business, political, academic) do if they find they are filling their affirmative action quotas with poorly qualified minorities?
3. How far should affirmative action go; that is, at what point should it stop? Should it be abolished? Should there be hiring quotas? Promotion advantages for minorities?
4. From the perspective of organizations, what are the benefits of affirmative action? In what ways is it a detriment?

A presentation of the historic development of legal applications of equal employ-ment opportunity laws to U.S. firms operating in other countries with an examina-tion of the economic, legal, ethical, and discretionary responsibilities of such firms.

Equal Employment Responsibilities
of Multinational Corporations

Patricia Feltes
Robert K. Robinson
Ross L. Fink

U.S. companies are advancing farther into the international marketplace to meet the threat of global competition. In an effort to ensure that all American workers receive as much protection as practical against employment discrimination when assigned to a foreign worksite, the U.S. Congress enacted a law directly affecting multinational employers. The act has significant economic, legal, ethical, and discretionary impact. By examining these four social responsibility categories, a multinational organization can now develop corporate guidelines to successfully address employee rights in an international context.

In 1988, 2,000 U.S. companies had a total of 21,000 foreign subsidiaries in 121 countries. It is unclear how many U.S. citizens are employed in those nonterri-torial outposts of American firms, but the State Department estimated that there were 2.2 million U.S. citizens living abroad that year.[1] Recently, an encompassing trade pact with Mexico is being considered. A potential result of the agreement is a projected increase in U.S. manufacturing subsidiaries in Mexico with a greater num-ber of U.S. citizen managers and staff assigned to them.

One dilemma facing U.S.-based international organizations is employee rights. In 1964, Congress enacted the Civil Rights Act of 1964 which provided spe-cific protection of individual rights in the workplace. Title VII of the act forbids an employer from discriminating on the basis of an employee's race, religion, gender, or national origin. The primary objective of this legislation was to achieve certain national socio-cultural objectives in the work environment. While bearing this in mind, successfully internationalizing organizations are equally aware of the de-mands of the host country's legal and cultural practices. The potential for conflict arises when the laws of many host countries do not provide the same level of protec-tion for employees as found in Title VII. Furthermore, accepted business practices in some countries may even be contrary to the values of U.S. business and society.

COURT ACTION

A case involving these conflicting issues was recently brought before the United States Supreme Court. Arguments were presented which called for the extension of Title VII protections to U.S. citizens who are employed by American companies

Reprinted with permission from *Business Forum*, Summer 1992.

outside of the territorial boundaries of the United States. The questions at the center of the Equal Employment Opportunity Commission (EEOC) versus Arabian American Oil Company case are:[2] Do U.S. equal employment opportunity laws protect an American expatriate employed by a U.S. firm from discrimination? Are U.S. firms bound to follow U.S. Congress directives in the midst of another country's culture?

The case was brought by Ali Boureslan, a naturalized U.S. citizen of Lebanese descent who joined the firm of Aramco Services Company of Houston, Texas, a subsidiary of the Arabian American Oil Company (ARAMCO) in 1979. He was transferred by ARAMCO from Houston to Dharan, Saudi Arabia. Shortly after his arrival, Boureslan claimed he became the victim of a harassment campaign initiated by his supervisor. He claimed the harassment took the form of racial, ethnic, and religious slurs, and led to his subsequent termination in 1984. Upon returning to the U.S., Boureslan filed a complaint with the Equal Opportunity Commission for the discriminatory treatment which he allegedly received in Saudi Arabia. He contended he was entitled to Title VII protection.

The defendants argued that Title VII did not afford extraterritorial protection to any American citizen, only to those who work within the boundaries of the U.S. Both the U.S. District Court and the U.S. Court of Appeals for the Fifth Circuit agreed with this argument and ruled against extraterritorial application. Concurring, the Supreme Court held that federal law does not prohibit U.S. companies from engaging in employment discrimination against American citizens abroad. Companies located in other countries are governed by the existing rules and laws of the host country, not the provisions of U.S. legislation unless Congress expressly declares otherwise.

CONGRESS RESPONDS

As a response to this Supreme Court finding, the Congress included provisions addressing this issue in the then proposed Civil Rights Act. The bill was passed and signed into law November 21, 1991.[3] Both inclusionary and exclusionary provisions were incorporated into the act.

The overseas extension of civil rights protections is not, however, universal or automatic. If a conflict between U.S. employment law and the host country's employment law arises in an overseas operation, then the U.S.-based employer is expected to comply with the host country's law. For example, assume that a company has an operation in a foreign country which has statutes prohibiting the employment of women in management positions. That company would be expected to follow the law of the host country and would not be liable for sex discrimination under Title VII of the Civil Rights Act of 1964.

However, if the host country has no employment laws which explicitly ban the employment of certain minorities, followers of particular religions, members of specific nationalities, or women, then the employer is expected to ensure the U.S.-mandated equal employment opportunities of its U.S. employees. In other words, U.S. citizens working for a U.S.-owned or controlled corporation's foreign operations are entitled to the same employment rights that they would enjoy had they been working at a domestic site belonging to that employee—unless these rights are prohibited by the laws of the host country.

Corporations are seen as major powers in the fabric of society. Their power is increased as their access to and use of the world's resources increases. Enhanced power is often identified with enhanced responsibilities. This is particularly true of multinational corporations which, with the possible exception of nations, are the most powerful organizations existent.[4]

The social responsibility of these organizations can be expressed as encompassing the economic, legal, ethical, and discretionary expectations that society has of them at a given point of time.[5] The following sections will consider the ramifications of the Supreme Court finding and the expectations of society in light of each of these four responsibilities.

ECONOMIC RESPONSIBILITY

The primary responsibility of a for-profit organization is to make a profit through the production and sale of socially desired goods and services. Some writers, for example Milton Friedman, may in fact limit the expectations appropriate for business to their economic contribution.[6]

At a time when internationalization and globalization are key concepts for survival in many industries, U.S. firms struggle to increase their worldwide revenues. To be economically successful, multinational firms have an obligation to consider the ramifications of host country laws and cultural norms. It may, in fact, be strategically imperative and financially advantageous for a firm to choose international locations in which various social costs including employee lawsuits, damage suits, etc. are low.[7] The recent extension of civil rights employment protections to a U.S. firms extraterritorial work force limits the organization from participating in those benefits. Congress has constrained the managerial rules and assignments the corporation may feel are necessary by expanding the potential of legal repercussions and expense. Firms may be faced with the dilemma of conflicting U.S. law and host country culture and work practices which are not codified into law.

However, another economic consideration is the effective use of the human resources within the firm. Research on internal process effectiveness has focused on both human resources approaches and economic efficiency.[8] Both approaches indicate that there is a relationship between employee loyalty (commitment) and overall organizational performance. By ignoring or blatantly disregarding employee rights, an organization could conceivably erode employee commitment. Following the tenets of the Civil Rights Act of 1991 may prove to be both legally sound and economically advantageous if seen as support of a company's employees.

LEGAL RESPONSIBILITY

Until passage of the Civil Rights Act of 1991, U.S. corporations had no legal responsibility to follow the anti-discrimination tenets of Title VII in their foreign plants and subsidiaries. With its passage however, U.S. corporations now may be sued by disgruntled employees in U.S. courts as a result of alleged bias in treatment, promotion, job assignment, or other conditions of employment in a nonterritorial corporate facility. The laws of the host nation will act as constraints on the legal protection possible to alleged victims of discrimination rather than as the only avenue of legal recourse available to them as in the past.

Over the years, some U.S. companies have been found in violation of Title VII in their domestic operations, and their attendant actions to comply with the law have set standards which have been accepted by their counterparts in other countries. These activities outside the United States, however, are predicated on moral suasion and the willingness of the relevant countries to accept Title VII concepts into their own legal systems. For example, the American Telephone and Telegraph Company in 1973 signed a consent agreement with the Department of Labor and the Equal Employment Opportunity Commission to begin a substantial affirmative action program for women in the United States. As a result of that consent decree, Canadian companies increasingly made a noticeable effort to provide similar programs for women in their organizations.[9]

ETHICAL RESPONSIBILITY

Although multinational companies do business in more than one country, they are inexorably tied to the home country through ownership and mores. They are generally chartered in a single country with ownership by home country nationals exceeding 90 percent. Invariably, the highest management levels tend to be dominated by home country managers.[10] Ethical responsibility expectations are, therefore, often predicated on those ethical standards that are acceptable in the home country rather than those in the host country.

The United States public through its democratic institutions has supported the Congressional stance regarding equal rights. The legal and moral status of the Civil Rights Act, including Title VII, has been reaffirmed since its passage in 1964 through numerous court hearings and Congressional discussions until the culmination in the Civil Rights Act of 1991. As a result of this continuing reaffirmation it may be assumed that U.S. societal standards include nonbiased workplace activity.

In addition to the expectations of the home country society, several multilateral accords adopted by governments over the past 40 years have included ethical guidelines in an attempt to influence the employment and trading practices of multinational companies.[11] These moral guidelines have been presented as a framework for internationally acceptable behavior.

Each of these accords is dependent on the concept of national sovereignty. In none of these multilateral compacts has an expression of willingness to depose the rights and laws of the host country been addressed. Therefore, the accords cannot be seen as a substitute for local law or as based on some superordinate legal system. They do, however, in the instances cited, press for social equity voluntarily defined and agreed upon by the parties involved.

Within these agreements, which cover many different moral issues, are those relevant to the concerns of employers and employees. Those issues of interest to this discussion may be described in three categories: equality of pay, nondiscriminatory

Accord	Equality of Pay	Nondiscriminatory Employment	Rights of Individuals Policies
United Nations Universal Declaration of "Human Rights, 1948"	Yes	Yes	Yes
"Helsinki Final Act, 1973"			Yes
OECD Guidelines to "Multinational Enterprises, 1976"		Yes	
International Labor Office Tripartite Declaration of Principles Concerning Multinational Enterprises and "Social Policy, 1977"	Yes	Yes	Yes

Figure 2.3 Rights covered by international accords.

Source: P. Feltes, R. K. Robinson, and R. L. Fink, "Equal Employment Responsibilities of Multinational Corporations," *Business Forum* (Summer 1992), p. 19. Reprinted with permission.

employment policies, and rights of the individual.[12] We define equality of pay as multinational companies providing equal pay for equal work, nondiscriminatory employment policies as multinational companies developing nondiscriminatory employment policies and promoting equal job opportunities, and rights of the individual as multinationals respecting the rights of all persons to equal protection of the law, work, choice of job, just and favorable work conditions, and protection against unemployment and discrimination.

Of the several accords described by researcher William C. Frederick, four specifically contain the relevant provisions[13] (Figure 2.3). They are: The 1948 United Nations Universal Declaration of Human Rights which addressed equality of pay, nondiscriminatory employment policies, and rights of the individual; the Helsinki Final Act of 1973 which addressed nondiscriminatory employment policies and the rights of the individual; OECD Guidelines for Multinational Enterprises in 1976 which covered non-discriminatory employment policies; and the International Labor Office Tripartite Declaration of Principles Concerning Multinational Enterprises and Social Policy in 1977 which focused on equality of pay, nondiscriminatory employment policies, and rights of the individual.

There is both domestic and international support for the furtherance of employment rights even without the specific sanction of law. As members of the global community, multinational companies have a moral interest in the observance of those rules. It is also within the power of the countries involved to make these guidelines mandatory within their borders. In particular, if the U.S. public perceives American multinational companies as not performing in the best interest of society and disregarding its standards, it may respond by seeking legislative redress.

DISCRETIONARY RESPONSIBILITY

There are some activities loosely considered social responsibilities that are not expressly expected of business firms. These are voluntary and occur more as a result of business owners and managers choosing to commit their organizations to perform them than from any economic, legal, or ethical responsibility.[14] Public expectations regarding them may, in fact, be unclear and divergent.

In the case of Title VII provisions, firms may choose to implement practices and policies which support antidiscrimination ideals beyond the legal requirement to do so. For example, a corporation may initiate a non-required affirmative action policy offering advanced placement or special benefits for women and minorities. Sensitivity training for managers, support groups for affected individuals, and philanthropic donations to relevant non-profit organizations, e.g., NAACP, are other discretionary activities in which firms may engage.

In the international arena, a firm may also look beyond its own internal boundaries. It could use its economic influence with the host country to publicize and promote its employment standards. This might result in governments contemplating more equitable treatment for workers under their legal system.

In all cases, these are discretionary options available to the firm. They are not required by law or by the expectation of society but are dependent upon the decisions made by the organization. A firm choosing to follow this voluntary path would need to be cognizant of the potential and actual costs and weigh these against the perceived benefits.

As corporations comply with the 1991 act, an offsetting benefit could be the gain of highly qualified employees or applicants who perceive the corporations as supportive and a desirable place in which to work.

NOTES

1. Wermiel, Stephen, "Supreme Court Rules Civil Rights Act Doesn't Bar Bias by U.S. Firms Abroad," *Wall Street Journal.* 72 (114), March 27, 1991, A18.
2. *EEOC* v. *Arabian American Oil Company*, 111 S. Ct. 1227, 1991.
3. Larson, Lex K., *Civil Rights Act of 1991*, Matthew Bender series, Times-Mirror Books, N.Y.
4. Donaldson, Thomas, *The Ethics of International Business*. Oxford University Press, New York, 1989.
5. Carroll, A.B., "A Three-Dimensional Conceptual Model of Corporate Performance," *Academy of Management Review*, 4 (4), 1978, 497–505.
6. Friedman, Milton, *Capitalism and Freedom*, University of Chicago Press, 1962.
7. Robinson, Richard D., *Internationalization of Business: An Introduction*, The Dryden Press, Chicago, 1983.
8. Argyris, Chris, *Integrating the Individual and the Organization*, John Wiley and Sons, New York, 1964. Likert, Rensis, *The Human Organization*, McGraw Hill, New York, 1967. Beckhard, Richard, *Organizational Development Strategies and Models*. Addison-Wesley Publishing Co., Reading, MA. Evans, William

M., "Organizational Theory and Organizational Effectiveness: An Exploratory Analysis," *Organization and Administrative Sciences*, 7, 15–28.

9. Adler, Nancy J., "Women in International Management: Where Are They?," *California Management Review*, 26, (4), 1984, 78–89.

10. Donaldson, Thomas, "Multinational Decision-Making: Reconciling International Norms," *Journal of Business Ethics*, 4, 1985, 357–366.

11. Frederick, William C., "The Moral Authority of Transnational Corporate Codes," *Journal of Business Ethics*, 10, 1991, 165–177.

12. *Ibid.*

13. *Ibid.*

14. Carroll, A.B., *op. cit.*

DISCUSSION QUESTIONS

1. Suppose a U.S. company has an overseas facility located in a country where the cultural norms dictate that it is socially unacceptable to put women or certain other nationalities in supervisory positions. Should the company honor local customs in this regard?

2. Suppose the company in question 1 chooses to hire or promote women or low-status minorities into supervisory positions. What business advantages might result? What business disadvantages might result?

3. Our laws clearly indicate that the U.S. believes in fair treatment and opportunity for all employees. Many countries; for historic, ethnocentric and/or economic reasons do not share these beliefs. If the host country has no regulations, do you think our companies located there should influence the host country to accept our beliefs? If the host country does have discriminatory laws, should our companies lobby for change toward our beliefs?

4. There are many U.S. organizations overseas that are nonprofit. Some are charitable and depend for success upon acceptance by, and close relations with the local people. Should these organizations be required to follow U.S. employment laws if the host country has strong prejudices against employing or promoting certain groups? Why or why not?

The Xerox Corporation is an example of an organization that is approaching diversity from a positive perspective. The corporation is inclusive of many groups, including white males, supportive of minority caucus groups, and has a 30 year history of trying to move beyond AA/EEO's legal requirements toward a strategy of managing diversity.

⧘ Xerox Makes It Work ⧙

Bruce D. Butterfield

Rochester, N.Y.—De Wayne McCulley grew up poor but ambitious in rural Farrel, Pa., one of the only young blacks in the town to make it through college.

But when he arrived at Xerox Corp. here to take an engineering job, he had no intention of conforming to the traditions of white corporate America.

Every day, he strode into meetings with white Xerox managers and executives wearing all-black clothes, dark sunglasses and a bushy Afro haircut. — *Resistance stage*

"I look back and say to myself, 'How did you survive?' I pushed the limits."

Except that it was 1974, and limits at Xerox were ready to be pushed. In the years since, McCulley has more than survived Xerox. He has thrived at the company, rising to head a 37-person department of engineers and designers. One reason, he notes: "The bottom line at Xerox was and is today, 'are you performing?' "

But equally as important to McCulley's success, Xerox has had another bottom line for the last two decades: an unshakable commitment to developing a diverse and fully integrated work force from entry-level clerks to top executives.

As much as any other major corporation in America, Xerox has succeeded in that goal—despite the doubts over affirmative action sweeping other companies today.

Like many companies, Xerox does not use formal "quotas" in hiring, and in the late 1980s shifted away from using the term "affirmative action" to describe its racial and gender equality programs. Unlike many companies, however, Xerox hasn't sought in recent years to distance itself from traditional affirmative action. Rather, it has used it to build a wider program called "Managing for Diversity."

Among its 56,000 U.S. employees, minority workers at Xerox today account for 25.7 percent and women make up 32.3 percent. More minorities and women are employed in lower and mid-level jobs as a percentage of the work force than upper-level jobs. But among company managers, more than 18 percent are minorities and over 23 percent are women.

The company's senior executives are 17 percent minority and 8.5 percent women. This relatively small percent of female top officers is one area Xerox says it has still to work aggressively to change.

But company officials insist they will near a "top to bottom" racially and gender-balanced work force by 1995. To guard against any "white backlash" among its

Reprinted courtesy of *Boston Globe*, October 20, 1991, pp. 33–37.

employees, the company's balanced work force concept includes a unique addition—affirmative action hiring for white males when, as has happened among its engineers, Xerox finds white males underrepresented in entry-level positions.

Not all company employees, meanwhile, are sold on its aggressive affirmative action posture, by whatever name it is called—including some who stand to benefit by it.

"All you hear about here is how affirmative action is wonderful," complained one white female professional, who maintained that many minorities and women were often looked on by colleagues as "special hires."

It is a designation she resents, asking: "Don't you think this creates discrimination?"

Still, Xerox's progressive policies in hiring, after more than two decades, appear to have more backers than critics among employees. "It's the right thing to do," Stephen Kennard, a white Xerox engineer. "And Xerox has made it work well, I think."

When a black or other minority applies for a job here, managers have a special incentive to hire them. A manager's own promotion and bonuses are tied, in part, to how well they integrate the work force under them and still maintain productivity.

Many companies aggressively hire minorities, particularly those with government contracts that have to show the Labor Department that they are doing something about Affirmative Action. At Xerox, however, a manager's performance is also judged on how well minorities and women—and white males, too—are trained, perform, and move up in the ranks to achieve balanced equality.

To ensure that managers—most still white males—are sensitive to discrimination and equipped to deal with it, Xerox often goes to elaborate lengths. Earlier this year, for example, it pulled more than 3,000 managers off the job to attend special "interactive" theatre productions around the country in which actors portrayed Xerox managers dealing improperly with minority and women employees under them.

The theater department at Cornell University was hired by Xerox to put the productions together, and managers were called on by the actors to participate. "Most of the problems we have are not issues of affirmative action. They are issues of poor management," insisted Deborah K. Smith, a vice president of human resources.

She said the Cornell productions were designed to confront managers in a dramatic fashion with bad choices they may make, and show them how to make better ones.

It also, she conceded, kept managers on notice that top officials at Xerox would tolerate no backsliding on racial gains.

The basis for the company's success dates back to the late 1960s, when chairman Joe Wilson and president Peter McColough sent a directive to all managers condemning racial discrimination, committing the firm to all out minority recruitment, and holding managers accountable for results.

By the beginning of the 1970s, Xerox had hired its first large group of black sales representatives, and began aggressive hiring in most other marketing fields. In the words of one black executive, the document company looked for the "best and the brightest" among minorities and generally got them.

It was typical affirmative action in its early stages. And there were problems.

Hiring minority workers was one thing. Xerox says it found holding onto them and ensuring they were promoted and treated fairly was another proposition. Black workers themselves—particularly those hired in the competitive sales field—soon realized there was more to corporate equality than a company identification card.

According to a study on Xerox done by professor Raymond Friedman of Harvard Business School, blacks at the company found themselves generally frozen out of the "informal" network of shared information and contacts so necessary for the success that white workers enjoyed. In some sales areas, black employees also found they were being systematically given the less productive sales areas to work. *Isolation stage*

Led by Barry Rand, then a young sales representative who today is president of Xerox Marketing and one of the nation's top black executives, along with a small group of other black employees, fought back—forming special black caucus groups at key locations around the country. It was the rise of these black caucuses at Xerox, Freidman and top company officials themselves concede, that sparked early successes.

"Racial equality doesn't happen because management decrees it or mandates it. This is where the black caucuses came into play," said Ted Payne, Xerox executive formerly in charge of affirmative action. "They were absolutely key."

More than gripe sessions, the caucuses developed around improving training, identifying problem areas in Xerox's affirmative action programs, and providing unofficial "mentors" for new black workers. *Adaptation stage*

But they also had a political side, with black leaders winning the confidence and access to top Xerox officials. David Kearns, now chairman of Xerox, threw his support behind the caucuses in the mid 1970s—giving them legitimacy throughout the company.

Many corporations—including giant International Business Machines—actively discourage such nonofficial company networks even today, seeing it as undermining management authority and creating something akin to a labor union .

But black Xerox managers say that largely due to Kearns—at the time a senior executive sent by the company to deal with the black caucus situation—Xerox decided to encourage the caucuses' independence and growth.

Through the 1980s in fact, Payne and other Xerox officials say, the company found the caucuses a valued addition to its own special training and minority tracking program, and a valuable way to help judge performance of its middle-level managers as well. *Coexistence stage*

"There was a lot of middle management not excited by all the caucus groups," observed Friedman of Harvard. But there was nothing they could do about it. Near the end of the 1980s, the black caucus groups had been so successful they led to similar groups at Xerox for Hispanics, Asians, and women—groups that continue today.

"When we started years ago at Xerox, I don't think we'd have made the progress if not for the support of the leadership," Rand said. But, in addition to what he calls the "enlightened" corporate philosophy of Kerns, Rand maintains that black employees like himself were successful at Xerox because they took control of their own affairs, and helped each other excel.

"Part of the philosophy of the black caucuses was performance," Rand added, "I believed I did not have the luxury of mediocrity. Blacks do not have the luxury to be mediocre."

"There are many leaders who profess support for equality of employment and for civil rights, and who even believe in civil rights. But they don't manage it at their companies," said Rand in a recent interview at corporate headquarters in Stamford, Conn.

DeWayne McCulley says he felt the same way when he joined Xerox in 1974. An honors graduate from Penn State, he arrived in Rochester after a brief stint as an engineer for Hughes Aircraft in California determined to show his stuff as an engineer charged with developing programs to troubleshoot Xerox's new wave of copying machines.

Rejection Stage

But he didn't look the part of a professional, and had no intention of taking on the dress and style of his white co-workers. Right from the start, things seemed tough. His first manager at Xerox was a Southern white, he says, clearly uncomfortable with McCulley's dress and style. He was also, McCulley says politely, "uninformed" about racial matters.

"He called people colored." I laughed, and told him: "You've got to get with the program. The word is black, and to make it more complicated, Afro-American."

To his surprise, McCulley said, the manager backed off, worked to change his attitudes, and gave McCulley "the opportunity to prove myself." Xerox itself, he added, proved a flexible and friendly place to work—providing you did your job.

"Just because you walk through the door here, racial prejudice doesn't go away. We have our problems here," he says. "What's different is that Xerox recognizes those problems, and they are proactive in working to change that."

"Everybody gets an opportunity. It's all we can ask."

Integration stage

Affirmative Action for White Males at Xerox

It might be called the nation's first affirmative action program for white males. After years of aggressively hiring women and minorities, Xerox Corp. looked over its list of entry-level engineers in Webster, N.Y., and discovered that white men were largely missing.

Committed to its program of "Managing for Diversity," Xerox has no intention of letting this "imbalance" continue.

"We are having absolutely no problem hiring minority engineers. The problem I have now is a white male problem," said Deborah K. Smith, a Xerox vice president. Few other companies in America, given the shortage of minority engineers, would likely consider that a problem. But at Xerox, Smith explains it this way:

"What happens is that Xerox people are great at following objectives. So if you tell people you want them to hire a certain group (of minorities), they'll go out and do that to a fault." Smith declined to talk about the numbers of white males that had to be hired in Xerox's group of about 250 engineers in Webster, but officials conceded it would not likely be difficult to find them.

While the white male shortage may be unique to Xerox, the issue of making sure white men don't feel left out in companies committed to "diversity" is not.

International Business Machines Corp., for example, has made sure it has a white male, along with a woman and two minorities, overseeing affirmative action. Says Ted Childs, the black executive who runs the program: "It's not uncommon for me to say to two people, 'make sure in this debate we're having, the white male point of view is presented.'"

DISCUSSION QUESTIONS

1. Make a list of the reasons, in addition to AA/EEO compliance, that could motivate a company like Xerox to take a proactive stance on diversity.
2. Evaluate your list in terms of some of the key factors currently associated with management today: total quality, productivity, globalization, and so on.
3. Prepare an argument that supports Rand's statement, "Blacks do not have the luxury to be mediocre."
4. The Xerox article illustrates that managing diversity can include white males in addition to minority workers. Why is it also important to address this often overlooked aspect of diversity?

CHAPTER

THREE

On the Dimensions of Diversity

You can't change what people think of you. People are what they are. But a time comes when you're defined by what you've done. People don't consider that 'the deaf Beethoven' wrote the Ninth Symphony, or that 'the blind Milton' wrote the later poems. It's a matter of what you achieve at the end of the road.[1]

Diversity can be seen as a challenge or as an opportunity; as an asset or as a liability; as adding richness or complexity. This chapter contains readings that explore in more depth four unchangeable, fixed aspects of difference: gender, race/ethnicity, physical challenge, and sexual orientation.

These four topic areas were chosen because they are the inborn dimensions that play the strongest role in determining how people experience life from birth to death. One's whole socialization process, self-image, and many of the opportunities experienced or denied on or off the job, are shaped and affected by these characteristics.

While other dimensions like age, marital status, income, social class, and religion may also set individuals apart as "others," these latter attributes are more changeable, often more easily concealed, and may be of more or lesser importance according to an individual's experience.

However, the use of this framework is not intended to imply that the individuals in these categories share identical characteristics, management styles, or experiences. There is a wide range of personal differences within these groups.

While these readings on selected aspects of difference are intended to provide a forum for exploration and discussion of how gender, race/ethnicity, physical challenge, and sexual orientation may affect one's experience in the workplace, one does not necessarily have to exhibit these characteristics in order to improve his/her understanding of how people with these differences experience the world. For example, male managers with working wives have more empathy toward employees who are working mothers. The siblings of gays or lesbians will be more sensitive and less tolerant of the homophobic remarks and jokes of co-workers.

Just as these experiences with differences can help our understanding of diverse employees and lead to more productive management styles, the readings that follow were selected to increase students' understanding and awareness of issues particular to these four aspects of the diverse experience: gender (Kanter, Gallese, Billard), race/ethnicity (McIntosh), physical challenge (Prince), and sexual preference (Hunt).

Kanter's article, *The Job Makes the Person*, explores the notion that women's lack of career progress is due more to the characteristics of the organization and the way that women experience these, than it is to having a different, more feminine, management style. Kanter argues that any employee, male or female, who is denied career opportunities, feels powerless, lacks self-confidence, and does not have a mentor, will have difficulty rising in the organization. When this experience is coupled with being different and being treated as a token, less productive behavior often results.

In *Why Women Aren't Making It to the Top*, Gallese uses a series of short cases to make the point that women can and do react differently to these organizational constraints. Some of the women in Gallese's examples overcame these obstacles by taking control of their lives, whereas others were less successful at overcoming obstacles.

In contrast, Billard takes a stand that is the subject of much controversy and debate today. In *Do Women Make Better Managers?*, she contends that women do manage differently than men. To Billard, women exhibit a more transformational, participative style that is more suitable for today's organizations than men's transactional more controlling style.

The McIntosh article develops perspective in two ways. First, it introduces the idea that being Caucasian is an ethnicity as well as a race, because there is a culture of privilege associated with this membership. For the Caucasian and for the male, many privileges are traditionally viewed as entitlements. In addition, McIntosh turns the tables on the general perspective of viewing other groups as "underprivileged" and focuses on being male and Caucasian as "overprivileged."

With the passage of the Americans with Disabilities Act (1990), the employment of more physically and mentally challenged workers became a reality and a legal right. Prince's *Aspirations and Apprehensions: Employees with Disabilities* provides an exploration of the ramifications of increasing numbers of physically challenged individuals in the workforce. The examples cited in this work show that differently abled workers can and do want to be productive workers.

In *Situating Sexual Orientation on the Diversity Agenda: Recent Legal, Social and Economic Developments* by Gerald Hunt, the author explores the recent changes that affect gays and lesbians in the workplace. He argues for their inclusion in the legal protection afforded to other types of diversity and for organizational considerations for the accommodation of their lifestyles. Readers will react to and experience these articles differently according to their degrees of association, involvement, and experiences with these aspects of difference. The progress that readers make toward understanding diversity is more significant than the understanding readers begin with. Although few would question the value of the contributions of the deaf Beethoven or the blind Milton, these examples from the opening quotation lead one to wonder what the world would be like if we could learn how to understand differences enough to fully utilize the talents and contributions of more of the women, racial/ethnic minorities, physically challenged individuals, and gays and lesbians who will be making up a large percentage of tomorrow's workforce.

NOTES

1. Mehta, Ved. quoted in a book review (by Marjorie Boone) of *What's That Pig Outdoors,* Henry Kisor. *SHHH Journal*, September/October 1990: 23.

An analysis of how opportunity, power, and tokenism explains common perceptions and stereotypes (as well as the behaviors) of women in organizations.

The Job Makes the Person

Rosabeth Moss Kanter

"I'd never work for a woman," a woman draftsman told me." "They are too mean and petty."

Research on female workers has for years looked for sex differences on the job. Women, the surveys show, have lower aspirations than men, less commitment to work, and more concern with friendships than with the work itself. And many people assume that women make poor leaders because their personalities do not allow them to be assertive. Women who do make it to management positions are presumed to fit the mold of the dictatorial, bitchy boss.

To explain why more women don't seek or find career success, many people concentrate on supposed personality differences between the sexes: women's "motive to avoid success" or incapacity to handle power. Or they look at childhood training and educational training: how women learn to limit their ambitions and hide their accomplishments. Because women learn that high achievement means a loss of traditional femininity, they choose to preserve the latter and sacrifice the former.

When I began to study women in work organizations three years ago, I also was looking for sex-related individual differences that would explain women's absence from high-status, powerful jobs. If women were ever going to make it in a man's world, the conventional wisdom said, we would have to get them when they're young and make sure they don't pick up any motives to avoid success or other bad habits. When I looked more closely at how real people in organizations behave, however, the picture changed. I could find nothing about women in my own research and that of others that was not equally true of men in some situations. For example, some women do have low job aspirations, but so do men who are in positions of blocked opportunity. Some women managers are too interfering and coercive, but so are men who have limited power and responsibility in their organizations. Some women in professional careers behave in stereotyped ways and tend to regard others of their sex with disdain, but so do men who are tokens—the only member of their group at work.

So I dropped my search for sex differences, and I concentrated instead on three aspects of a business organization that do the most to explain the conventional wisdom about women: opportunity, power, and tokenism.

OPPORTUNITY

Are women less ambitious and committed to work than men? According to one large corporation I investigated, they are. This company has surveyed 111 hourly employees in white-collar jobs about their attitudes toward promotion. Sure enough, the men showed greater motivation to advance in rank than the women, and the men had higher self-esteem, considering themselves more competent in the skills that would win them promotions. The women seemed much less interested in advancement, sometimes saying that they cared more about their families.

Yet in this company, like many, there were dramatic differences in the actual opportunities for promotion that men and women had. Men made up only a small proportion of white-collar workers; most were clustered in professional roles with steps toward management positions. Over two thirds of the women were secretaries or clerks in dead-end jobs. They could hope to advance two or three steps up to executive secretary, and there they would stop. Only rarely had a secretary moved up into professional or managerial ranks. No wonder the women found promotion a far-fetched idea.

If the company had looked at women in high-ranking jobs, the apparent sex difference in work attitudes would have vanished utterly. In my interviews, I found that ambition, self-esteem, and career commitment were all flourishing among women in sales jobs, which are well-paid and on the way to top management. Indeed, one successful young woman in the sales force told me she hoped someday to run the company.

Lack of opportunity to succeed, not a personality style that shuns success, is often what separates the unambitious from the climbers—and the women from the men. The great majority of women hold jobs that have short, discouraging career ladders—secretarial, clerical, factory work. When the jobs include opportunities for advancement, women want to advance. But jobs without such opportunities depress a person's ambition and self-esteem, for men as well as women.

The early research that first specified the circumstances under which workers are not highly committed to work or hungry for promotion was all focused on men. Social scientists Eli Chinov (who studied auto workers), Harry Purcell (meat-packers), and Robert Dublin (factory workers) concluded that the men in these routine jobs behaved just like the typical woman, they defined their jobs as temporary and dreamed of leaving. They claimed to have little interest in climbing to a higher-status job, preferring, they said, "easy work." And they placed a higher value on family life than on their careers. In effect, they adopted values that rationalized the reality of their roles.

GOSSIP AT THE DEAD END

Opportunity also determines what kinds of relationships a person forms on the job. Workers who have few prospects of moving up and out compensate by making close friends. The very limitations of the job ensure that those friends will be around for a while, and one better make sure that at least the social side of an unchallenging job is pleasurable. Being well-liked becomes another meaning of success to people in dead-end work, and if you've got the best stories to offer the office, you can add a bit of excitement to mundane work. So it often looks as if women are "talk-oriented," not "task-oriented," in their jobs. Some employers point to the gossipy office coffee klatch as a direct result of women's natural concern with people, rather than with achievement. Instead, I think it is more accurate to say that female socializing reflects the jobs they have.

Highly mobile jobs demand that a person be most concerned with the work. Such jobs make close friendships with co-workers less likely. The corporate world requires its participants to be willing to relocate, to surpass rivals without hesitation, to use other people to advance in status. The aggressive, striving junior executive is as much a creation of his place in the organization hierarchy as is the talkative, unambitious secretary.

A laboratory study by Arthur Cohen clearly showed what happens to young men when their opportunity for advancement is varied. He set up some groups to be highly mobile, with a strong potential for individual promotions, and he set up other groups to believe they had no such potential. The highly mobile groups quickly became more involved with the task they had to do. They dropped irrelevant chatter, and reported later that they cared more about the high-power people who were supervising them than about each other. The nonmobile group members, by contrast, concentrated on each other. They virtually ignored the powerful supervisors, because they had nothing to gain from them anyway. They were more openly critical and resentful of people with power.

THE FRUSTRATED FOX

People who are placed in dead-end jobs set a self-fulfilling prophecy in motion. Such workers cope with career limitations by giving up hope; like the frustrated fox, they decide they don't want the grapes after all. Instead, they create peer groups that give them moral support for not seeking advancement, and develop a hostility to outsiders and power figures. Peer groups make a bad job endurable or even fun, but they also put pressure on an individual to stay put. To leave would be a sign of disloyalty. For this reason, the rare man who is offered a promotion out of a dead-end factory slot feels the same ambivalence as the rare secretary who gets a chance at management.

When workers lower their aspirations, their employers logically conclude that they don't have the right attitudes for promotion. The organization decides to invest less of its resources in developing people who seem uninterested, and this decision reenforces the workers' perceptions of blocked opportunity. The vicious circle is complete.

POWER

One of the reasons given to explain why so few women have organizational authority is that people don't like female bosses. In a 1965 *Harvard Business Review* survey of almost 2,000 executives, few respondents of either sex said that they or others would feel comfortable about working for a woman, although the women were more ready to do so than the men. Over half of the men felt that women were "temperamentally unfit" for management, echoing the stereotype of the ineffective lady boss who substitutes pickiness about rules for leadership.

In fact, there is no solid evidence of lasting differences in the leadership styles of men and women. Nor is there evidence that people who work for women have lower morale. Research points in the other direction: those who have worked for a woman boss are much more likely to be favorably disposed toward female leaders.

One clear factor distinguishes good leaders from bad, effective from ineffective, liked from disliked. It is not sex, but power. It is not a matter of personality, but of clout.

Just because people have been given formal authority by virtue of position and title, they do not necessarily have equal access to power in the organization. It is not enough to be the most skillful handler of people in the world. One also needs system-granted power to back up one's demands and decisions and to ensure the confidence and loyalty of subordinates.

System power comes from having influence in the upper echelons of the organization, through membership in informal inner circles and by having high status. As a number of social-psychological studies have shown, people who bring such signs of status and influence into a group tend to be better liked—not resented—and to get their way more often. Organization members, as my interviews revealed, prove to be very knowledgeable about who is in and who is out, and when I asked them to describe desirable bosses, they decidedly preferred those with power to those with style or expertise.

That preference carries real as well as symbolic payoffs. Powerful leaders get more rewards and resources to dispense, and their own mobility promises advancement for the subordinates they bring along. Powerful leaders on the move also pick up a few practices that make them admired. As sociologist Bernard Levenson suggests, promotable supervisors generally adopt a participatory style in which they share information with employees, delegate responsibility, train successors, and are flexible about rules and regulations. They also want to show that they are not indispensable in their current jobs, and they seek to fill the vacancy created by their own advancements with one of their own lieutenants. Since highly mobile people also want to please those above them more than nonmobile people do, they effectively build the relationships that ensure system power.

PUNITIVE, PETTY TYRANTS

Now consider again the stereotype of the bossy woman boss, who is supposedly rigid, petty, controlling, and likes to poke her nose into the personal affairs of employees. This image is the perfect picture of the powerless. Powerless leaders, men and women alike, often become punitive, petty tyrants. Psychologically, they expect resistance from subordinates. And because they have fewer organizational rewards to trade for compliance, they try to coerce employees into supporting them. Blocked from exercising power in the larger hierarchy, they substitute the satisfaction of lording it over subordinates. Unable to move ahead, they hold everyone back, and praise conformity to rules rather than talent and innovation.

Burleigh Gardner, a human-relations consultant, reviewed the experiences of women who took over supervisory jobs from men during World War II. He concluded: "Any new supervisor who feels unsure of himself, who feels that his boss is watching him critically, is likely to demand perfect behavior and performance from his people, to be critical of minor mistakes, and to try too hard to please his boss. A woman supervisor, responding to the insecurity and uncertainty of her position as a woman, knowing that she is being watched both critically and doubtfully, feels obliged to try even harder. And for doing this she is said to be 'acting just like a woman.'" In truth, she is acting just as any insecure person would.

We again come full circle. Those who have a favorable place in the power structure are more likely to become effective leaders, to be liked, and thus to gain more power. Sponsorship, for example, is a typical road to the top for many men. The protégé system, whether in academia, politics, or business, is a tough and informal way of keeping outsiders out, and making sure the best insiders keep on the fastest track. For this reason, it has been almost impossible for a woman to succeed in business without sponsorship or membership in the company's ruling family. But when women do get real power, whether in politics like Indira Gandhi or in business like advertising executive Mary Wells, they behave just as well—or badly—as men do.

TOKENISM

I studied what happens to women when they do manage to get closer to the top, and I uncovered a range of familiar situations. Male managers who could not accept a woman as a colleague without constantly reminding her that she was "different." Women who could not make themselves heard in committee meetings and who felt left out. Bright women who hid their accomplishments. A female sales executive who felt that most women should not be hired for jobs like hers. A woman scientist who let another woman in her unit flounder without help. A woman faculty member who brought cookies to department meetings and mothered her colleagues.

All the characters were there, dressed in their sex roles. Yet I saw that even so the play was not about sex. It was about numbers. These women were all tokens, alone or nearly alone in a world of male peers and bosses. When people take on a token status—whether they are female scientists or male nurses or black executives in a white company—they share certain experiences that influence their behavior.

Tokens, by definition, stand out from the crowd. In one company I studied, the first 12 women to go to work among 400 men set the rumor mill in motion. They caused more talk and attracted more attention, usually for their physical attributes, than new male employees. The men tended to evaluate the women against their image of the ideal female rather than the ideal colleague, and the women, under relentless scrutiny, felt they could not afford to make mistakes.

When the token is a black man among whites, a similar reaction occurs. Shelly Tayler and Susan Fiske of Harvard set up an experiment in which they played a tape of group discussions to students. Then they showed pictures of the group and asked the students for their impressions of the discussants. Sometimes the photos showed a lone black in an all-white group and sometimes a mixed black-white group. Taylor and Fiske found that the students paid disproportionate attention to the token: they overemphasized his prominence in the group and exaggerated his personality traits. But when the students responded to integrated groups, they were no more likely to recall information about blacks than about whites, and they evaluated the attributes of the blacks as the same of those of the whites.

HOSTILE, RAUNCHY TALK

Tokens get attention, but they are isolated on the outskirts of the group. They are reminded constantly of how different they are, and what their proper place should be. Other employees sometimes respond to tokens by closing ranks and exaggerating the in-group culture. In several groups of sales trainees I observed, the men's talk got raunchier when token women were present, though they also added elaborate apologies and bows in the women's direction. Tokens have to listen to jokes about people like them, and they face the subtle pressures to side with the majority against their kind. Male nurses report the same kind of disguised hostility from the women they work with, who constantly remind them that they do not belong and pose loyalty tests to see if they will side with women against other men. The token is never quite trusted by the rest of the group.

To win the group's trust, tokens often resort to acting out the stereotypical role that members of their sex or race are supposed to play. These roles require them to deny parts of themselves that don't fit the majority group's assumptions, and they make it difficult for the tokens to be ordinary workers doing their jobs. Token women, for instance, may wind up playing mother, sex object, pet, or iron maiden. Token men get caught, too. Lone blacks in groups of white workers, sociologist Everett Hughes found, may play the comedian. Taylor and Fiske's students saw the solo black as taking on special roles in the group, often highly stereotyped. And male nurses, according to Bernard Segal, get inveigled into doing the distasteful chores that the women didn't want to do, which were considered "men's work."

Tokens face additional pressures because they must work doubly hard to prove themselves. "Women must work twice as hard as men to be thought half as good," wrote suffragist Charlotte Whitton; "Luckily, this is not difficult." But it *is* difficult, and takes its psychological toll in emotional stress. Tokens have a shaky identity because of their precarious position; they can't behave in a totally natural way because they are on display all the time.

Many of the supposed personality traits of minority people in white male organizations, then, simply reflect their token status. To avoid the glare of visibility, some tokens try to hide themselves and their achievements. To escape the feeling of being outsiders, some tokens go overboard in adopting the attitudes of the insiders. To win trust and the comfort of being accepted, some play the stereotype that is expected of them.

Yet all these reactions—which are not necessarily conscious or intentional— are exactly those that prove to the majority that they were right all along. So tokens are kept to a numerical minimum, and another vicious spiral continues.

THE JOB MAKES THE WOMAN

What I am suggesting is that the job makes the man—and the woman. People bring much of themselves and their histories to their work, but I think we have overlooked the tremendous impact of an organization's structure on what happens to them once they are there.

If my approach is right, it suggests that change will not come from changing personalities or attitudes, and not from studying sex or race differences. Change will come only from interrupting the self-perpetuating cycles of blocked opportunity, powerlessness, and tokenism.

Take the case of Linda S., a woman who had been a secretary in a large corporation for 16 years. Five years ago, she would have said that she never wanted to be anything but a secretary. She also would have told you that since she had recently had children she was thinking of quitting. She said secretarial work was not a good enough reason to leave the children.

Then came an affirmative-action program, and Linda was offered a promotion. She wavered. It would mean leaving her good female friends for a lonely life among male managers. Her friends thought she was abandoning them. She worried whether she could handle the job. But her boss talked her into it and promised to help, reassuring her that he would be her sponsor.

So Linda was promoted, and now she handles a challenging management job most successfully. Seeing her friends is the least of her many reasons to come to work every day, and her ambitions have soared. She wants to go right to the top.

"I have 15 years left to work," she says. "And I want to move up six grades to corporate vice president—at least."

DISCUSSION QUESTIONS

1. What would you do if you were a manager and you wanted your people to be more task-oriented?
2. In view of the Kanter findings, what advice would you give to anyone entering (or already in) an employment situation in which they are a minority?
3. Employees who are critical and resentful are often frustrated and blocked people who are not very productive and who act as depressors on others. What might be done to improve their morale and productivity?
4. Talent, innovation, and creativity are immensely important to organizations today. How do you develop managers who will reward these qualities? Under what circumstances do managers suppress or fail to reward these qualities?
5. Often in organizations minorities don't exhibit much ambition and they seem to "stick together." Apply Kanter's observations about women to such minorities. Relate this to Rivera's discussion of Hispanic traditional values.

A series of cases of women in the senior ranks of organizations and their problems gaining power.

Why Women Aren't Making It to the Top

Liz Roman Gallese

Blame male managers, of course, who won't give women a fair shot. But could it also be that women don't crave power enough?

In the 1970s, women first began entering managerial and professional jobs in substantial numbers. Two decades later, not one has reached the top rung of a major publicly held company by rising through the ranks. Katharine Graham, chairman of the Washington Post Company, inherited the position upon her husband's death. The retired Elisabeth Claiborne Ortenberg had founded Liz Claiborne Inc.

The prevailing wisdom holds that women aren't as ambitious or as qualified for top jobs, or that there is a point—a "glass ceiling"—beyond which discrimination hampers their advancement. But in a five-month, intensive study of 24 corporate women that I recently undertook, another theory emerged: What holds women back, at least in part, is the way they and their male peers perceive women's capacity for attaining and exercising power.

Men, say women, are ambivalent about women's ability to fight for and wield power. Women, the women themselves admit, aren't as forthright as men about doing so. And misconceptions on the part of both men and women create a vicious cycle that holds back even the most talented women.

Women's inability to get to the top "isn't inherent in the woman," asserts Christina Brown, a 53 year-old head-hunter who was recently forced out of an upper-middle-level line job in finance when her former employer was taken over. "It is well accepted that women are smart," she explains. "In other words, I Mr. Biggie Corporate, am happy for it to be a woman who handles a job that involves *thinking power*. I'm happy for it to be a woman who makes the presentation, showing me the results of the market research. Florence Skelly gets the same respect as Daniel Yankelovich.

"But what no one has bought into yet is that women can exercise power. When it's guts-balls leverage, when it's fighting, when it's playing poker, when it's 'I bet my $4 zillion on this deal, where are you?' the world doesn't think women can do that. And I don't know how many women think women can do that."

The thesis framed by Brown's words surfaced again and again in the course of my study. The 24 women interviewed were among the most highly placed—and in some cases, highly visible—female executives in America. Two are themselves chief executive officers, albeit not of publicly held concerns. Eight hold jobs in

"Why Women Aren't Making It to the Top," by Liz Roman Gallese. Reprinted from *Across the Board* (April 1991); The Conference Board, 845 Third Avenue, New York, NY 10022.

which they report directly to the CEO; eight are in positions in which they have frequent and substantive contact with the CEO. Of the remaining six, all had held senior-level corporate jobs—and had failed to advance further. Two of these women (Brown being one) switched careers as a result. Two founded their own businesses. Two took early retirement.

During our conversations, each woman told me what had happened at each stage of her career. When taken in aggregate, their stories point to a clear pattern.

Specifically, those women who broke into the senior ranks did so because male bosses didn't allow common misconceptions about women's capacity for power to cloud their judgment, and because the women were themselves comfortable with pursuing power. The women who failed, by contrast, were held back by male superiors, and didn't scramble as aggressively for power. What follows are the stories of four of the women whom I interviewed—two who failed to reach senior positions, and two who succeeded. The names have been changed to protect their identities.

PEG SIMPSON: TRIPPED AT THE FINISH LINE

What does it mean for a woman to fail to advance because her male superiors stack the deck against her—in other words, refuse to cede power to a woman?

The answer to that question became clearer when I met 59-year-old Peg Simpson. Seated in her spacious corner office atop a brand-new building in midtown Manhattan, a spectacular silver necklace adorning her royal-blue dress, Simpson had all the trappings of the arrived corporate executive. Yet there was something awry: The big desk was devoid of paper, not a single book graced the coffee table. This was, I realized, the room where dreams die. Peg Simpson had been in the race for the presidency of this service-industry corporation, and she had lost. Now she was preparing to take early retirement.

"There are glass ceilings for women because women won't fight in the same way that a man will fight," Simpson was saying. "Women won't demand the same things. Even more importantly, the male hierarchy doesn't expect women to demand the same things."

On the surface, the facts were simple enough. Having risen through the ranks thanks to her superb technical skills, Simpson was named one of the firm's two executive vice presidents and was put in charge of one of the two major business lines. Both Simpson and her male peer were candidates for the presidency, she was told by the chairman.

But then came the stacked deck: Her peer was paid more than she, and was named to the board of directors. Inexplicably, Simpson wasn't—and her pleas for an explanation were stonewalled. "I was told that the board wanted to reduce the number of inside directors," she says, "I said, 'I understand that, but what are you going to do for me?'"

On paper, the firm's chairman was a forthright supporter of women's advancement. In fact, the company had been cited by women's groups as a superb employer for women. And the chairman had come to Simpson's own defense earlier in her career when she had been up against a boss who wasn't supportive.

Yet when she edged closer to a job at the very top—the presidency—the chairman had set up an unequal race. Why hadn't he met her halfway?

Simpson theorizes that he is supportive of women's advancement *intellectually*, but not *emotionally*; in other words, it's okay in theory, but not in his backyard. "In his gut, he isn't supportive," she says. "I think he didn't want me as a major contender because he was uncomfortable thinking a woman would be president of this company."

Simpson's case exemplifies a phenomenon noted by many other women interviewed: Women move easily within the lower ranks of the corporate world because men have no trouble with women displaying technical expertise, as is required at the bottom and middle rungs. It's at the higher levels, when the game becomes exercising raw power that apprehensions arise.

Another subtlety of corporate power noted by the women in my study was that jobs at the upper middle level—which usually involve the exercise of autonomous line authority over a chunk of business—are the most typical point of derailment for women in corporations. One explanation is that jobs at the next higher level—those in the senior circle—suddenly require far different skills: that of deference to the chief executive officer, support for his goals, and the building of consensus among both the top people and the troops. A man's ability to perform these functions is highly valued by other men, say the women in the study, but in a woman, the same ability is perceived as weakness. For men, a female executive exhibiting the kind of deferential behavior that characterizes high-level jobs triggers associations with other women in their lives—wives, mothers, daughters, secretaries, and more recently, executive assistants—among whom deference often denotes powerless helpmates.

One woman in the study, for example, brought her high evaluation of a female subordinate to the attention of her male boss, telling him that the young woman was promotable because she was "smart, attractive, articulate, and presented herself well." Her boss replied: "It's interesting you speak highly of her. I always think of her as. . . I mean, she could be married to my brother."

By and large, the male response to women on the issue of deference remains subconscious and conflicted. As a result, female executives often receive mixed signals from men about how they are expected to behave. One woman in the study, who had recently advanced from an upper-middle-level job into the senior ranks, says she frequently runs into this problem at corporate parties. "On one hand, the men want you to be like a wife at a cocktail party and stand a half pace behind," she says, "On the other hand, they want you to be one of the boys and contribute to the conversation."

Peg Simpson's case begs an intriguing question: Was the chairman trying to test her ability to demand the power due her—her seat on the board? Simpson admits she could have done more to that end. A popular executive with underlings, Simpson says she "could have traveled around the country, making myself visible," and that she could have strengthened alliances with other powerful board members, then threatened the chairman with an appeal to the board if the two of them were unable to resolve the problem.

"A man would have done that," Simpson speculates, including the peer to whom she lost the race. ("He's a tough guy," she says.) "But I couldn't be the person saying, 'Slit that other guy's throat to give me what I want'."

Simpson's inaction in this situation gives one pause, but backs right up against a brick wall when one considers that a man at Simpson's level wouldn't have been denied the board seat in the first place. The issue is not just deference but fairness.

For a woman, moreover, deference holds yet another subterfuge. As is the case for many women, Peg Simpson had always been promoted a step or two behind similarly able men, and so had come to believe that patience was an ally in her climb to the top. When first denied the board seat, she says, her reaction was, "In time this too will be corrected." Yet the race at this ultimate level was different. Indeed, Simpson's career was short-circuited because of a discrepancy on the part of her male superior between what was promised—a shot at a top job—and what was delivered—an unequal race. And in her spectacular empty office, Simpson is left to speculate about the reasons for the chairman's misconceptions about women and power.

CHRISTINA BROWN: OUTSIDE THE IN-GROUP

In her home Manhattan office, Christina Brown is analyzing her failure to survive at the upper-middle-level job she had held at a top financial corporation. In some respects, it's an old story: A takeover occurs, the new team comes in, and out goes the old management.

Yet for Brown there's another dimension to the tale—the issue of the way female executives are treated in the aftermath of a power play. She speaks matter-of-factly about her demise, though her brow furrows slightly under carefully combed blond hair. For the new management team, she asserts, "maleness equaled money equaled power." The new chairman was so "uncomfortable" with women as equals that he "went out of his way to make staff meetings formal agenda-type stuff," she says. He held the real meetings on Sunday mornings at his home so that he could decide for himself whom to include.

Brown was quickly swept out of the inner circle. The revenue level for divisions to be included was upped, so that the division she ran no longer qualified. Unlike Peg Simpson's case, Brown's new superiors seemed to be treating her in the same way as her male peers. Numbers are numbers, after all.

But the kicker was that a male colleague, whose division was smaller than hers, was awarded part of another unit so that he could still be part of the circle. The male hierarchy took care of their own, Brown says, while women were left to fend for themselves. According to Brown, her male peers are still at the company, "and, for the most part, very rich now."

Brown didn't depart immediately. She hung on until she had "almost no will but to get out," she says. Indeed, she seems a bit proud when noting the chairman himself was surprised by her tenacity. Yet given that the situation was untenable, why didn't Brown bail out sooner? Could it have been that she was ambivalent about demanding the power due her? Did she actually want peace instead? "I bought peace rather than power," she responds, "because I decided I couldn't get power."

JOAN PRENDERGAST: AN OBJECTIVE APPOINTMENT

Joan Prendergast is one of the few women who have achieved both peace and power in a corporate setting. Hunched over her big desk, the gray drapes in her office drawn as if to focus her attention on the task therein, Prendergast, the newly appointed president of a large Midwestern bank, appears to blend with her environment. She wears a gray banker's suit, sturdy low-heeled shoes, and a stoic can-do expression.

Why was she able to get to the top when both Simpson and Brown fell short? "The chairman of my company has a very interesting way of making decisions" about whom to appoint to top jobs, Prendergast begins.

The chairman bases his selection on criteria that are as objective as possible. To select a candidate, he draws a matrix, listing down the side the qualifications necessary for the job, and across the top the candidates. To each box on the chart, he assigns a score. When Prendergast scored highly on all, he knew he "had to consider my candidacy seriously," she says.

How simple, how right, one is compelled to think. But in the real world of corporate baton-passing at the highest levels, how rarely done. Prendergast's champion himself was no doubt aware of that, for in presenting her as his candidate to the full board, he made his case judiciously.

Asking her to wait outside, he addressed his fellow board members without naming her or in any way indicating that she was a woman. Rather, he carefully reviewed all the criteria the board had agreed were necessary for the job, then the scores he had assigned to each prospect. "The board went through in a very careful way, what they had agreed were the qualifications," says Prendergast, then "they went through my candidacy relative to the requirements."

Only then did the chairman announce that his nominee for the position was a woman. Prendergast also happened to be six months pregnant at the time. "From the moment I walked in, the atmosphere was friendly and relaxed," she says. "Maybe the board was incredulous about meeting a pregnant woman—I don't know."

Other factors may also have contributed to the unbiased manner in which Prendergast was treated. For one, the bank was in trouble and needed help fast. The chairman couldn't easily afford to differentiate between male and female candidates—he simply needed to find the best possible person. On another level, the job itself was perceived by the board of directors as more technical in nature than the top jobs at most corporations. Indeed, one requirement was an advanced academic degree.

In many respects, the Prendergast case was an exception. At the highest corporate levels, the emphasis on technical skill—which seems to make a female candidate far more acceptable to men—is downplayed, if raised at all. Technical competence has long been assumed. Typically, the issue at the upper echelon is an individual's capacity to wield power over others: Can candidate A set goals and motivate subordinates to achieve them?

Another common requirement, infrequently acknowledged, is a proper chemistry between chairman and candidate. The strictly objective way in which the chairman in the Prendergast case zeroed in on his candidate is rare.

SUSAN APPEL: LAYING CLAIM TO POWER

Susan Appel, like Joan Prendergast, was brought into her organization at a senior level rather than promoted from within. Hired by a major communications corporation to head a new venture, which was the chairman's pet project, Appel, 45, has risen swiftly to a position of even greater power. She is the only woman in the study to have been appointed to her company's board.

Like other women in the study, Appel had to fight for the power due her. The test for Appel came shortly after she arrived when a subordinate told her that the chairman had indicated that he wouldn't have to answer to her. According to Appel, the chairman had said, "She's coming in, but life goes on as usual, and she really isn't your boss."

In her characteristically direct and efficient manner, Appel "fixed that pretty quickly," by having the man transferred to another department. But she was appalled that the chairman would try to undermine her in such a way. It was a "dirty trick," she maintains.

Put in the best light, the chairman might have been trying to ease tensions among the troops, she concedes. But asked whether it might also have been an oversight on his part, she refuses to let him off the hook: "There are no oversights for the chairman of this company."

Misconceptions about women's capacity to achieve and exercise power hurt women in a number of insidious ways. One surprise in the study was that women at the highest levels—like their entry-level counterparts in generations past—are underpaid relative to their male peers. Most hadn't complained, preferring to hold the inequity as a card to play when combating what they viewed as more treacherous discrimination. Besides, as one woman put it: "I like my $120,000."

Impolitic as it may be to fight the salary issue, a more disheartening finding was the lowering of expectations on the part of the most capable women. One such woman, a 45-year-old banker, spoke of being named by her boss to a senior-level line job, which would have put her in the running for the presidency in the years ahead. The day her appointment was to be announced, her boss's boss—the chairman of the company—called her into his office and asked her to decline the position. What he offered instead was a senior staff job.

Although the staff job had both visibility and influence—it came with the fillip of appointment to the bank's policy-making inner circle—it was still a staff job. It didn't involve the exercise of power. It wouldn't test her ability to run a major unit of the bank. Without such responsibility, her chances for the presidency of the company were virtually nil. "I had major misgivings about taking this role," she concedes, "but when the chairman asks you to do something, you do it."

Asked about her future, she appears a bit wistful. "I think about career achievement in terms of enrichment and enjoyment rather than just sheer power," she says.

While women with thwarted ambitions and cheated careers may now be the evident casualties of the power imbalance in corporate America, it will ultimately be American business that suffers most if the imbalance continues uncorrected. The global challenges of the 1990s require that companies choose from the full spectrum of executive talent. To those corporate officers contemplating the task of bringing women in from the cold, Susan Appel offers a few words of advice: "Go the extra mile. Take the risk. And don't let the woman executive sit out there and freeze. See to it that your support is verbal, clear, and positive."

Liz Roman Gallese, who writes from Wellesley, Massachusetts, is a frequent contributor to *The New York Times, Forbes*, and other publications. She is author of *Women Like Us: What Is Happening to the Women of the Harvard Business School. Class of '75—the Women Who Had the First Chance to Make It to the Top* (William Morrow).

DISCUSSION QUESTIONS

1. None of the women in this article cited other women as mentors or role models. How do you account for this?
2. Make a list of the possible factors that may account for the "glass ceiling" that keeps women from top corporate jobs. Divide the list into the factors that women can and cannot control. Is there any disagreement between the men and women in the class about which factors women cannot control? How do you account for these differences in perception?
3. How can a woman be her own worst enemy in terms of career advancement? Cite specific examples from the cases, articles, or your own work experiences.
4. Assess Joan Prenderville's boss's method of presenting her candidacy to the board. Was it fair, clever, realistic, deceitful? Explain your answer.
5. In terms of effective management, contrast Prenderville's boss's method of approaching the board with Peg Simpson's boss's failure to appoint her to the board.

Discussion of controversy surrounding differences in male and female management styles.

Do Women Make Better Managers?

Mary Billard

ROBIN ORR THINKS THE "ETHIC OF CARE" is a feminine concept. Whereas the medical profession traditionally approaches the body as a machine, Orr wants to bring intuition and personal relationships to hospital care. As national director of hospital projects at Planetree, a consumer health-care organization in San Francisco, she has designed a system that gives patients greater control in their treatments. They are allowed to read and write on their medical charts; nursing stations, the physical barrier between patients and care givers, have been banished; family members are encouraged to administer drugs, change bandage dressings, and stay overnight in hospital rooms. "Here sick people are empowered to work and get well," explains Orr.

An independent, nonprofit corporation, Planetree teams up with existing hospitals to create patient-centered services. Five hospitals have affiliated with the program since 1981, and Orr is consulting with at least 10 others interested in instituting the Planetree method. "We try not to seem like an outside force imposing our will to effect change," she says. "Many men make a mistake that leadership means control. Management is about inspiration and influence."

Orr's approach is at the center of an issue that is hotly debated these days by executives, academics and the media. Do women have a different management style than their male counterparts, and if so, do the consensus-building, participatory methods that are largely attributed to women work better than the hierarchical, quasi-militaristic models? The subject has become increasingly controversial and has in turn raised many more questions. Do participatory styles work in most corporate settings and situations? How does such a manager deal with the realities of increased competition and downsizing? And does labeling any style as distinctly female promote sexism and encourage stereotyping?

The theory that there is a style of management particular to women gained widespread attention in a 1990 article in the Harvard Business Review by Judy Rosener, professor of management at the University of California at Irvine. Entitled "Ways Women Lead," the piece argued that women are more likely than men to manage in an interactive style—encouraging participation, sharing power and information, and enhancing the self-worth of others. Rosener claimed that women tend to use "transformational" leadership, motivating others by transforming their self-interest into the goals of the organization, while men use "transactional" leadership, doling out rewards for good work and punishment for bad.

First appeared in *Working Woman*, March 1992, written by Mary Billard. Reprinted with permission of *Working Woman* Magazine. Copyright © 1992 by *Working Woman, Inc.*

Rosener sent an eight-page questionnaire to all members of the International Women's Forum, an association of women leaders, and asked each of the 465 respondents to supply the name of a man with similar responsibilities. She then sent the men the questionnaire, which asked, in part, about leadership style.

Rosener's findings immediately sparked a controversy and the letters in response to her article filled nine pages in the Harvard Business Review. Professor Cynthia Fuchs Epstein of the City University of New York criticized Rosener's decision to ask managers to describe their management style rather than observing the managers at work and drawing her own conclusions. She argued that much current research, hers included, shows that men and women tend to stereotype their own behavior according to cultural views of gender-appropriate behavior. Other letter writers supported Rosener's view. One was Bernard Bass, a professor of management at the State University of New York at Binghamton, who studied subordinates of both men and women managers. Like Rosener, Bass found that women bosses were more often described as possessing transformational leadership qualities.

As the idea of a women's style of management gained momentum, it plugged into a larger body of work outside the world of business management. Psychologist Carol Gilligan has been exploring how women's model of moral development differs from that of men. The recent book *Brain Sex* argues that men's and women's brains are biologically different, while sociolinguist Deborah Tannen, in her bestselling book, *You Just Don't Understand: Women and Men in Conversation*, persuasively shows how men and women communicate differently.

While advocates of these theories argue that women's strengths should be tapped—even celebrated—critics counter that any stereotyping by gender is a form of sexism, one that will only shackle women to their traditional role as nurturer. Replace the word "woman" with "black," they say, and most people would see racism. Susan Faludi, author of the critically acclaimed book *Backlash: The Undeclared War Against American Women*, is worried by the demarcations. "I'm really torn," she says. "I agree that the workplace needs to be transformed and humanized, but it makes me nervous when men are seen as being one way and women are seen as sugar and spice."

Dee Soder, president of the Endymion Company, which advises senior corporate executives on their managerial strengths and weaknesses, believes the distinctions are irrelevant. "I think there is a higher proportion of participative women managers than there is men." she says, "but the crossover is so high it is a moot point."

DAMN THE HIERARCHIES

Whether or not this management philosophy is distinctly female, a lot of women embrace it. Many say they feel relieved not to have to strain to become carbon copies of men in order to succeed in business. "When the idea was first discussed, I felt like I belonged—I wasn't a little crazy," says Barbara Grogan, founder and president of Western Industrial Contractors in Denver. Grogan started with $50,000 in 1982 and has built a thriving $6 million company. She credits her success to high levels of staff productivity. Her strategy: Flatten the corporate hierarchy and make sure that information flows freely to all staff members. Toward that end, she had Western's new 7,000-square-foot office building constructed without any doors. "I do not have six levels of staff," she says. "And I don't have any organizational chart. If I did, it would be flat."

Grace Pastiak, director of manufacturing for a division of Tellabs, Inc., Ill., believes her participatory style of management has helped her meet her production targets 98 percent of the time (the industry standard is only 90 percent). Like Grogan, Pastiak advocates cutting out layers and making information widely available. She currently teaches a problem-solving class in which her student-employees have come up with suggestions that have saved the company $160,000. Pastiak, who overseas 200 people, has also eliminated a level of management and regularly rotates managers from production control to manufacturing to saleslike jobs in a factory. "It has more a cross-functional structure than a hierarchy," she says.

Perhaps the most successful example of this kinder, gentler style of management is that of Anita Roddick, owner of the Body Shop skin and hair-care stores. The chain now has over 600 stores in 37 countries and, at the end of fiscal year 1991, reported pretax profits of $215 million. "It's just a family here," says Roddick. "We like to say, 'Partnerships, not power trips.' Even the language we use is feminine—things like 'gut feeling' and 'instinct.'" Roddick solicits information by rotating the board-of-directors meetings to different shops in order to meet with workers. "Every boss goes through a two-way assessment with workers," she says. "I even sit down with the tea lady. It is a breakdown of power—very feminine."

THE TEST OF TOUGH TIMES

As the recession and the realities of the '90s hit American businesses, the unexplored question is how well these participatory styles deal with layoffs and restructuring. Harvard Medical School psychologist Steven Berglas thinks the female style of leadership is better positioned for hard times. "In an era when the need to motivate is so important, women will do better because they are nurturers and value driven," he says. "And at a time when the corporation needs restructuring, women will be able to do so because they operate in webs rather than pyramid-shaped hierarchies." But John Whitney, former president of Pathmark, who successfully turned around the ailing drugstore company in 1972, argues that there are times when participatory management just doesn't work. "If an organization is in crisis, it needs a period of authoritative management styles," he says. "People will be dazed. They need someone to say, 'I'm going to take control.'" Whitney quotes Theodore Levitt, professor emeritus at Harvard, who says that effective leaders concentrate on producing consent, not seeking consensus.

Orr believes that even in a crisis situation "employees should be polled and talked to on a personal level." But when she needs to act quickly, she does take control. "Things move too fast sometimes, and decisions need to be made," she says. "You don't bother asking 15 people what they think." When the Denver economy went sour in 1987, Grogan had to cut employees. Although she consulted staffers about the cuts, she admits it was one instance: changes were instituted in 1983, productivity has gone up 300 percent. This year Stayer reached the ultimate conclusion and abolished his job as president. "Now I consult for other companies," he says.

James Autry, former president of the magazine group at Meredith Corporation in Des Moines, also embraces participatory management. Last November he carried out a salary freeze at the company. "The traditional way would have been to make the decision and send out a memo," he says. "Instead, I started talking about such a possibility months beforehand. In meetings I would say, 'Hey, what do you think?'" Because they had been involved, Autry says, his employees supported the move. He also believes that women do "get it" quicker than men when it comes to employee empowerment. "Women think of themselves as affiliated with their people—men think of themselves as the boss," he says.

WHAT'S REALLY AT STAKE

The fiercest polarity on this issue is marked by those who wish to celebrate gender differences and those who are wary of such a move. Author Faludi is concerned about the implications of claiming a women's style of management. "It's a soothing message—no one has to change," she says. "Women can be Mommy, and men don't have to change." Anthropologist Louise Lamphere, a professor at the University of New Mexico who has studied women in the workplace, agrees. "Women may be embracing this idea because they are recognized as having something of value," she says. "Men can embrace it because it offers a way of dealing with women." The liability, according to Lamphere, is the potential for ghettoizing.

Supreme Court justice Sandra Day O'Connor echoed that concern in a lecture at New York University last year. "More and more writers have suggested that women practice law differently than men," she said. The early women lawyers had to fight the notion that they were too "compassionate, selfless, gentle, moral and pure. . . for adversarial litigation."

Others see no danger. "It is not 'betters' or 'worsers.' It is not a gender-limited thing. It is a question of what you lead with," says Saatchi's Forman. "I can be as tough as the men in my office, but I apply it differently, say it differently. Men and women can learn from each other." Sherry Suib Cohen, author of *Tender Power*, an early book on the subject, agrees: "It is the next stage to the feminist movement. It's not reactionary. It is that we no longer have to ape the male."

Whether it's a matter of gender or not, everyone involved in this debate agrees on one thing: It's time to expand the old management model. Global competition is changing the rules and norms of business. But as GE's Welch has said, "Change in the marketplace isn't something to fear; it's an opportunity to shuffle the deck." That doesn't mean throwing out all the old ideas. It means introducing some new ones—rocking the boat a little. The women and men exploring and defining transformational leadership are offering a vital and increasingly successful option for change. As a growing number of companies embrace these ideas, what's emerging is a more productive and humane workplace. And that's worth stirring up a little controversy.

DISCUSSION QUESTIONS

1. Do you agree or disagree that women make better managers for today's organizations? Cite specific examples from your work experience to back up your answer.
2. Explain the major differences between "transformational" and "transactional" leaders. Which of these styles are you most comfortable working under? Why? Which of these styles would you feel most comfortable using as a manager? Why? Do you think that your answers to these questions were influenced by your gender? Why or why not?
3. How do people develop different management "styles"?
4. What can female managers learn from men and what can male managers learn from women?
5. What factors in an organization's cultures could account for one style working better than the other in that particular organization?

An examination of why males and whites are reluctant to recognize they have special unearned privileges that give them advantages, concluding with an extensive list of everyday, taken-for-granted, white privileges.

White Privilege and Male Privilege:
A Personal Account of Coming to See
Correspondences Through Work
in Women's Studies

Peggy McIntosh

Through work to bring materials and perspectives from Women's Studies into the rest of the curriculum, I have often noticed men's unwillingness to grant that they are over-privileged in the curriculum, even though they may grant that women are disadvantaged. Denials which amount to taboos surround the subject of advantages which men gain from women's disadvantages. These denials protect male privilege from being fully recognized, acknowledged, lessened, or ended.

Thinking through unacknowledged male privilege as a phenomenon with a life of its own, I realized that since hierarchies in our society are interlocking, there was most likely a phenomenon of white privilege which was similarly denied and protected, but alive and real in its effects. As a white person, I realized I had been taught about racism as something which puts others at a disadvantage, but had been taught not to see one of its corollary aspects, white privilege, which puts me at an advantage.

I think whites are carefully taught not to recognize white privilege, as males are taught not to recognize male privilege. So I have begun in an untutored way to ask what it is like to have white privilege. This paper is a partial record of my personal observations, and not a scholarly analysis. It is based on my daily experiences within my particular circumstances.

I have come to see white privilege as an invisible package of unearned assets which I can count on cashing in each day, but about which I was "meant" to remain oblivious. White privilege is like an invisible weightless knapsack of special provisions, assurances, tools, maps, guides, codebooks, passports, visas, clothes, compass, emergency gear, and blank checks.

Since I have had trouble facing white privilege, and describing its results in my life, I saw parallels here with men's reluctance to acknowledge male privilege. Only rarely will a man go beyond acknowledging that women are advantaged to acknowledging that men have unearned advantage, or that unearned privilege has not been good for men's development as human beings, or for society's development, or that privilege systems might ever be challenged and *changed*.

I will review here several types or layers of denial which I see at work protecting, and preventing awareness about, entrenched male privilege. Then I will draw parallels, from my own experience, with the denials which veil the facts of white privilege. Finally, I will list 46 ordinary and daily ways in which I experience having white privilege, within my life situation and its particular social and political frameworks.

Writing this paper has been difficult, despite warm receptions for the talks on which it is based.[1] For describing white privilege makes one newly accountable. As we in Women's Studies work reveal male privilege and ask men to give up some of their power, so one who writes about having white privilege must ask, "Having described it, what will I do to lessen or end it?"

The denial of men's overprivileged state takes many forms in discussions of curriculum-change work. Some claim that men must be central in the curriculum because they have done most of what is important or distinctive in life or in civilization. Some recognize sexism in the curriculum but deny that it makes male students seem unduly important in life. Others agree that certain *individual* thinkers are blindly male-oriented but deny that there is any systemic tendency in disciplinary frameworks or epistemology to overempower men as a group. Those men who do grant that male privilege takes institutionalized and embedded forms are still likely to deny that male hegemony has opened doors for them personally. Virtually all men deny that male overreward alone can explain men's centrality in all the inner sanctums of our most powerful institutions. Moreover, those few who will acknowledge that male privilege systems have over-empowered them usually end up doubting that we could dismantle these privilege systems. They may say they will work to improve women's status, in the society or in the university, but they can't or won't support the idea of lessening men's. In curricular terms, this is the point at which they say that they regret they cannot use any of the interesting new scholarship on women because the syllabus is full. When the talk turns to giving men less cultural room, even the most thoughtful and fair-minded of the men I know well tend to reflect, or fall back on, conservative assumptions about the inevitability of present gender relations and distributions of power, calling on precedent or sociobiology and psychobiology to demonstrate that male domination is natural and follows inevitably from evolutionary pressures. Others resort to arguments from "experience" or religion or social responsibility or wishing and dreaming.

After I realized, through faculty development work in Women's Studies, the extent to which men work from a base of unacknowledged privilege, I understood that much of their oppressiveness was unconscious. Then I remembered the frequent charges from women of color that white women whom they encounter are oppressive. I began to understand why we are justly seen as oppressive, even when we don't see ourselves that way. At the very least, obliviousness of one's privileged state can make a person or group irritating to be with. I began to count the ways in which I enjoy unearned skin privilege and have been conditioned into oblivion about its existence, unable to see that it put me "ahead" in any way, or put my people ahead, overrewarding us and yet also paradoxically damaging us, or that it could or should be changed.

My schooling gave me no training in seeing myself as an oppressor, as an unfairly advantaged person, or as a participant in a damaged culture. I was taught to see myself as an individual whose moral state depended on her individual moral will. At school, we were not taught about slavery in any depth; we were not taught to see slaveholders as damaged people. Slaves were seen as the only group at risk of being dehumanized. My schooling followed the pattern which Elizabeth Minnich has pointed out: whites are taught to think of their lives as morally neutral, normative, and average, and also ideal, so that when we work to benefit others, this is seen as work which will allow "them" to be more like "us." I think many of us know how obnoxious this attitude can be in men.

After frustration with men who would not recognize male privilege, I decided to try to work on myself at least by identifying some of the daily effects of white privilege in my life. It is crude work, at this stage, but I will give here a list of special circumstances and conditions I experience which I did not earn but which I have been made to feel are mine by birth, by citizenship, and by virtue of being a conscientious law-abiding "normal" person of good will. I have chosen those conditions which I think in my case *attach somewhat more to skin-color privilege* than to class, religion, ethnic status, or geographical location, though of course all these other factors are intricately intertwined. As far as I can see, my Afro-American co-workers, friends, and acquaintances with whom I come into daily or frequent contact in this particular time, place, and line of work cannot count on most of these conditions.

1. I can if I wish arrange to be in the company of people of my race most of the time.
2. I can avoid spending time with people whom I was trained to mistrust and who have learned to mistrust my kind or me.
3. If I should need to move, I can be pretty sure of renting or purchasing housing in an area which I can afford and in which I would want to live.
4. I can be pretty sure that my neighbors in such a location will be neutral or pleasant to me.
5. I can go shopping alone most of the time, pretty well assured that I will not be followed or harassed.
6. I can turn on the television or open to the front page of the paper and see people of my race widely represented.
7. When I am told about our national heritage or about "civilization," I am shown that people of my color made it what it is.
8. I can be sure that my children will be given curricular materials that testify to the existence of their race.
9. If I want to, I can be pretty sure of finding a publisher for this piece on white privilege.
10. I can be pretty sure of having my voice heard in a group in which I am the only member of my race.
11. I can be casual about whether or not to listen to another woman's voice in a group in which she is the only member of her race.
12. I can go into a music shop and count on finding the music of my race represented, into a supermarket and find the staple foods which fit with my cultural traditions, into a hairdresser's shop and find someone who can cut my hair.
13. Whether I use checks, credit cards, or cash, I can count on my skin color not to work against the appearance of financial reliability.

14. I can arrange to protect my children most of the time from people who might not like them.

15. I do not have to educate my children to be aware of systemic racism for their own daily physical protection.

16. I can be pretty sure that my children's teacher and employers will tolerate them if they fit school and workplace norms; my chief worries about them do not concern others' attitudes toward their race.

17. I can talk with my mouth full and not have people put this down to my color.

18. I can swear, or dress in second hand clothes, or not answer letters, without having people attribute these choices to the bad morals, the poverty, or the illiteracy of my race.

19. I can speak in public to a powerful male group without putting my race on trial.

20. I can do well in a challenging situation without being called a credit to my race.

21. I am never asked to speak for all the people of my racial group.

22. I can remain oblivious of the language and customs of persons of color who constitute the world's majority without feeling in my culture any penalty for such oblivion.

23. I can criticize our government and talk about how much I fear its policies and behavior without being seen as a cultural outsider.

24. I can be pretty sure that if I ask to talk to "the person in charge," I will be facing a person of my race.

25. If a traffic cop pulls me over or if the IRS audits my tax return, I can be sure I haven't been singled out because of my race.

26. I can easily buy posters, post-cards, picture books, greeting cards, dolls, toys, and children's magazines featuring people of my race.

27. I can go home from most meetings of organizations I belong to feeling somewhat tied in, rather than isolated, out-of-place, outnumbered, unheard, held at a distance, or feared.

28. I can be pretty sure that an argument with a colleague of another race is more likely to jeopardize her chances for advancement than to jeopardize mine.

29. I can be pretty sure that if I argue for the promotion of a person of another race, or a program centering on race, this is not likely to cost me heavily within my present setting, even if my colleagues disagree with me.

30. If I declare there is a racial issue at hand, or there isn't a racial issue at hand, my race will lend me more credibility for either position than a person of color will have.

31. I can choose to ignore developments in minority writing and minority activist programs, or disparage them, or learn from them, but in any case, I can find ways to be more or less protected from negative consequences of any of these choices.

32. My culture gives me little fear about ignoring the perspectives and powers of people of other races.

33. I am not made acutely aware that my shape, bearing, or body odor will be taken as a reflection of my race.
34. I can worry about racism without being seen as self-interested or self-seeking.
35. I can take a job with an affirmative action employer without having my co-workers on the job suspect that I got it because of my race.
36. If my day, week, or year is going badly, I need not ask of each negative episode or situation whether it has racial overtones.
37. I can be pretty sure of finding people who would be willing to talk with me and advise me about my next steps, professionally.
38. I can think over many options, social, political, imaginative, or professional, without asking whether a person of my race would be accepted or allowed to do what I want to do.
39. I can be late to a meeting without having the lateness reflect on my race.
40. I can choose public accommodation without fearing that people of my race cannot get in or will be mistreated in the places I have chosen.
41. I can be sure that if I need legal or medical help, my race will not work against me.
42. I can arrange my activities so that I will never have to experience feelings of rejection owing to my race.
43. If I have low credibility as a leader I can be sure that my race is not the problem.
44. I can easily find academic courses and institutions which give attention only to people of my race.
45. I can expect figurative language and imagery in all of the arts to testify to experiences of my race.
46. I can choose blemish cover or bandages in "flesh" color and have them more or less match my skin.

I repeatedly forgot each of the realizations on this list until I wrote it down. For me, white privilege has turned out to be an elusive and fugitive subject. The pressure to avoid it is great, for in facing it I must give up the myth of meritocracy. If these things are true, this is not such a free country; one's life is not what one makes it; many doors open for certain people through no virtues of their own. These perceptions mean also that my moral condition is not what I had been led to believe. The appearance of being a good citizen rather than a troublemaker comes in large part from having all sorts of doors open automatically because of my color.

A further paralysis of nerve comes from literary silence protecting privilege. My clearest memories of finding such analysis are in Lillian Smith's unparalleled *Killers of the Dream* and Margaret Andersen's review of Karen and Mamie Fields' *Lemon Swamp*. Smith, for example, wrote about walking toward black children on the street and knowing they would step into the gutter; Andersen contrasted the pleasure which she, as a white child, took on summer driving trips to the south with Karen Fields' memories of driving in a closed car stocked with all necessities lest, in stopping, her black family should suffer "insult, or worse." Adrienne Rich also recognizes and writes about daily experiences of privilege, but in my observation, white women's writing in this area is far more often on systemic racism than on our daily lives as light-skinned women.[2]

In unpacking this invisible knapsack of white privilege, I have listed conditions of daily experience which I once took for granted, as neutral, normal, and universally available to everybody, just as I once thought of a male-focused curriculum as the neutral or accurate account which can speak for all. Nor did I think of any of these perquisites as bad for the holder. I now think that we need a more finely differentiated taxonomy of privilege, for some of these varieties are only what one would want for everyone in a just society, and others give license to be ignorant, oblivious, arrogant, and destructive. Before proposing some more finely-tuned categorization, I will make some observations about the general effects of these conditions on my life and expectations.

In this potpourri of examples, some privileges make me feel at home in the world. Others allow me to escape penalties or dangers which others suffer. Through some, I escape fear, anxiety, or a sense of not being welcome or not being real. Some keep me from having to hide, to be in disguise, to feel sick or crazy, to negotiate each transaction from the position of being an outsider or, within my group, a person who is suspected of having too close links with a dominant culture. Most keep me from having to be angry.

I see a pattern running through the matrix of white privilege, a pattern of assumptions which were passed on to me as a white person. There was one main piece of cultural turf; it was my own turf, and I was among those who could control the turf. I could measure up to the cultural standards and take advantage of the many options I saw around me to make what the culture would call a success of my life. *My skin color was an asset for any move I was educated to want to make.* I could think of myself as "belonging" in major ways, and of making social systems work for me. I could freely disparage, fear, neglect, or be oblivious to anything outside of the dominant cultural forms. Being of the main culture, I could also criticize it fairly freely. My life was reflected back to me frequently enough so that I felt, with regard to my race, if not to my sex, like one of the real people.

Whether through the curriculum or in the newspaper, the television, the economic system, or the general look of people in the streets, we received daily signals and indications that my people counted, and that others *either didn't exist or must be trying, not very successfully, to be like people of my race.* We were given cultural permission not to hear voices of people of other races, or a tepid cultural tolerance for hearing or acting on such voices. I was also raised not to suffer seriously from anything which darker-skinned people might say about my group, "protected," though perhaps I should more accurately say *prohibited*, through the habits of my economic class and social group, from living in racially mixed groups or being reflective about interactions between people of differing races.

In proportion as my racial group was being made confident, comfortable, and oblivious, other groups were likely being made inconfident, uncomfortable, and alienated. Whiteness protected me from many kinds of hostility, distress, and violence, which I was being subtly trained to visit in turn upon people of color.

For this reason, the word "privilege" now seems to me misleading. Its connotations are too positive to fit the conditions and behaviors which "privilege systems" produce. We usually think of privilege as being a favored state, whether earned, or conferred by birth or luck. School graduates are reminded they are privileged and urged to use their (enviable) assets well. The word "privilege" carries the connotation of being something everyone must want. Yet some of the conditions I have described here work to systemically overempower certain groups. Such privilege simply *confers dominance*, gives permission to control, because of one's race or sex. The kind of privilege which gives license to some people to be, at best, thoughtless and, at worst, murderous should not continue to be referred to as a desirable attribute. Such "privilege" may be widely desired without being in any way beneficial to the whole society.

Moreover, though "privilege" may confer power, it does not confer moral strength. Those who do not depend on conferred dominance have traits and qualities which may never develop in those who do. Just as Women's Studies courses indicate that women survive their political circumstances to lead lives which hold the human race together, so "underprivileged" people of color who are the world's majority have survived their oppression and lived survivor's lives from which the white global minority can and must learn. In some groups, those dominated have actually become strong through *not* having all of these unearned advantages, and this gives them a great deal to teach the others. Members of so-called privileged groups can seem foolish, ridiculous, infantile, or dangerous by contrast.

I want, then, to distinguish between earned strength and unearned power conferred systemically. Power from unearned privilege can look like strength when it is in fact permission to escape or to dominate. But not all of the privileges on my list are inevitably damaging. Some, like the expectation that neighbors will be decent to you, or that your race will not count against you in court, should be the norm in a just society and should be considered as the entitlement of everyone. Others, like the privilege not to listen to less powerful people, distort the humanity of the holders as well as the ignored groups. Still others, like finding one's staple foods everywhere, may be a function of being a member of a numerical majority in the population. Others have to do with not having to labor under pervasive negative stereotyping and mythology.

We might at least start by distinguishing between positive advantages which we can work to spread, to the point where they are not advantages at all but simply part of the normal civic and social fabric, and negative types of advantage which unless rejected will always reinforce our present hierarchies. For example, the positive "privilege" of belonging, the feeling that one belongs within the human circle, as Native Americans say, fosters development and should not be seen as privilege for a few. It is, let us say, an entitlement which none of us should have to earn; ideally it is an *unearned entitlement*. At present, since only a few have it, it is an *unearned advantage* for them. The negative "privilege" which gave me cultural permission not to take darker-skinned Others seriously can be seen as arbitrarily conferred dominance and should not be desirable for anyone. This paper results from a process of coming to see that some of the power which I originally saw as attendant on being a human being in the U.S. consisted in *unearned advantage* and *conferred dominance*, as well as other kinds of special circumstance not universally taken for granted.

In writing this paper I have also realized that white identity and status (as well as class identity and status) give me considerable power to choose whether to broach this subject and its trouble. I can pretty well decide whether to disappear and avoid and not listen and escape the dislike I may engender in other people through this essay, or interrupt, take over, dominate, preach, direct, criticize, or control to some extent what goes on in reaction to it. Being white, I am given considerable power to escape many kinds of danger or penalty as well as to choose which risks I want to take.

There is an analogy here, once again, with Women's Studies. Our male colleagues do not have a great deal to lose in supporting Women's Studies, but they do not have a great deal to lose if they oppose it either. They simply have the power to decide whether to commit themselves to more equitable distributions of power. They will probably feel few penalties whatever choice they make; they do not seem, in any obvious short-term sense, the ones at risk, though they and we are all at risk because of the behaviors which have been rewarded in them.

Through Women's Studies work I have met very few men who are truly distressed about systemic, unearned male advantage and conferred dominance. And so one question for me and others like me is whether we will be like them, or whether we will get truly distressed, even outraged, about unearned race advantage and conferred dominance and if so, what we will do to lessen them. In any case, we need to do more work in identifying how they actually affect our daily lives. We need more down-to-earth writing by people about these taboo subjects. We need more understanding of the ways in which white "privilege" damages white people, for these are not the same ways in which it damages the victimized. Skewed white psyches are an inseparable part of the picture, though I do not want to confuse the kinds of damage done to the holders of special assets and to those who suffer the deficits. Many, perhaps most, of our white students in the U.S. think that racism doesn't affect them because they are not people of color; they do not see "whiteness" as a racial identity. Many men likewise think that Women's Studies does not bear on their own existences because they are not female; they do not see themselves as having gendered identities. Insisting on the universal *effects* of "privilege" systems, then, becomes one of our chief tasks, and being more explicit about the *particular* effects in particular contexts is another. Men need to join us in this work.

In addition, since race and sex are not the only advantaging systems at work, we need to similarly examine the daily experience of having age advantage, or ethnic advantage, or physical ability, or advantage related to nationality, religion, or sexual orientation. Prof. Marnie Evans suggested to me that in many ways the list I made also applies directly to heterosexual privilege. This is a still more taboo subject than race privilege: the daily ways in which heterosexual privilege makes married persons comfortable or powerful, providing supports, assets, approvals, and rewards to those who live or expect to live in heterosexual pairs. Unpacking that content is still more difficult, owing to the deeper imbeddedness of heterosexual advantage and dominance, and stricter taboos surrounding these.

But to start such an analysis I would put this observation from my own experience: The fact that I live under the same roof with a man triggers all kinds of societal assumptions about my worth, politics, life, and values, and triggers a host of unearned advantages and powers. After recasting many elements from the original list I would add further observations like these:

1. My children do not have to answer questions about why I live with my partner (my husband).
2. I have no difficulty finding neighborhoods where people approve of our household.
3. My children are given texts and classes which implicitly support our kind of family unit, and do not turn them against my choice of domestic partnership.
4. I can travel alone or with my husband without expecting embarrassment or hostility in those who deal with us.
5. Most people I meet will see my marital arrangements as an asset to my life or as a favorable comment on my likability, my competence, or my mental health.
6. I can talk about the social events of a weekend without fearing most listeners' reactions.
7. I will feel welcomed and "normal" in the usual walks of public life, institutional, and social.
8. In many contexts, I am seen as "all right" in daily work on women because I do not live chiefly with women.

Difficulties and dangers surrounding the task of finding parallels are many. Since racism, sexism, and heterosexism are not the same, the advantaging associated with them should not be seen as the same. In addition, it is hard to disentangle aspects of unearned advantage which rest more on social class, economic class, race, religion, sex and ethnic identity than on other factors. Still, all of the oppressions are interlocking, as the Combahee River Collective statement of 1977 continues to remind us eloquently.[3]

One factor seems clear about all of the interlocking oppressions. They take both active forms which we can see and embedded forms which as a member of the dominant group one is taught not to see. In my class and place, I did not see myself as racist because I was taught to recognize racism only in individual acts of meanness by members of my group, never in invisible systems conferring unsought racial dominance on my group from birth. Likewise, we are taught to think that sexism or heterosexism is carried on only through individual acts of discrimination, meanness, or cruelty toward women, gays, and lesbians, rather than in invisible systems conferring unsought dominance on certain groups. Disapproving of the systems won't be enough to change them. I was taught to think that racism could end if white individuals changed their attitudes; many men think sexism can be ended by individual changes in daily behavior toward women. But a man's sex provides advantage for him whether or not he approves of the way in which dominance has been conferred on his group. A "white" skin in the United States opens many doors for whites whether or not we approve of the way dominance has been conferred on us. Individual acts can palliate, but cannot end, these problems. To redesign social systems we need first to acknowledge their colossal unseen dimensions. The silences and denials surrounding privilege are the key political tools here. They keep the thinking about equality or equity incomplete, protecting unearned advantage and conferred dominance by making these taboo subjects. Most talk by whites about equal opportunity seems to me now to be about equal opportunity to try to get in to a position of dominance while denying that *systems* of dominance exist.

It seems to me that obliviousness about white advantage, like obliviousness about male advantage, is kept strongly inculturated in the United States so as to maintain the myth of meritocracy, the myth that democratic choice is equally available to all. Keeping most people unaware that freedom of confident action is there for just a small number of people props up those in power, and serves to keep power in the hands of the same groups that have most of it already. Though systemic change takes many decades, there are pressing questions for me and I imagine for some others like me if we raise our daily consciousness on the perquisites of being light-skinned. What will we do with such knowledge? As we know from watching men, it is an open question whether we will choose to use unearned advantage to weaken hidden systems of advantage, and whether we will use any of our arbitrarily-awarded power to try to reconstruct power systems on a broader base.

NOTES

1. This paper was presented at the Virginia Women's Studies Association conference in Richmond in April 1986 and the American Educational Research Association conference in Boston in October 1986 and discussed with two groups of participants in the Dodge Seminars for Secondary School Teachers in New York and Boston in the spring of 1987.
2. Andersen, Margaret, "Race and the Social Science Curriculum: A Teaching and Learning Discussion." *Radical Teacher*, November 1984, pp. 17–20. Smith, Lillian, *Killers of the Dream*, New York, 1949.
3. "A Black Feminist Statement," The Combahee River Collective, pp. 13–22 in Hull, Scott, Smith, eds., *All the Women Are White, All the Blacks Are Men. But Some of Us Are Brave: Black Women's Studies*. The Feminist Press, 1982.

DISCUSSION QUESTIONS

1. What does the author mean by the concept of "white privilege"?
2. Reread the author's list of 46 examples of white privilege. Select the five examples that seem the most significant in helping you to understand that white people are privileged. Explain your selections.
3. In addition to white privilege, the author also cites examples of heterosexual privilege. Develop a list of privileges that the able bodied enjoy that the physically challenged do not experience.
4. Most of us have experienced privilege in some form. Describe an example from your experience.
5. How does this article help you to understand the oppression that members of other groups may experience?

A description of the current status of employment of the disabled using biographic sketches of disabled employees, employment statistics, and an analysis of factors changing the employability picture.

Aspirations and Apprehensions: Employees with Disabilities

Bonnie Prince
Hocking College

Amy: "I have a strong will to be independent."

"It means a lot to anybody, just to get your pay check. No one can take that away from you. I have a strong will to be independent. I've pushed myself." This was Amy's response when asked why she wanted to have a job when she could probably be on disability funds indefinitely.

On her high school graduation day in June, Amy attended the ceremony, went home, packed her bags and was admitted to the hospital the next day for diagnostic tests. The following September, she had surgery for a brain tumor, creating a chronic hormonal deficiency and emotional impact on her life. A six-month hospitalization was followed by a two-year convalescence and years of intermittent illness, doctor visits, medications, conflict at home until she moved out, new diagnoses and returns to the hospital for treatments. Her unsteady waitress jobs proved to be too stressful and she turned to the community mental health clinic where she was assisted in applying for Social Security disability funds.

While Social Security Disability Insurance (SSDI) benefits stabilized the roller-coaster of finances, they did little for Amy's personal esteem or need to make a contribution. As Amy described it, "all I was doing was going to the doctor, taking medication, and that's all that was in my life. I was wanting something else to be more rewarding, so I could be worth something. With everything in my life, it's always been half done. It means an awful lot to me to have something in black and white stating that I'm worth something. Stating that *I did it*. The doctors didn't help me do it. I did it on my own." Amy desired not to be labeled "disabled," to "get the label off my back." She enrolled in college, earned a degree in Secretarial Science and became employed at a small, energetic insurance office. When asked about support for her disability since she's been employed, she said, "they're friendly and understanding here, if I need to be off to go to the doctor. Because of my disability, I had to have my upper teeth pulled, right as I started here. I thought, these people aren't going to want me coming in with no teeth, not knowing how to speak. But they've been super. I've taken the time off, and I've come back the next day, like I've never left."

This article is based on a research demonstration project conducted at Hocking College, Nelsonville, Ohio and funded by the Social Security Administration. While their names have been changed, these are true stories of persons with disabilities who participated in the project.

Phil, Amy's boss, who hired her directly from a college internship, stated, "We've been really pleased with Amy. We're really glad for the help. It came at a good time." When asked how he had become aware of her disability, Phil said, "Amy explained to us in the beginning [when she came in for the internship]. But prior to that, we weren't aware she had a disability. We did not have any outside knowledge of her disability. It doesn't affect her job in any way. Even if it did, as long as a person can perform her job, we are open to any idea." When asked, Phil said he believed that employers don't take a chance on hiring persons with disabilities because they're afraid it's going to cost them lots of dollars, especially if there is a costly training period, or if the person doesn't work out. He also thought employers would be concerned about the appearance of employees with disabilities who work directly with the public, although Amy's teeth apparently did not concern him.

Pete: "Everyone needs a job."

At the country club kitchen where he prepares Italian cuisine and fancy pastries, Pete was interviewed about why he felt he needed a job, since he could continue drawing his disability benefits. "It helps your self esteem," he replied. "Before, I didn't have any confidence at all. None. I just felt useless. You need a job. Everyone needs a job. You know, disability benefits are a trap. You get stuck in it. There's no incentive that I know of. It makes sense to get off."

Pete had started many jobs over the years, most them low paying and only moderately challenging, including construction work and blueprint reading. His resumé, had he had one, would have read like Swiss cheese—no job for more than 90 days, quitting several times after finding a job too stressful. Pete stated, "When I worked before, I had no stability. I never was actually fired, but I had no confidence. I couldn't hang on to jobs. I thought they were going to fire me, and I would just leave. Would just walk off the job and wouldn't even get my money."

When asked about these short, unproductive jobs and how he survived financially, Pete said, "when you are a transient, that's about the only thing you can get. You work spot labor, you live out of rescue missions, skid row, that sort of thing, the Salvation Army. Who do you think most of your homeless are? They're ex-mental patients. They are."

Currently twenty-nine years old and a banquet prep cook at a prestigious country club in Ohio, Pete had spent fifteen years in and out of a state mental hospital, with several inconclusive diagnoses labeling him, as he puts it, everything from schizophrenic, to alcoholic, to having bipolar disorder, to being a victim of child sexual and physical abuse. Never graduating from high school, Pete finally obtained a G.E.D. at a Job Corps center. Soon after his last release from the hospital, Pete enrolled in a two-year college program that retrains persons with disabilities where he completed an associate degree in Culinary Arts. The college experience developed him personally as well as occupationally, he said. "I started out [when I went to college] just like I was a teen-ager, a 14 year-old. They worked with me. Now I'm an adult. I just started driving in January. I even bought a car. This is as long as I have been out in my life, outside of any kind of controlled environment." Pete's long range goal is to become a fully credentialed chef.

Discussing the prospects and best procedures for persons with disabilities to become employed, Pete noted, "there's lots of discrimination. Because a lot of people treat us like children. And we're not. Brian [his boss at the country club] had his doubts at first. He was going to give me some old crappy job, on the grill or something. But he didn't, and now he says he's glad he didn't."

When asked whether people with a disability who are looking for a job should disclose their disability, Pete said, "you play it by ear. You let them talk. You just give them so much. Myself, I've always been frank with them. I've just told them. Because they're going to find out anyhow, when you set up therapy, or sometimes if you act funny if you're on new medication. I would be up front. If they are going to hire you, they are; if they aren't, they aren't, you know. I laid it all on the line with Brian." When questioned about any job difficulties due to his disability, he said that his boss, Brian, "understands my condition. I'm not treated differently than anyone else. If I'm messing up, he lets me know right away. He's got a lot of patience. He takes the time to show me." Asked about the job accommodations that persons with disabilities may need, Pete stated, "we need flexible jobs, flexible hours. We need a good boss who can help schedule your hours around therapy and getting adjusted with medications."

Pete's supervisor, Brian, said that during the initial interview, Pete had been "up front" with him, telling him he had spent time in the state mental hospital. Pete had given him the name of his counselor to call. Brian said his main concern had been whether there was a potential danger to his other employees. When he was assured by Pete's counselor that there was no danger, he hired him, since he "thought Pete would be an asset to our team here. And he has been." When asked about Pete's job performance, Brian said that only once had the disability interfered when he had not taken his medication and was a little lethargic. "The next day, he came in and he was going like gangbusters. He's a good worker. Dependable. I'd like to have four or five Petes."

When Brian was questioned about the apprehensions managers generally harbor about hiring persons with disabilities, he said that managers are mainly afraid of "problems." When asked what kinds of problems, he said, "you name it," suggesting that an amorphous fear of unidentified issues, rather than a knowledge of specific concerns drives this uncertainty. He noted that managers may fear expensive or complicated accommodations, but then described his own experience when hiring dishwashers who were deaf. Although their initial attendance had been irregular, they performed very well after a simple accommodation was worked out, replacing a bell with a light to signal the need for their services. He added that excessive absenteeism is another fear employers may have. He noted that it's hard to find good help these days. Hiring someone who may not initially seem to be a 'model' employee can actually reap benefits for the organization. You can turn that employee into a model employee, he suggested, assisting that person in developing good work habits, building loyalty to your company at the same time.

THE CONTEXT: NEW FACES IN UNACCUSTOMED PLACES

The "disability minority" faces issues that are both different and similar to those of other underrepresented groups in the work force. Similar to race, gender or ethnic background, persons with disabilities carry their condition with them, without choice, to the table of employment. Like those in other groups, society has assumed the disabled will not perform adequately in the work place or will cause difficulties for the organization and therefore should be excluded, or included only if restrictions are applied.

Traditionally, persons with disabilities have found great difficulty in becoming part of the labor force. According to the U.S. Bureau of Census' March 1988 Current Population Survey, 32 percent of adults with disabilities who are of working age (16 to 64) and are available for work (i.e., not living in an institution) are working or seeking employment, while 79 percent of non-disabled adults in the same age range are involved in similar employment activities (Bowe, 1990). Groups which have traditionally been discriminated against who also have a disability are even less likely than their non-disabled counterparts to be working. Only 27 percent of women with disabilities work compared to 69 percent of all women; 22 percent of blacks with disabilities compared to 79 percent of non-disabled blacks; 23 percent of disabled persons of Hispanic origin compared to 74 percent of non-disabled persons of Hispanic origin. Amazingly, these numbers represent a decrease from previous years. Bowe (1990) notes that in 1970, the percentage of working age persons with disabilities was 41 percent and cites several factors that contribute to this decline: the nation's economic recessions during the 1970s and 80s which placed persons with disabilities into last-hired, first-fired status; the use of SSI benefits which were slightly better than minimum wage jobs; and the poor educational preparation which many persons with disabilities have, with only 15 percent seeking post-secondary education and only 2 percent enrolled in four year colleges in the late 1980s. To this might be added the difficulty persons with disabilities find in obtaining adequate health insurance from employment sources compared to disability medical benefits.

Bowe (1990) also notes that unemployment for persons with disabilities (14.2 percent in 1988) is two to three times as high as that of non-disabled persons (6.2 percent for men and 5.2 percent for women in March 1988). The kinds of jobs held by persons with disabilities are considerably more likely to be blue collar and less likely to be managerial or professional. Earnings by workers with disabilities averaged slightly over $12,000 in 1987, 35 percent less than the almost $19,000 of non-disabled workers, though these figures improve to 16 to 19 percent if disabled persons who work year-round full-time are compared to non-disabled persons of the same work level. Nevertheless, economic inequality permeates the lives of working persons with disabilities.

It comes as little surprise that American employers are ill-prepared to accept persons with disabilities into the norms of the work place. Early legislation and initiatives to "hire the handicapped" were, at best, ineffective and at worst demeaning. Often persons with disabilities were relegated to menial, less demanding or unimportant levels of employment, in the back rooms of businesses or public sector jobs, where they would not be seen and therefore would not endanger the public image or profits of an organization. Often "sheltered" jobs in segregated work places were the places society designated as appropriate for persons with disabilities. Media-based stereotypes of persons with disabilities in non-fiction and fiction alike have also been mixed, often labeling such persons as "special," or presenting stories of "courageous," "inspiring" or "admirable" persons who beat the odds to become unrealistic heroes or deserving of our sympathy or charity. In these images, disability is usually represented only by persons with white canes, wheel chairs or Down's Syndrome characteristics. Such tales are often sentimental and inaccurate. Seldom have the media included persons with disabilities without fanfare among the wide cross-section of real or fictional characters they generate, without special comment, simply showing their "regular" participation in our lives, without the focus of the story being the disability itself.

THE CHANGING ISSUES

Recent changes are making equal employment for persons with disabilities far more promising. First, a significant shift has occurred from the view that persons with disabilities belong in segregated classrooms and work places to a new emphasis on deinstitutionalization and the "least restrictive" environment. The children of "mainstreamed" education settings who entered school in the mid 1970s are just now becoming young adults, ready to enter college or the work force. Years of rights-focused schooling have made them (and their parents) assertive consumers of the systems that non-disabled citizens expect. Persons with disabilities are now provided with individualized plans for work, education, rehabilitation and transition to the regular environments of society by their teachers, counselors and service providers. Most importantly, persons with disabilities have become their own best advocates, sponsoring their own conferences, organizations, on-line computer bulletin boards, and outspoken media (see *Mouth: The Voice of Disability Rights*, for example).

Job accommodations that address specific functional limitations (rather than generic categories of disability) have become an expected practice for employers. Earlier expectations set forth by the Rehabilitation Act of 1973 specified that employers who contracted with the federal government at certain levels were required to provide "reasonable" accommodations for qualified handicapped persons, including providing physical access to facilities, restructured jobs, modified work schedules, use of special equipment, devices, readers or interpreters.

As of 1990, the Americans with Disabilities Act (A.D.A.), certainly the most far-reaching legislative recognition of this population, supersedes previous legislation by assuring access and accommodations for persons with disabilities to all citizenship arenas of employment, public buildings, public transportation and telecommunications. No longer are private employers or facilities exempt from providing access. Any organization which opens its business to the public must, as a matter of assuring the civil rights of persons with disabilities, offer its services, activities and facilities in an accessible and nondiscriminatory manner to all.

Also, employers have at their disposal an increasing number of technical systems, devices and support services to assist them in providing successful accommodations. Computers and other electronic technologies now offer effective bridges between a person with a disability and the work to be done. Physical accessibility goes hand and hand with renovation and new building construction. Vocational rehabilitation agencies can be called upon to assist with a smooth transition from training or home environments to the work place for persons with disabilities. The national Job Accommodation Network (JAN) offers a "hot line" telephone system for employers and disability professionals to seek or share information and consulting services when they plan for the employment of persons with disabilities.

The A.D.A. has expanded our definitions of "disability." While most of us conceive of persons with disabilities as having physical mobility needs (wheelchairs!), A.D.A. covers persons with communication disorders (blind, deaf, impaired for vision or hearing), mental health disorders, learning disabilities, cosmetic disfigurements and serious diseases (AIDS, epilepsy, cancer, etc.). Additionally, even if a disability never occurred or currently does not exist, discrimination in employment practices is prohibited in persons who: have a record or history of impairment; are regarded as disabled; have an association or relationship (family, dating partner) with a disabled person; have suffered from drug addiction (in the past) or currently suffer from alcoholism. Employers may not discriminate between disabled and non-disabled persons in their hiring practices (hiring, promoting, demotion, discharge, insurance and other benefits, etc.), nor in the insurance or other benefits they normally offer, nor in pre-employment medical tests or other screening procedures.

A disabled person may expect job accommodations such as facility or work station modification, or job transfer or re-assignment of tasks they can no longer perform to others. "Essential functions" of a job, functions which can be performed by a person with a disability with or without job accommodation, have become a key concept for determining job capabilities. Employers are advised to rewrite job descriptions to specify the essential functions. An employer may, however, limit the employment of a person with a disability if there is "substantial probability" that the disability would pose a "significant risk" to the health and safety of others. Also, providing "reasonable" job accommodations is required unless it can be shown that this would create "undue hardship" for the employer. Unfortunately, none of these terms is well defined at the moment.

> William: "I want to make something of my life."

> "To me, I'm just like everyone else. I have to do things just a little bit different. I would like to work because I'm not one to sit around and do nothing. I want to make something of my life. Contribute something with my life. I think as long as I work that I will feel better, and I think I will live longer than if I just sit around. And I've always helped people, no matter what I've done. If I can help somebody that's in the position I am, and just make their life a little bit easier, then that's my goal."

William is quadriplegic. His career goal is to become a disability advisor and advocate, ideally in a state government office that assists persons who have disabilities locate appropriate services for themselves. His condition resulted from surgery on his spinal chord at the base of his neck when he was in his early 40's. William volunteered for the surgery, knowing that his surgeons offered only a small chance for correcting his condition, also knowing that he risked complete paralysis if the procedure failed. He awoke to find that immediately he was without any control of physical movement below his neck.

William had graduated from high school at the usual age, served in Vietnam, then worked at several jobs back in his home community as a factory employee. The concept of returning to school, becoming academically proficient, attaining the knowledge and skills for using a computer, and developing the counseling abilities and legal knowledge for assisting others was certainly not a career goal he ever envisioned for himself. But neither was the prospect of spending more than half a lifetime in a wheelchair, watching television, living as a "patient" among elderly, often dying, residents in a nursing home. William made a decision to enter college to train as a disability advisor.

Currently, William is completing courses at a two-year college to prepare for his new career, combining self-sufficiency with support from assistants. He manages his own life choices, independently conducting his own personal and financial decisions. Though he relies on a care attendant to drive his van, he personally handles many physical logistics with skill, maneuvering the bulky chair in almost any interior environment, driving his own wheelchair throughout the college with a mouth stick, for example. Prior to attending the college, William spent hours digesting disability legal issues through a correspondence school training program in which he had enrolled independently. Over the last two years at the college, he has become trained to tackle a variety of business operations which can be performed using a computer. To accomplish this, he first mastered the sophisticated Dragon Dictate voice-activated software system for IBM PCs, "training" the "Dragon" to recognize and respond to his voice, a laborious process of repeating words and codes into a microphone headset linked to the computer. He also proceeded to gain an understanding of general computer "literacy" functions and specific IBM PC concepts. Finally he learned Word Perfect and Lotus 1-2-3 through regular college courses with additional tutoring outside of class.

William has also completed courses in writing, algebra, psychology, group counseling techniques and human relations, using a mechanical page turner and tape recorder. Note-taking and oral testing are provided by college staff. As part of his training, he participated in an on-the-job student practicum, consisting of seventy hours during a three month period at a disability agency similar to the employment he will eventually seek. During this work experience, William handled both inbound and outbound calls on an adapted telephone, conducted verbal interactions with clients and fellow workers, and performed assigned duties like any able-bodied employee.

Sometime in the next twelve months, William will be seeking permanent employment. Among the many accommodations he will need are a care attendant to transport him in his van between his home in the independent living center where he plans to live and his place of work, and to assist with personal needs such as eating and elimination systems. While he will bring the Dragon software with him to his job, he will require that an IBM PC be made available by the employer for his exclusive, personal use so that he can operate this system himself. He also will require a specially adapted work station and telephone, plus assistance from fellow workers for a few operations which the computer cannot handle. Most of his job functions, however, will be completely handled by himself.

Based on his patterns of college attendance, it appears that William will have periods of good health, and also some periods of poor health, a condition his future employer will have to accept if William is to be hired. As he moves into employment, he will be covered by Medicare through his SSDI status for a few years after he is hired, but this will eventually be discontinued. He will then require other health insurance, something which his employer will be required by law to provide at the same level as all other employees. Given both these assets and limitations, there are questions about whether current American social, employment, and economic structures will support or deter William in becoming a contributor to the work force and the society.

REFERENCES AND RESOURCES

Bowe, F. (1990). Employment and people with disabilities: Challenges for the nineties. *OSERS News in Print*, Vol. III, No. 3. Washington, DC: U.S. Department of Education: Winter, 1990.

Job Accommodation Network (JAN). Toll-free Number: 1-800-JAN-PCEH or, in West Virginia, 1-800-JAN-INWV, by both voice or TDD, 8:00 a.m. to 8:00 p.m.

Kiernan, W.E., Schalock, R.L. & Knutson, K. (1989). Economic and demographic trends influencing employment opportunities for adults with disabilities. In W.E. Kiernan & R. L. Schalock, *Economics, industry, and disability: A look ahead*. Baltimore: Paul H. Brookes, 1989.

Mouth: The Voice of Disability Rights. 16 Brighton Street, Rochester, NY 14607.

Prince B., Philips-Carmichael, I., and Shaner, K. F. (1993). *Individual technical training and placement program: The Accent Program at Hocking College*. Final report. Nelsonville, OH: Author.

Bonnie L. Prince, Ph.D., Dean of Alternative Education, Hocking College, Nelsonville, Ohio.

DISCUSSION QUESTIONS

Assume you are an employer with a position opening for which William may be suitable. Consider the following questions. Also examine the issues in the context of other kinds of disabilities. For example, ask the same questions for persons who have sensory, mobility, or communication limitations; for persons with a guide dog, care attendant, or assistive technology device such as a talking computer; for persons who do not appear to be disabled, but announce they have a mental health or learning disability or a chronic illness; and for persons who specify a kind of accommodation they will need for the job.

1. What are the misunderstandings or biases that employers might have about hiring a person like William? What are some legitimate concerns? What are positive reasons or advantages for hiring persons with disabilities?

2. What should William (or anyone with a disability) put on a resumé when seeking a position from an employer who does not know about his condition? How should such a person refer to the disability during the interview, if at all?

3. If you know in advance that a person like William will require special access for the interview, what sort of preparations, if any, should you make? If a person with a disabling condition appears for an interview without your advanced knowledge, what should you do?

4. What questions are appropriate for the employer to ask during the interview? What questions are inappropriate or illegal? Are special interviewing techniques called for? What are some mistakes an interviewer might make? How do job descriptions fit into the picture?

5. What issues can be applied to the final decision about whether or not to hire William? What issues are not legitimate? What are some "gray areas"? How does the Americans with Disabilities Act apply?

6. What approach should managers take to providing job accommodations? What kinds of accommodations are suitable for William? Or for other kinds of disabilities? Where can a manager get technical information or assistance about accommodations?

7. How should a manager cope with a disability acquired by an existing employee?

8. For persons with disabilities, how should a manager handle organizational systems of feedback and coaching, performance evaluation, job descriptions, promotion, or dismissal?

An outline of the growing forces that are coalescing to make sexual orientation an important form of diversity requiring corporate attention.

Situating Sexual Orientation on the Diversity Agenda: Recent Legal, Social, and Economic Developments

Gerald Hunt

Increasingly supportive public attitudes, significant changes in the legal environment, expanding marketplace activity, growing union pressures, and the emergence of activist employee groups, provide persuasive evidence that sexual orientation is now firmly situated on the corporate diversity agenda. The implications for educators and managers are discussed.

Although there is a growing management literature concerned with diversity and equity in the workforce, almost none of it deals with the issue of sexual orientation. This oversight is unfortunate because gay men and lesbian women are becoming more open about their sexuality and more assertive in their demands for equal treatment at work. Also, in the past couple of years there have been important changes in the social, legal, and economic environments to do with gay rights in many parts of the world, with the result that the rights of gays and lesbians in the workplace are finding a place on the corporate agenda to a degree that would have been unimaginable a few years ago.

Organizational leaders and management educators can no longer afford to ignore the issue of sexual orientation, and need more and better information if they are to understand this new diversity challenge. Toward this end, this paper examines the kind of changes that gays and lesbians want in the workplace, and then assesses some of the recent legal, social, and economic developments that are exerting pressure for change in the status quo. The paper concludes by recommending a proactive rather than reactive strategy, and by offering a few suggestions for creating a gay-positive work environment.

GAYS AND LESBIANS AT WORK

It is generally believed that 10 percent of the population is predominately homosexual, and that considerably more are bisexual (Kinsey, 1953). Unlike most other minority groups, however, homosexuals are not readily visible, and many have chosen to remain invisible, especially at work, because they fear the negative consequences that might result from revealing their sexual orientation. This is with good reason: In Nazi Germany, homosexuals were rounded up and forced into concentration camps where many died in the gas chambers (Plant, 1986); and throughout history there have been many examples of organizations harassing and dismissing employees when it became known, or even when it was suspected, that they were homosexual (the United States military being one of the more blatant examples) (Shilts, 1993).

Nevertheless, in recent years, more and more gays and lesbians have decided it is time to come out of the "closet" and fight for equal rights in the workplace (Cruikshank, 1992; Blumenfeld, 1992). Indeed, it now appears that gay and lesbian activists in western democracies such as Canada, the United States, Australia, and most parts of western Europe, have targeted the workplace as one of the main foci of activity in the 1990s. The *New York Times*, for example, recently told its business section readers to get ready because gay rights at work was going to be the "issue of the '90s" (Deutsch, 1991). A recent edition of the business journal *Fortune* reported in a very positive cover story titled "Gay in Corporate America" that, "In the company closet is a big, talented group of men and women. They want out—and are making the workplace the next frontier for gay rights. That has important implications for your company" (Stewart, 1992:42).

What is it that this minority group wants? In fact, the demands gays and lesbians are making for equality in the workplace closely mirror the demands made by women and other minorities: they do not want extraordinary rights or privileges, merely the same rights and protection enjoyed by others. One activist group in Canada, for example, included the following in its list of demands made to the government.

> Nondiscriminatory procedures must extend to areas such as recruitment, hiring, benefits, promotion. . . .Three things are necessary to change workplaces for the better: topline management support, clearly expressed and publicized; the provision of resources to fight prejudice; and good educational programs (CLGRO: 1991:1, 2, 9).

Similarly, at the 1993 gay and lesbian March on Washington, a march believed to be one of the largest ever mounted on the Capital, the extensive platform of demands included many items calling for equal treatment at work. Interesting as well, not only did the organizers of the march demand change in Federal, State and Municipal legislation dealing with fairness and equity in civil rights generally and employment legislation specifically, they also demanded full and equal inclusion of gay and lesbian concerns in workplace-sponsored diversity training initiatives (Committee for the March on Washington, 1993).

In other words, spokespersons for this minority offer a clear message: gays and lesbians believe they are discriminated against and treated inequitably at work. They seek change in institutional policies and practices to do with recruiting, hiring, promotion, discipline, and employee benefits (specifically to include same-sex partners), and look to organizational leaders to foster and promote an environment that is positive and supportive of human difference and diversity. Ultimately, they want employers to initiate education and training programs that foster positive and supportive work environments where such things as jokes, sexual harassment, negative stereotyping, and acts of omission on the basis of sexual orientation would be deemed unacceptable and cause for disciplinary action—demands that closely parallel the demands being made by women and other minorities. Implicit in these demands is a perception that the majority of organizations continue to discriminate, openly or subtly, on the basis of sexual orientation. While some universities, several cities and municipalities, and a few private sector companies, such as Lotus and Levi Strauss, are noted for taking positive steps in response to the issues raised by gay and lesbian activists, it is probably safe to say that very few organizations currently could be described as "gay-positive."

SOCIAL, LEGAL, AND ECONOMIC DEVELOPMENTS

In the past couple of years, in tandem with more gays and lesbians openly making demands for equality at work, there has been a number of important developments heightening the potential for change in the area of gay rights in the workplace. Specifically, a changing social, legal, and economic context, combined with pressure from unions and the emergence of gay and lesbian employee groups, are having the effect of exerting considerable pressure on organizational leaders to rethink and change their policies and practices to do with their gay and lesbian workers.

Social Forces

In recent years, gays and lesbians have acquired a higher and more positive public profile. In the United States, for example, there are two openly gay Congressmen (Barney Frank and Gerry Studds), and the number of gay or lesbian mayors, county supervisors, and city councilors continues to rise each year. Similar developments have taken place in Canada, Britain, and Australia. Perhaps the greatest change that has taken place, though, has been the way in which the devastating impact of AIDS has given the gay community a much stronger presence and voice in society. It has become increasingly harder and harder for others to suggest they have never seen or talked to a gay man or a lesbian woman, or to suggest they are unaware of the changes this minority group seeks.

Over the past couple of decades, public opinion polls have shown a steadily increasing tolerance toward homosexuals in general, and gay rights in the workplace in particular. A comprehensive review of public opinion polling in Canada, Britain, and the United States, for example, found that by 1988 most people supported gay equality rights, leading the authors to conclude that, "over the course of a generation, a major shift towards a more liberal position on the principle of equality rights for lesbians and gay men has been evident" (Rayside and Bowler, 1988:649). Since 1988, polling results indicate that public support for homosexual rights has if anything been increasing, with a corresponding decrease in moral disapproval. A recent *Newsweek* poll found that 78 percent of Americans believed homosexuals should have equal rights in job opportunities, while only 58 percent believed that homosexuality was in some way not an acceptable lifestyle alternative (Newsweek, 1992). In other words, while there may not be widespread public involvement in fighting for homosexuals rights, there does appear to be little basis for believing that the citizens of western democracies continue to support either overt or covert discrimination in the workplace on the basis of sexual orientation.

Legal Forces

According to some legal experts, the law is in a process of fundamental change, albeit it slow and haphazard, on the issue of gay rights. A study undertaken by Harvard University, for example, found that "there have been a number of significant legal developments regarding the rights of lesbian and gay people," even though they also found that "discrimination on the basis of sexual orientation persists throughout American society and the American legal system" (*Harvard Law Review*, 1990: 162, 170). In fact, over eighty American cities have now enacted gay rights laws, whereas in 1969 there were none; only twenty-five states now have sodomy laws compared to forty-eight in 1969; and a growing number of cities, as diverse as Ann Arbor, Michigan, and Takoma Park, Maryland, have now introduced gay rights ordinances (Cruikshank, 1992). These advances, however, do have to be counter-balanced against states such as Colorado which have recently overturned gay rights initiatives, and by other jurisdictions that continue to discriminate actively and openly against homosexuals.

Western democracies other than the United States have shown even more leadership on this particular human rights issue. In Canada, for example, the Charter of Rights and Freedoms (roughly equivalent to a Constitution) has been interpreted by the courts to include sexual orientation as a protected grounds, and the provinces of Nova Scotia, New Brunswick, Quebec, Ontario, Manitoba, British Columbia, and the Yukon all specifically include sexual orientation in their Human Rights Codes—legislation that overrides all other statutes.

Economic Forces

Building on increased public tolerance, and in tandem with increased court activity, gay and lesbian activists are also targeting the marketplace as a focal point for exerting pressure on corporations to change. In a recent American survey, the average annual household income for gay men was found to be $51,624, and $42,755 for lesbian women. Although the results of this survey were based on readers of an up-market gay lifestyle magazine, other more general marketing surveys have found gay men in particular to be consumers with higher-than-average incomes, and ones that are more willing than average to spend and invest their money (Nelson, 1992). Not surprisingly, activists see this financial strength as a source of considerable clout in the marketplace, and the gay and lesbian community has become much more aware of the financial pressure they can bring to bear on institutions. Activists in the United States for example, recently announced a three-pronged attack for dealing with anti-gay companies and institutions: waging proxy contests against homophobic companies, urging public institutions to buy the shares of companies that prohibit anti-gay discrimination and to sell the shares of companies that do not, and lobbying for legislation that would prohibit states and municipalities from purchasing products and services from companies that discriminate against their homosexual employees, and/or against lesbians and gay men more in general (Wall Street,

1992). This new, countrywide, centralized initiative builds on earlier boycotts of anti-gay companies such as Coors Beer and the Cracker Barrel chain of restaurants. One recent example is a boycott organized in response to the State of Colorado's anti-gay initiative. By one estimate, this boycott has already cost the City of Denver more than $33 million in lost business and canceled conventions (Gallagher, 1993).

In related initiatives, the gay press now regularly publishes the names of companies thought to be gay-positive, encouraging readers to favor these companies when making consumer and investor decisions. One American bimonthly magazine, *The Advocate*, now publishes an annual listing of the top ten corporations for gay and lesbian workers, and another magazine, *Genre*, publishes an annual listing of the names of the top ten companies with the best records for not discriminating against gay people. Both lists included high profile, international firms such as Lotus, Digital, and Levi Strauss (Katzeff, 1992; Nelson, 1992). Given the financial and organizing strength of the gay community, being on these lists, and equally importantly, not being on lists of the "worse" companies, may well have a very direct impact on the corporate bottom-line in years to come.

As well, a growing number of companies are coming out of the corporate closet in order to curry the loyalty of gay consumers (Kilgour, 1991). For example, many large cities hold an annual gay pride day and these events are often partially sponsored by high profile corporations such as breweries and clothing manufacturers, who obviously view the gay community as a legitimate and profitable target group for their advertising dollars. And, in similar developments, gay- and lesbian-focused events, such as the gay games held in Vancouver in 1990 and in New York in 1993, receive significant corporate sponsorship. In fact, more and more corporations are beginning to realize that gays and lesbians represent an important and lucrative marketing niche. Assessing the actual impact of these marketplace initiatives is not straightforward, but one thing is certain: in return for "gay bucks," businesses can expect to be closely scrutinized by activists regarding their policies and practices toward gays in general and their gay employees in particular.

Other Forces

Other forces are also beginning to exert an influence on how gays and lesbians are treated at work. Two important ones have to do with unions and the recent emergence of activist gay and lesbian employee groups.

Unions
As long ago as 1983, a lesbian active in the North American labor movement noted that, "Although the question of gay rights has only been raised in the last few years, a great deal of progress has already been made. . . the response to gay issues has been positive" (Genge, 1983:170). Even though this might have been a somewhat overly optimistic perspective, as many unions have proved to be reluctant to take on the issue of gay rights, it is true that by the 1990s many labor organizations had adopted formal non-discriminatory clauses that include sexual orientation. As

well, increasing numbers of collective agreements now have specific language and provisions that protect employees on the basis of sexual orientation (Frank and Holcomb, 1990). The American Postal Workers Union and the United Food and Commercial Workers, for example, have non-discriminatory clauses, and in 1989 the American Federation of Labor adopted a resolution prohibiting discrimination on the grounds of sexual orientation. As well, a growing number of unions and union locals have formed subcommittees and caucuses focusing on issues of concern to gay and lesbian workers.

Additionally, a small but expanding number of unions are even more actively tackling specific issues of concern to gays during contract negotiations. Unions such as the Oil, Chemical and Atomic Workers in the United States, and the Canadian Union of Public Employees in Canada, are publicly committed to bargaining for same-sex partner benefits in areas such as health care insurance, bereavement leave and pension coverage, and to providing their membership with sensitivity training sessions.

Gay and lesbian employee groups

Action-oriented coalitions of gay and lesbian employees are becoming a more and more common occurrence in both public and private institutions. Estimates are that there may be as many as a hundred such groups in the United States, based in companies such as Apple Computer, AT&T, Chevron, Hewlett Packard, United Airlines, Walt Disney Studios, Wells Fargo, IBM and Xerox (Workplace Issues Conference, 1992; Pegis, 1992). Although these groups do have a social component, most have issued public statements indicating that their primary goal is to lobby inside and outside their institutions for an end to discrimination on the basis of sexual orientation, as well as for increased tolerance and visibility for gays and lesbians within the workplace. A Vancouver-based spokesperson for GALAXE (Gays and Lesbians at Xerox) for example, indicates that the group's goal is "to improve dialogue with Xerox's senior management on long-standing issues relating to same sex partner benefits and diversity awareness" (Perrault, 1992:3). Similarly, a spokesperson for a group based in a telecommunications company, indicates that gay and lesbian employees are not only determined to press for equal spousal benefits, but that,

> As far as the corporations should be concerned, it's a rational management of human resources. Employees are more productive when they can be who they are at work and aren't treated like second-class citizens (Perrault, 1992:3).

Given the relative newness of these groups, combined with the absence of research, the corporate response to these employee activists is difficult to gauge accurately. As one example, though, a spokesperson for the IBM group suggests the computer giant has been somewhat ambivalent. Even though there appeared to be a general reluctance to change policies to do with same-sex partner benefits, and even though the official response from corporate headquarters was that "IBM does not choose to assume a leadership role on this issue at this time," the company did welcome and honor the group's request to have gay and lesbian issues included in company-wide diversity training initiatives (Workplace Issues Conference, 1992). At

the very least, these groups herald a new crop of gay and lesbian activists determined to work for change from within their organizations and professions, a development that represents an important shift in gay activism, and one with potentially
important implications for the gay rights movement in years to come. In particular,
if these groups become aligned with other civil rights activists and union leaders inside their organizations, they will almost certainly become a force that management
will not be able to ignore.

CONCLUSIONS AND DISCUSSION

The demands of gays and lesbians for equality and recognition in the workplace are
similar to the recent demands made by women and other minorities. What appears
to be happening is that the gay rights movement is only now catching-up with other
human rights movements. Collectively, women and minority groups seek fairness
and justice in such things as recruitment, hiring, promotion, discipline, and employee benefits, and look to organizational leaders to foster and promote an environment that is positive and supportive of human difference and diversity. Although
there are differences within and between the experience of women, racial minorities,
the disabled, homosexuals, and other minorities, many individuals from all of these
groups do come together in sharing a history of various forms of prejudice and
workplace disadvantage. While some gay men and lesbian women have been able to
avoid the sting of workplace discrimination by remaining invisible, more and more
members of this minority group have decided that this option is either not available
to them or is too high a price to pay for success.

A dominant theme in the management literature is that organizations must continually monitor their internal and external environments, and develop appropriate adaptation
strategies if they are to maintain their vitality and effectiveness. Increasingly supportive
public attitudes, significant changes in the legal environment, expanding marketplace activity, growing union pressures, and the emergence of activist employee groups, all provide persuasive evidence that sexual orientation is now firmly situated on the corporate diversity agenda as an issue requiring action. As the business press has already noted, gay
rights is poised to occupy a key place on the corporate agenda for the 1990s. Clearly, the
time has arrived for most organizations to begin rethinking and altering their discriminatory policies and practices toward gay and lesbian workers. Nevertheless, homosexuality
continues to be a controversial issue, one that makes some people feel extremely uncomfortable. Some people might even suggest that overt and covert discrimination against gay
men and lesbian women should not only be continued, but should be entrenched even
more assertively. Religious and moral arguments suggest that homosexuality goes against
the teachings of some religious doctrines or moral codes. However, in countries based on
a notion of secular government, and on the idea that various religious and spiritual traditions should co-exist (many of which are not opposed to homosexuality), the idea that the
religious or moral philosophy of one group should override all others, and directly influence the State and workplace, becomes intolerable. Ultimately, the foundation of democ-

racy is the celebration of tolerance, diversity and individual rights; without this, all persons run the risk of falling from favor and bearing the brunt of discriminatory forces.

In general, then, how might a progressive organization respond to this diversity challenge? Writers concerned with workforce diversity issues, such as Fernandez (1991) and Kirchmeyer and McLellan (1991), strongly recommend a management approach that is proactive, values diversity, celebrates differences, and seeks to maximize the creative potential of human differences, and there is no rational reason why this philosophical approach should be altered when dealing with sexual orientation. In support of a proactive strategy, the experience at those few companies that have taken a leadership role on gay rights at work, seems to have been almost entirely positive: at Lotus, for example, there has not been a customer backlash or boycott, heterosexual employees have taken the changes in their stride, and the financial costs have been low (Kronenberger, 1991). Ideally, if it is not already there, sexual orientation should be added to all non-discriminatory policy statements that cover such things as sexual harassment, hiring, promotion, employment equity and purchasing policies. Effort should be made to ensure that all the benefits, rights, and obligations of heterosexual and homosexual employees are the same. In particular, spousal benefits for same-sex domestic partners should be offered at every level of organizational life, whether it be pension plans, access to the company gym, discounted loans, or invitations to the annual Christmas party. Although some critics might argue that opening up pension and benefit plans to same-sex partners would lead to abuse, there is no reason to believe that gays and lesbians would abuse these perks any more or less than other groups. Others have argued that extending benefits to gay partnerships would be prohibitively expensive, but again there is no reason to believe that such arrangements would break the bank. As Gibb-Clark (1992) points out, compensation and benefits experts have estimated that the additional costs for company pension plans that included gay and lesbian employees would be less than 1 percent.

As well as implementing policy changes, an approach that values human diversity must also combat negative attitudes and stereotypical ways of thinking. In most organizations, educational workshops and sensitivity training would be required to deal with ingrained prejudice and misconceptions about homosexuality, just in the same way that educational sessions are often required around gender, racial, ethnic and religious differences. Some heterosexual workers might even require off-site, "safe" settings in which to express their confusion and anger about homosexuality. Ultimately, though, a progressive organization would need to make clear through its disciplinary policies that anti-gay behavior and actions would no more be tolerated than would sexist or racist behaviors.

REFERENCES

Blumenfeld, W. (ed.). (1992). *Homophobia: How We All Pay the Price*. Boston: Beacon Press.

(CLGRO) Coalition for Lesbian and Gay Rights in Ontario. (1991). *Submission to the Ontario Legislature Concerning Employment Equity Initiatives*. October.

Committee for the March on Washington. (1993). *Program Guide of the Committee for the March on Washington for Lesbian, Gay and Bi Equal Rights and Freedoms*. Washington.

Cruikshank, M. (1992). *The Gay and Lesbian Liberation Movement*. New York: Routledge.

Deutsch, C. (1991). "Gay Rights, Issue of the 90s." *New York Times*, 28 April, p. F23.

Fernandez, J. (1991). *Managing a Diverse Workforce*. Lexington: Lexington Books.

Frank, M., and Holcomb, D. (1990). *Pride at Work: Organizing for Lesbian and Gay Rights in Unions*.

New York: Lesbian and Gay Labor Network.

Gallagher, J. (1993). "Boycott Blues." *The Advocate*, 4 May, p. 27.

Gibb-Clark, M. (1992). "Gay-couples Ruling Won't Break the Bank." *Globe and Mail*, 7 September, B4.

Genge, S. (1983). "Lesbians and Gays in the Union Movement." In Briskin, L., and Yanz, L. (eds.), *Union Sisters*. Toronto: The Women's Press.

Harvard Law Review. (1990). *Sexual Orientation and the Law*. Cambridge: Harvard University Press.

Katzeff, P. (1992). "The Top Ten." *The Advocate*, 16 June.

Kirchmeyer, C., and McLellan, J. (1991). "Capitalizing on Ethnic Diversity: An Approach to Managing the Diverse Workgroups of the 1990s." *Canadian Journal of Administrative Sciences*, 8(2), pp. 72–79.

Kilgour, K. (1991). "Stirring Up The Marketing Mix." *Marketing*, 10 June, p. 1.

Kinsey, A., Pomeroy, W., Martin, C., and Gebhard, P. (1953). *Sexual Behavior in the Human Female*. New York: Simon and Schuster.

Kronenberger, G. (1991). "Out of the Closet." *Personnel Journal*, 70(6), pp. 40–44.

Nelson, B. (1992). "Gay Money: Who's Got it? Who Wants It?" *Genre*, Oct/Nov, Issue 8, p. 20.

Newsweek. (1992). "Gays Under Fire." *Newsweek*, 14 September, pp. 35–40.

Pegis, J. (1992). "Corporate Canada Feels the Pinch." *Xtra*, Issue No. 210, (13 November), p 7.

Perrault, J. (1992). "Knocking On the Glass Ceiling." *Xtra (XS supplement)*, Issue No. 34 (August), p. 3.

Plant, R. (1986). *The Pink Triangle: The Nazi War Against Homosexuals*. New York: Henry Holt.

Rayside, D., and Bowler, S. (1988). "Public Opinion and Gay Rights." *Canadian Review of Sociology and Anthropology*, 25(4), pp. 649–660.

Shilts, R. (1993). *Conduct Unbecoming: Gays and Lesbians in the U.S. Military*. New York: St. Martin's Press.

Stewart, T. (1991). "Gay in Corporate America." *Fortune*, 124(14), 16 December, pp. 42–55.

Wall Street Project. (1992). "Wall Street Project Mobilizes Investor Dollars to Fight Homophobia." *Wall Street Project* position paper.

Workplace Issues Conference. (1992). Unpublished notes from Second Annual Lesbian and Gay Workplace Issues Conference, held at Stanford University, Palo Alto, California, October 2–3, 1992.

Dr. Gerald Hunt is an assistant professor in the Administrative Studies Program at Nipissing University in North Bay, Ontario, Canada, where he teaches courses in Organizational Behavior and Industrial Relations. Currently, he is involved in a research project considering the degree to which labor unions have taken an active role in fighting for minority issues in the workplace.

DISCUSSION QUESTIONS

1. What factors or forces might continue to discourage some organizations from taking on the issue of gay and lesbian rights in the workplace? How might these factors or forces be overcome?
2. What suggestions do you have for designing an effective, in-house training program on diversity, one designed to incorporate gay and lesbian issues, along with gender and racial issues?

C H A P T E R

FOUR

On Experiencing Diversity: Cases

Application is the highest level of learning. Concepts have to be very well under-stood to apply them to the real world. . . . Learning to understand and apply con-cepts can be effectively and pleasantly accomplished through case study.[1]

Diversity is a complex topic that often instigates debate and disagreement. The cases in the following section were selected to illustrate the complications of work-ing in and managing an increasingly heterogeneous workforce. These cases offer a variety of perspectives on issues of diversity in large and small organizations in terms of gender, race, ethnicity, physical challenge and sexual preferences. How-ever, all the cases share one common element—they present an opportunity to think about diversity, not in isolation, but within the complexity of trying to manage di-versity in changing organizations.

The first case, *Continental Airlines* (Sadd), illustrates the intricacy of manag-ing a more diverse workforce and of implementing new policies, when assumptions are made about the homogeneity of demographic groups of employees. Continen-tal's management issued new appearance regulations developed by a panel that in-cluded seven women, and one female employee chose to resist the new standards. Supported by special interest groups and skillfully interacting in the public forum, she managed to have a major effect on the organization's policies.

In contrast to a woman successfully asserting power against the organization, the following two cases—*Al the Joker* (Crowner and Pryciak) and *Briarwood Indus-tries* (Harvey)—examine the situations of two women who have difficulties coping effectively with their situations in their workplaces. In *Al the Joker*, a young worker is subject to sexual harassment and receives little support from either the organiza-tion or her peers. In the *Briarwood* case, a successful female manager does not re-ceive an expected promotion. Instead of trying to work this problem through, she re-signs.

The *Freida Mae Jones* case (Mosler) illustrates the multiplicity of problems experienced by a woman who is both the first female and the first black executive in her branch bank. Although she is very intelligent and highly educated, her boss does not offer her the same opportunities and level of experience as a white male co-worker. Her frustration with his paternalistic treatment is interpreted by him as over sensitivity rather than discrimination.

Starting one's own business is a path often taken by qualified women and mi-norities who feel frustrated in their jobs. The *Emanuel Company* (Thomas), once one of the top 100 black-owned businesses in the United States, is the story of a black man, Don Emanuel, whose business initially benefitted from being minority owned, just as minority workers may get entry level jobs due to government man-dates. Later, as his company grew, Don found himself up against a "glass ceiling" of opportunity, much like the barriers experienced by minority employees in large or-ganizations.

When a large corporation builds a manufacturing plant in another country, they may expect to adjust their management styles to the cultural differences. The *General Dynamics in the Navajo Nation* case (Winfield), however, illustrates that there are cultural differences to adapt to even within the United States and business advantages that make such change profitable and worthwhile.

In the *Mail Management Systems: The Karin Hazam Case* (DiBiasio), the entrepreneur, a woman who never spoke until she was in her twenties and who has only 28 percent hearing capacity, shows what can be done when you have never heard the word *no*. Karin built a successful business that employs a majority of physically challenged workers. Her company enables many differently abled individuals to be productive and less dependent on government assistance.

The *Cracker Barrel Restaurants* case (Howard) illustrates the problems that lesbians and gays experience in the workplace. Homosexuals have less legal protection under Civil Rights statutes than any of these other groups. The Cracker Barrel Corporation adopts an anti-homosexual policy that subjects them to discriminatory treatment and costs lesbians and gays their jobs.

The last case, The *Mobil Oil Corporation* (Hogan) presents an opportunity to analyze how a major corporation is attempting to deal with diversity in two major divisions that are structurally different and have taken two very different approaches to managing diversity.

Cases have much in common with diversity issues. Both cause students frustration because they are complex, often lack sufficient information to make decisions, and may offer no clear cut right or wrong answers. However, cases, like diversity, force us to take an objective view of a new situation in an unfamiliar area and to make a decision, just as we have to do in life.

NOTES

1. Schuller, Randall, S. *Case Problems in Management and Organizational Behavior,* 4th ed., St. Paul Minnesota: West, 1991, p. xi.

"Ticket Agent Fired over Makeup Policy": Continental Airline's Appearance Standards Policy

William C. Sadd

Assumption College

In the Spring of 1991, Houston-based Continental Airlines was struggling for its survival. The domestic airline industry was experiencing near-record losses. The economy was in an extended recession. Weaker carriers were being absorbed by stronger airlines, or, like Eastern Airlines, ceasing operations and liquidating their assets. Continental itself had declared bankruptcy under Chapter 11 in December 1990.

For 1991, Continental lost $306 million, mostly from operations, on revenues of $5,550 million. This loss came on the heels of prior year's losses of $2,344 million (which included significant bankruptcy-related charges) and $886 million in 1990 and 1989, respectively. These losses resulted in a negative retained earnings of $4,824 million at the end of 1991, and a negative net worth of $3,740 million.

During 1990, Continental had operated with a passenger load factor of 60.4 percent, about 11 percent (or about 4,500 million passenger miles) below their break-even point of 67.2 percent. In short, Continental was in serious financial condition. The auditor's opinion for 1991 "raised substantial doubt about the ability of the Company to continue as a going concern." The airline was listed last in *Fortune* magazine's 1991 *Most Admired Corporations* annual rankings. Management was focusing on a number of strategies aimed at assuring its survival and returning the airline to profitability.

THE NEW PERSONAL APPEARANCE STANDARD

Clearly a critical factor in returning to profitability would be Continental's ability to increase their passenger load factor and get revenue passenger miles back above the 67 percent break-even point. Management decided to institute a number of major actions to improve its image in terms of its aircraft, facilities, and service to its customers, according to Arthur Kent, Continental's vice president of corporate communications.

"There was a change in the uniform worn by all ground personnel from a sort of aubergine color to a more professional navy blue. As part of that process, professional standards were chosen and an appearance standard was established," said Kent.

The new appearance standards for "customer contact personnel" were developed by a sixteen-person Professional Standards Committee which had been chosen by the Company's Employee Council, a body elected by the other employees to, among other things, help decide upon new standards. The seven women who were on the Committee which wrote the standard, insisted that a minimum amount of makeup be included in the standard, which also covered hairstyles and facial hair for men.

In March 1991, Continental unveiled the new appearance code which was to become effective on May 1.

TERESA FISCHETTE'S BACKGROUND

Unbeknownst to Continental, Teresa Fischette's whole life appeared to have been a rehearsal for her confrontation with Continental. Once, in the middle of the night, she spent two hours at a highway rest stop trying to rescue a stray cat. When she had a chance to help bring Romanian orphans to the United States, she changed her wedding plans at the last minute.

Terri was born in the early 1950s in the small town of Newark in upstate New York. She seemed to challenge authority from the beginning, both at home and in school. Social responsibility quickly became an ingrained value. Her father, an accountant, went back to school so he could learn to teach the disabled. Her mother wrote for the local paper, and her older sister, an affirmative action administrator for the state of New York, pursues sex discrimination cases as part of her job.

During the 1960s, the Fischette home was an open forum with police bulletins occasionally interrupting mealtime debates. It was not uncommon for the two sisters to accompany their mother to local crime scenes and drug busts. In the early 1970s, Terri spent a few semesters at Potsdam State University. After an early marriage ended in divorce, she moved to Florida and went to work for an airline.

In Miami, Fischette met her guru, hunger activist Sam Harris who had established RESULTS, a nonprofit group that lobbies Congress for famine relief. A favorite RESULTS word is *"trimtab,"* the small rudder used to turn a big ship. As a principle of advocacy, *trimtabbing* means finding the points of institutional vulnerability in a nonconfrontational way which seeks a common ground and provides for face-saving options. Nudging those points can lead to significant results.

In the early 1980s, Fischette began switching airlines and climbing the corporate ladder. She worked in Chicago and Washington, DC, often putting in long hours. Burned out and dissatisfied, she decided to go part time and devote more energy to her causes. With its free travel passes and flexible hours, the airline business was an ideal vocation for a budding social activist.

She had spent the last decade on the edges of the world hunger and animal rights issues. She helped activist friends lobby Congress. She participated in letter-writing campaigns and candlelight vigils, was taught how to write op-ed pieces, how to speak "laser-talk" and how to pressure newspaper editorial boards. "She knows where all the levers of power are," says Henry Spira, an animal-rights activist who has advised her.

In 1984, Terri moved to Boston and fell in love with Pat Marz, an affluent Logan-based consultant for charter airlines, and they soon married. She continued her part-time routine, working mornings for Continental. During her free time, she assisted animal-rights activist Henry Spira, listened to WRKO talk-show host Gene Burns, or button-holed Rep. Joseph P. Kennedy, Jr., for some save-the-wetlands laser-talk.

REACTION TO THE NEW APPEARANCE STANDARD

When Continental unveiled its new appearance standards in March, Terri opposed the requirement that women must wear makeup. Her first move was to call her sister, the affirmative action specialist. She also asked Continental to reconsider their position. Although many fellow employees at Logan Airport signed a petition that she drew up, corporate headquarters in Houston remained adamant.

On April 5, realizing that a confrontation might be inevitable, she contacted the League of Women Voters, the National Organization for Women, the Civil Liberties Union of Massachusetts, and several labor groups.

Meanwhile, Fischette continued to hope that a quiet, amicable solution would be possible. She wrote six letters to Continental. She assembled copies of company records that showed her to be a model employee, including the monthly report cards that airlines issue on personal appearance.

"Continental should not be mixing their perception of attractiveness with professionalism," Fischette said. "Makeup should be a personal choice. It's not fair to ask women in the workplace to adorn themselves with makeup when it's not part of the job. You wouldn't ask a man to wear a toupee because he's losing his hair. They have to get into the '90s."

On April 29, three days before the mandatory makeup rule was to go into effect, Fischette flew to Washington on a company pass and visited NOW headquarters, the RESULTS office, and Susan Shure, a public relations specialist who advised her to call Ellen Goodman and Oprah Winfrey, Ms. Magazine and Lear's.

On May 3, Terri was fired for refusing to wear makeup and because she "did not fit in with Continental's new image." She had refused a transfer to a "non customer-contact position" on the ramp, handling baggage.

IN THE AFTERMATH OF THE FIRING

On Saturday, May 11, Fischette's story was reported on the front page of *The Boston Globe*. The next day, 78 reporters called her home. She had started a national letter-writing campaign to get her message across and to educate Continental. She was heard on 20 radio talk shows and taped an appearance on the "CBS Nightly News."

Several organizations that she had contacted previously offered help and legal assistance, calls came in from around the country offering a show of support. One call came from a machinist in San Francisco who said that he and 50 other guys wanted to do something to show their support. He had sent a letter to Continental.

Continental also received a number of calls at their Houston headquarters, "not all negative and not all positive." Oprah Winfrey asked Terri to appear on her television show and had taped a segment that was scheduled to air on May 24.

Sarah Wunsch, a staff attorney at the Civil Liberties Union, said that Fischette's colleagues at Logan Airport considered her to be a highly professional, personable, and attractive worker. "Continental is making a terrible, terrible mistake," said Wunsch. "If they think the public cares more about a ticket agent than customer service, then they have sadly misjudged what the public wants. We care about safety, we care about good service, and we care about getting there on time. We could care less about makeup."

Fischette, through her counsel Wunsch, filed a sex discrimination complaint with the Massachusetts Commission Against Discrimination and the Federal Equal Employment Opportunity Commission, and was preparing to bring suit in federal court.

In the past, courts had ruled that employers could have reasonable appearance or dress codes as long as they were consistent with community standards and applied uniformly to all employees. Within the last decade, however, federal judges have ruled that such regulations can be discriminatory unless the employer can demonstrate a clear job-related requirement. Over the past few years, courts have struck down a number of stereotypical or gender-biased airline rules, including standards prohibiting flight attendants from wearing eye glasses, getting married, becoming pregnant or working past the age of 35.

On Tuesday, May 14, Terri received a letter from Continental stating that it planned to stand firm on its decision to fire any female ground personnel who did not adhere to the new appearance rules. That night, while sitting in for Johnny Carson, comedian Jay Leno focused national attention on Fischette's firing when he produced a skit about the fired ticket agent. In one scene, an actress with layers of makeup and a revealing uniform posed as Fischette's replacement.

CONTINENTAL'S REVERSAL

The next day, on May 15, Continental Chairman Hollis Harris held a press conference where he acknowledged that the company had made a mistake and would make its mandatory appearance rules on makeup, hairstyles and facial hair optional. Harris also made a public apology to Fischette and offered to reinstate her with back pay. "One of Continental's new corporate themes is that one airline can make a difference," Harris said. "In line with that, in a letter to me, Miss Fischette noted that one person can make a difference. She was right."

REFERENCES

Diane Lewis, "Continental fires agent who won't wear makeup," *The Boston Globe,* May 11, 1991, pp. 1, 4.

Diane Lewis, "Continental makes up," *The Boston Globe,* May 16, 1991, pp. 1, 24.

Chris Reidy, "Facing down Continental," *The Boston Globe,* May 21, 1991, pp. 53, 56.

——, *Moody's Transportation Manual,* 1992, pp. 731–736.

William C. Sadd is an Assistant Professor of Management at Assumption College, Worcester, MA, and holds an MBA from the Amos Tuck School of Business Administration at Dartmouth College. He spent 23 years in a variety of management positions, principally in the consulting and computer industries, prior to making a career shift into teaching in 1986.

DISCUSSION QUESTIONS

1. Assess Continental's development of its new appearance standards. To what extent were the concepts of *diversity* and *otherness* applicable or incorporated into the process?
2. Were there problems with Continental's appearance standards themselves, or with the way in which they were implemented? Identify changes in both which would have improved the likelihood of a successful implementation.
3. Assess Teresa Fischette's relative power in this situation, relative to Continental, and identify the principal sources of this power.
4. Assess Teresa's response to Continental's new policy. Why was she successful? What could she have done differently?
5. Describe Teresa's use of the *trimtabbing* technique, citing specific examples, and assess its effectiveness and the reasons therefore.
6. Why did Continental reverse its position with such suddenness, making their mandatory appearance policy optional, after having been so adamant against changing it?

Al the Joker

Robert P. Crowner
Jeannette Pryciak

In mid-1990, Jackie sat at her desk watching the treatment the other employees in the department were giving Christy. Ever since Christy filed the complaint against Al the other employees were no longer friendly to her. Jackie could not understand everyone's reaction to Christy. She knew that Christy was justified in her complaint against Al, but Jackie didn't know what she should do.

THE COMPANY

A.C. Insurance Company's home office had approximately 600 employees. A majority of the employees, at least 90 percent, were women. The company provided a variety of jobs to women of various ages and skills. It had a comfortable working environment for women to work in and provided them with training if they wished to advance in the company.

Many of the women in the company had little or no college education and needed a job while their children were in school. A growing number were younger women who either did not wish to go to school or were trying to work their way through school.

The company provided good health, dental, optical and life insurance for its employees. It was a good place to work for anyone who needed a flexible schedule, benefits and room for advancement. Since a majority of the employees were women, the company seemed dedicated to help women, who might normally not work, find a place in the working world.

AL

When Al first came to the company everybody liked him. He was young, charming and had a great personality. Al was one of four male employees in a department of forty. He became friendly with everyone in the department and very "buddy-buddy" with the department manager, Cheri. In everyone's eyes, Al could do no wrong; he was a fun-loving guy who kept the department from getting boring.

Al loved to tell jokes and kept everyone laughing. Some of his jokes were distasteful but everyone just took them as fun. Besides, just about everyone knew or told a dirty joke once in awhile. However, Al started taking his joking too far.

His joking became too sexually related and aimed at certain women in the department. These jokes were not the standard "dirty jokes" but rather were explicit and personal.

Christy was one of the targeted women. At eighteen, she was the youngest woman in the department and had started working right out of high school. She soon became the victim of Al's "jokes."

Al would "jokingly" say things that he wanted to do to her sexually and he would not stop with a "Shut-up" or "Leave me alone." Ignoring him did not do much good either for he would just keep right on talking. Christy could not even wear a skirt to work without Al saying something disgusting to her.

CHRISTY'S COMPLAINT

Christy began to complain to other employees in the department about Al's so-called "jokes." All she was told was that she was overreacting and that what Al was doing was "no big deal." She also knew that she could not go to Cheri, the departmental supervisor, for help because Cheri and Al were too close.

After a few weeks Christy got sick of Al's "jokes" and she could not take it anymore. She went up to the Human Resources department and complained about the treatment she was getting from Al. The company did absolutely nothing about the accusation. Christy's complaint was simply ignored.

When word got back to the department that Christy had made a complaint, many of the other employees looked down on Christy. They told her that she should have never said anything against such a wonderful guy like Al. "Al was only joking," "That's just the way he is" and "You should not make a big deal out of nothing" were a few of the comments thrown Christy's way. Al told her that she was just flattering herself if she took his joking seriously. All of these remarks just made Christy feel worse.

JACKIE'S THOUGHTS

Jackie thought about what was happening. She knew what Christy was going through because Al acted exactly the same with her. Jackie wanted to slap Al in the face many times. Most of the time though, Jackie just tried to ignore him and get her work done. But, it was hard to get anything done when Al sat next to her.

Jackie talked to her friend Sue, a woman from another department, about the situation. Jackie wanted advice about what to do about Al. Sue told her she should just be quiet if she wanted to keep her job and not cause any trouble for herself.

Jackie was confused. She knew that what Al was doing to her and to Christy was wrong, but she did not want what happened to Christy to happen to her also. She needed to come to a conclusion about what to do.

DISCUSSION QUESTIONS

1. Does this situation constitute sexual harassment? Why or why not?
2. What was wrong with the way the company handled Christy's complaint?
3. What was wrong with the attitude of the other employees?

4. What was wrong with the advice received from her friend Sue?
5. What should Jackie do?

Briarwood Industries

Carol P. Harvey
Assumption College

Diane Williamson sat at her desk at Briarwood Industries aimlessly staring out of her office window. Today was to be her big day, she expected to be promoted to vice-president of marketing. Instead, she just wrote her letter of resignation. Impeccably dressed in her best navy blue suit, Diane looked successful but felt like a total failure.

When Diane came to Briarwood in 1980 as an experienced furniture sales rep, the company was already one of the largest manufacturers of upholstered living room furniture in the United States. Assigned to the west coast region, Diane soon became one of the top sales reps in the country. She recognized the potential of warehouse merchandising and capitalized on having one of the major chain's national headquarters in her territory, by securing a multi-million dollar contract to supply them with sofas and chairs.

In recognition, Diane was promoted to sales manager of the Seattle office in 1983 and to manager of new product and market development at corporate headquarters in North Carolina in 1986.

But the vice-president's job went to Larry Jaccobi, a twelve-year veteran of the company, who had the reputation of being efficient but not very creative in his management style. Larry was best known for implementing the company's order-entry system which equipped the sales reps with portable computers that sent order data directly back to the plant. Having order data rapidly enabled Briarwood to implement a Just-in-Time inventory system that was projected to save the company millions of dollars over the next five years. Diane felt that Larry, although excellent at implementing others ideas, lacked broad-based experience and the vision to lead the department.

Diane was startled by a knock at her office door. Sandy McBride, the advertising manager, and Diane's closest confidant at the company, heard through the office grapevine that Diane did not get the vice-president's job. "What's plan B?" McBride asked. Welcoming the opportunity to talk, Diane expressed her shock and hurt at not getting the promotion. "I just don't understand how this could have happened," Diane lamented. "I came up through the sales ranks. I was the one who had the vision to diversify into office furniture, our most profitable product line. I wrote the marketing plan for our expansion into Canadian and European markets. What else could I have done?"

"Well, Diane it was well known around here that Larry really wanted to be a vice-president. He felt that he had paid his dues and that it was the next logical step. He never missed an opportunity to make his ambition very clear, or his work visible to the top brass. Remember that presentation he gave on Just-In-Time at the national sales meeting? Then there was the time that he volunteered to represent the company at the labor negotiations with the truck drivers union. Those reports went right to the top. I know that you and Larry never really got along. . . "

Diane abruptly cut Sandy off. "I don't work like that," Diane said. "I wouldn't want to take all the glory for something that was the product of a team effort. Larry looks out for Larry. My style is to do the best job that I can for the company. Good work gets noticed and rewarded. Look at the profit margins for the office furniture division. Everyone knows that I am the brains behind that plan.

"And what about the year that I spent in charge of production at the Atlanta plant. I filled in when the company was short-handed. I am not interested in running a manufacturing facility but when the manager had a heart attack, I did it. I never complained about the assignment or about living away from my family for a year. Fine thanks I get.

"Well, it is too late now. I have resigned. It's Briarwood's loss. I am going to hand deliver this letter this morning."

An hour later Diane sat in Gary Logan's office. As the retiring vice-president of marketing, and Diane's current boss read the letter, he expressed his surprise at Diane's action. "I think that you might want to reconsider your resignation, Diane. Although you have done a fine job here, quite frankly, your name was not even among the three top contenders for my job.

"We see you as a hard working, loyal employee but not as corporate level material. You seem to lack the ambition, self-confidence and level of comfort with risk that this job requires. In fact, this is the first time that you have even expressed an interest in being promoted to my job and I announced my planned retirement date three months ago."

Diane felt her anger building and said. "You can't be serious? Why wouldn't you realize that I considered myself a viable candidate to move into your position? I hinted at it during my last review interview. I clearly remember saying that I have done everything that this company has asked of me and you agreed with me.

"What about the fact that I know that I am making $5,000 a year less than the other managers at this level? I never complained about the salary differences. In fact, I never even brought it up. Maybe I should see the Affirmative Action officer, and I just might call my lawyer." With that statement, Diane left Gary's office but left her letter on his desk.

Gary was glad that he had a lunch appointment with a good friend, Chris Wesley, the Vice-President of Finance at Briarwood. Chris had a lot of female employees. Maybe Chris could explain Diane's behavior.

DISCUSSION QUESTIONS

> NOTE: You will be given special directions by your instructor for the discussion of this case.

1. Is Diane's reaction to Larry's promotion justified? Why or why not?
2. Does Diane have legal grounds to sue the company?
3. Who is mainly at fault for this situation? Why?
4. If Diane leaves Briarwood, what does she stand to lose? What will the company lose?
5. If you were Diane's best friend, Sandy, what advice would you give her about this situation?

6. If you were Gary Logan's best friend, Chris, what advice would you give him about this situation?
7. What can Diane learn from this experience?
8. What can Gary learn from this experience?
9. What are the lessons from this case for men and women working together in organizations?

Freida Mae Jones: Racism in Organizations

Martin R. Moser

University of Lowell

BACKGROUND

Freida Mae Jones was born in her grandmother's Georgia farmhouse on June 1, 1949. She was the sixth of George and Ella Jones' ten children. Mr. and Mrs. Jones moved to New York City when Freida was four because they felt that the educational and career opportunities for their children would be better in the North. With the help of some cousins, they settled in a five-room apartment in the Bronx. George worked as a janitor at Lincoln Memorial Hospital, and Ella was a part-time housekeeper in a nearby neighborhood. George and Ella were conservative, strict parents. They kept a close watch on their children's activities and demanded they be home by a certain hour. The Joneses believed that because they were black, the children would have to perform and behave better than their peers to be successful. They believed that their children's education would be the most important factor in their success as adults.

Freida entered Memorial High School, a racially integrated public school, in September 1963. Seventy percent of the student body was Caucasian, 20 percent black, and 10 percent Hispanic. About 60 percent of the graduates went on to college, of which 4 percent were black, Hispanic and male. In her senior year, Freida was the top student in her class. Following school regulations, Freida met with her guidance counselor to discuss plans upon graduation. The counselor advised her to consider training in a "practical" field such as housekeeping, cooking, or sewing, so that she could find a job.

George and Ella Jones were furious when Freida told them what the counselor had advised. Ella said, "Don't they see what they are doing. Freida is the top-rated student in her whole class and they are telling her to become a manual worker. She showed that she has a fine mind and can work better than any of her classmates and still she is told not to become anybody in this world. It's really not any different in the North than back home in Georgia, except that they don't try to hide it down South. They want her to throw away her fine mind because she is a black girl and not a white boy. I'm going to go up to her school tomorrow and talk to the principal."

As a result of Mrs. Jones' visit to the principal, Freida was assisted in applying to ten Eastern colleges, each of which offered her full scholarships. In September 1966, Freida entered Werbley College, an exclusive private women's college in Massachusetts. In 1970, Freida graduated summa cum laude in history. She decided to return to New York to teach grade school in the city's public school system. Freida was unable to obtain a full-time position, so she substituted. She also enrolled as a part-time student in Columbia University's Graduate School of Education. In

Reprinted with permission of the author, Martin R. Moser, Ph. D., Associate Professor of Management, College of Management, University of Lowell, Lowell, Massachusetts.

1975 she had attained her Master of Arts degree in Teaching from Columbia but could not find a permanent teaching job. New York city was laying off teachers and had instituted a hiring freeze because of the city's financial problems.

Feeling frustrated about her future as a teacher, Freida decided to get an MBA. She thought that there was more opportunity in business than in education. Churchill Business School, a small, prestigious school located in upstate New York, accepted Freida into its MBA program.

Freida completed her MBA in 1977 and accepted an entry-level position at the Industrialist World Bank of Boston in a fast-track management development program. The three-year program introduced her to all facets of bank operations, from telling to loan training and operations management. She was rotated to branch offices throughout New England. After completing the program she became an assistant manager for branch operations in the West Springfield branch office.

During her second year in the program, Freida had met James Walker, a black doctoral student in business administration at the University of Massachusetts. Her assignment to West Springfield precipitated their decision to get married. They originally anticipated that they would marry when James finished his doctorate and could move to Boston. Instead, they decided he would pursue a job in the Springfield-Hartford area.

Freida was not only the first black but also the first woman to hold an executive position in the West Springfield branch office. Throughout the training program Freida felt somewhat uneasy although she did very well. There were six other blacks in the program, five men and one woman, and she found support and comfort in sharing her feelings with them. The group spent much of their free time together. Freida had hoped that she would be located near one or more of the group when she went out into the "real world." She felt that although she was able to share her feelings about work with James, he did not have the full appreciation or understanding of her co-workers. However, the nearest group member was located one hundred miles away.

Freida's boss in Springfield was Stan Luboda, a fifty-five-year-old native New Englander. Freida felt that he treated her differently than he did the other trainees. He always tried to help her and took a lot of time (too much, according to Freida) explaining things to her. Freida felt that he was treating her like a child and not like an intelligent and able professional.

"I'm really getting frustrated and angry about what is happening at the bank," Freida said to her husband. "The people don't even realize it, but their prejudice comes through all the time. I feel as if I have to fight all the time just to start off even. Luboda gives Paul Cohen more responsibility than me and we both started at the same time with the same amount of training. He's meeting customers alone and Luboda has accompanied me to each meeting I've had with a customer."

"I run into the same thing at school," said James. "The people don't even know that they are doing it. The other day I met with a professor on my dissertation committee. I've known and worked with him for over three years. He said he wanted to talk with me about a memo he had received. I asked him what it was about and he said that the records office wanted to know about my absence during the spring semester. He said that I had to sign some forms. He had me confused with Martin Jordan, another black student. Then he realized that it wasn't me, but Jordan he wanted. All I could think was that we all must look alike to him. I was angry.

Maybe it was an honest mistake on his part, but whenever something like that happens, and it happens often, it gets me really angry."

"Something like that happened to me," said Freida. "I was using the copy machine, and Luboda's secretary was talking to someone in the hall. She had just gotten a haircut and was saying her hair was now like Freida's—short and kinky—and that she would have to talk to me about how to take care of it. Luckily, my back was to her. I bit my lip and went on with my business. Maybe she was trying to be cute, because I know she saw me standing there, but comments like that are not cute, they are racist."

"I don't know what to do," said James. "I try to keep things in perspective. Unless people interfere with my progress, I try to let it slide. I only have so much energy and it doesn't make sense to waste it on people who don't matter. But that doesn't make it any easier to function in a racist environment. People don't realize that they are being racist. But a lot of times their expectations of black people or women, or whatever, are different because of skin color or gender. They expect you to be different, although if you were to ask them they would say that they don't. In fact, they would be highly offended if you implied that they were racist or sexist. They don't see themselves that way."

"Luboda is interfering with my progress," said Freida. "The kinds of experiences I have now will have a direct effect on my career advancement. If decisions are being made because I am black or a woman, then they are racially and sexually biased. It's the same kind of attitude that the guidance counselor had when I was in high school, although not as blatant." In September 1980, Freida decided to speak to Luboda about his treatment of her. She met with him in his office. "Mr. Luboda, there is something that I would like to discuss with you, and I feel a little uncomfortable because I'm not sure how you will respond to what I am going to say."

"I want you to feel that you can trust me," said Luboda. "I am anxious to help you in any way I can."

"I feel that you treat me differently than you treat other people around here," said Freida. "I feel you are over-cautious with me, that you always try to help me, and never let me do anything on my own."

"I always try to help the new people around here," answered Luboda. "I'm not treating you any differently than I treat any other person. I think you are being a little too sensitive. Do you think that I treat you differently because you are black?"

"The thought has occurred to me," said Freida. "Paul Cohen started here the same time that I did and he has much more responsibility than I do." [Cohen was already handling accounts on his own, while Freida had not yet been given that responsibility.]

"Freida, I know you are not a naive person," said Luboda. "You know the way the world works. There are some things which need to be taken more slowly than others. There are some assignments for which Cohen has been given more responsibility than you, and there are some assignments for which you are given more responsibility than Cohen. I try to put you where you do the most good."

"What you are saying is that Cohen gets the more visible, customer contact assignments and I get the behind-the-scenes running of the operation assignments," said Freida. "I'm not naive, but I'm also not stupid either. Your decisions are unfair.

Cohen's career will advance more quickly than mine because of the assignments that he gets."

"Freida, that is not true," said Luboda. "Your career will not be hurt because you are getting different responsibilities than Cohen. You both need the different kinds of experiences you are getting. And you have to face the reality of the banking business. We are in a conservative business. When we speak to customers we need to gain their confidence, and we put the best people for the job in the positions to achieve that end. If we don't get their confidence they can go down the street to our competitors and do business with them. Their services are no different than ours. It's a competitive business in which you need every edge you have. It's going to take time for people to change some of their attitudes about whom they borrow money from or where they put their money. I can't change the way people feel. I am running a business, but believe me I won't make any decisions that are detrimental to you or to the bank. There is an important place for you here at the bank. Remember, you have to use your skills to the best advantage of the bank as well as your career."

"So what you are saying is that all things being equal, except my gender and my race, that Cohen will get different treatment than me in terms of assignments," said Freida.

"You're making it sound like I am making a racist and sexist decision," said Luboda. "I'm making a business decision utilizing the resources at my disposal and the market situation in which I must operate. You know exactly what I am talking about. What would you do if you were in my position?"

DISCUSSION QUESTIONS

1. Do you think that the Jones' were being realistic or overly sensitive in their belief that their children would have to work harder to be successful because they were black? Explain your answer.
2. If you were Freida, what else could you have done? If you were Mr. Luboda, what else could you have done?
3. Do you think that Luboda was discriminating against Freida? Why or why not?
4. Does Freida have legal grounds to sue the bank for discrimination? Why or why not?
5. What role did the bank's upper management play in the managing diversity process? What could they have done differently?
6. Luboda's arguments for his decisions about Freida's responsibilities seemed to be based on the idea that the bank's customers might be uncomfortable with a black female in a position of authority. Is this a valid argument? Why or why not?

"the way for evil to triumph is for good people to do nothing"

The Emanuel Company

Carole Copeland Thomas
C. Thomas & Associates

"I am willing to take risks. Other people need a cushion between them and real business liabilities. They are afraid of assuming responsibilities and taking on contingent liabilities." After thirteen years in the making, and unable to sell the company to his key employees because of their fear of assuming possible liabilities from previously completed projects, The Emanuel Company officially shut its doors in November 1986.

The phase out would be gradual, having established itself as the largest minority-owned construction company in the state of Michigan. The time Don would now have would be well spent, taking piano lessons, learning French, painting, and traveling. Understandably burned out after years of handling the day to day activities of entrepreneurship, Don would spend four years exploring the world and pursing these other cultural interests before relaunching his business in 1990.

THE EARLY YEARS—1939 TO 1961

Donald Frank Emanuel was born in Birmingham, Alabama in 1939, and was reared in Detroit, Michigan. Interested in drawing and drafting as a young student, Don's interest in these subjects was furthered by a woodshop instructor in middle school. Combining his two favorite activities, Don decided to become an architect, studying it and drafting in high school. He graduated from Cass Technical High School and continued his education at Lawrence Institute of Technology in Detroit, majoring in architectural engineering. Marrying while at Lawrence Tech, he worked during the day and attended classes in the evening. (He divorced shortly after his daughter was born.) After four years as a part-time student, he left school and began working for an architect.

RACIAL BARRIERS IN THE INDUSTRY—1961

Don Emanuel's experience level grew during his early years. After a short period of unemployment he almost joined the Air Force. Just before enlisting, Don was hired by a local building products manufacturer, The Fenestra Company. They were looking for a registered architect; however, due to his experience and background, they decided to hire Don even though he was not registered. He started working for the firm as a draftsman, and soon became a popular employee among some of the administrators, because he quickly proved that he could handle the responsibilities they initially felt only a registered architect could handle.

Fenestra closed their Detroit offices and offered Don the opportunity to join the Buffalo, New York offices—an offer he accepted willingly. The staff members in the Buffalo office were unaware that their newly transferred draftsman was black, because Don's complexion is very fair, and his facial features resembled that of whites. He was placed in a supervisory position in charge of a drafting department of five employees at the age of 21.

Housing patterns, divided along racial lines in Buffalo were similar to those in other urban areas, and Don boarded with an elderly couple in Buffalo's African-American community. His job progressed well until someone in Fenestra discovered where Don was living. Unusual pressure was then placed on him, and his relationship with the firm became quite uncomfortable. Six months after transferring to the Buffalo office, he quit his job and returned to Detroit.

THE SHIFT TO CONSTRUCTION—1962 TO 1965

Upon returning home, Don joined the firm of Pioneer Detroit, a manufacturer of building products. He was hired in 1962 as a draftsman and soon moved up to serve as a product engineer from 1963–1965. In 1965 he was hired by The Walbridge-Aldinger Company, one of Michigan's largest general contractors. Like The Finestra Company, Walbridge was looking for an estimator—a position Don was not technically qualified for. He mailed them a resume, they were impressed and hired him as a job coordinator. In this position, he was responsible for delivery of building materials and coordinated the scheduling of subcontractors hired by the company to complete projects.

RACE AND THE WALBRIDGE YEARS—1965 TO 1973

Again, race was an issue. "It is obvious now. . . and it was obvious several months after I took the job. . . that they thought I was white," he states. And using his fair complexion worked to his advantage at times. "It was a game I could play. Very few (black) people could play this game, but I enjoyed it. One colleague actually thought my name was Dom—as in Dominique Emanuel and believed me to be Spanish. I never corrected him."

At times this color deception worked against Don. An incident occurred during a social event in an Allen Park, Michigan bar/restaurant involving white male Walbridge employees, who knew Don was black and other male business guests who didn't. The conversation gradually shifted from business to one ethnic joke after another. First were a round of Polish jokes, and ultimately a steady stream of black jokes. "It wasn't fun, and I didn't know how to deal with it," Don says. The level of discomfort rose for each Walbridge employee as the comic outpouring continued. One by one each Walbridge employee excused himself and headed for the restroom, never to return. Don was the only remaining company member left sitting with the guests. When he looked around, all of his Walbridge colleagues had reseated themselves at another table. When he joined his colleagues at the new table, they apologized profusely for what they had just witnessed.

Although blacks were hired for lower level construction jobs (like laborers), very few held supervisory or management positions at that time. It became clear to Don that many at Walbridge had accepted him on the basis that he was a white man. It was his association with a darker-skinned black friend who visited him at work that revealed his real ethnic identity. "It was very unusual for blacks to be involved in the construction business in that capacity (job coordinator) in those days," Don adds. After discovering that he was black, his relationship with his superintendent deteriorated, bringing back haunting memories of his days at The Fenestra Company. After three months on the job, Don decided to quit, hoping to find another firm that would accept him regardless of his ethnic background.

It was a series of work-related events that impacted the future of Don's career at Walbridge. Those in the company who had recognized his talent and ability to get the job done with efficiency and accuracy asked him to remain on his job until a replacement could be found. An exit interview was then arranged by the firm's owner, John Rakolta, Sr. While waiting to see him, Don was called into the project manager's office to resolve some material delivery scheduling problems. He made a series of telephone calls to solve the problem. Unbeknownst to him, the intercom system had been deliberately left on, and his conversations were broadcasted throughout the offices. Shortly thereafter, Rakolta, who had nothing to do with the broadcasted conversation, entered the room, introduced himself, expressed satisfaction on how Don had handled himself on the phone and turned off the intercom. The practical joke that was meant to embarrass Don, had backfired.

Impressed with Don's performance, Rakolta persuaded him to remain with the company and work in his office as a job coordinator. "He gave me every opportunity to learn," Don states, "and as I would learn more and more, other opportunities would open up." Walbridge was known as a company of very proud people who performed and delivered with professionalism and skill, and Don continued to prove his ability by focusing on his performance. His success continued, and on many occasions, Don wore the title of project manager, overseeing job sites throughout Michigan and as far south as Louisville, Kentucky.

In 1968, Walbridge entered into a joint venture with Huber, Hunt and Nichols in the largest contract ever awarded by the Ford Motor Company. As project manager, Don was given full exposure, later becoming one of the principal candidates Huber, Hunt and Nichols considered for their international operations. "I would have had the opportunity of international travel, prestige and more money," Don reflects. He decided instead to decline the offer and began setting his sights on becoming an entrepreneur.

"I told Rakolta about my goal of owning my own business on the night the Detroit Tigers won the Pennant in 1968." While dining with him on that evening and joining in the Tigers' festivities, Don discussed his future plans. His boss expressed surprise, not because of learning about Don's entrepreneurial interest, but rather of hearing of Don's decision not to pursue the international assignment with Huber, Hunt and Nichols.

Don stayed with Walbridge for five more years as an estimator and project manger on client assignments including Ford Motor Company's Paint Plant in Mount Clemens, Michigan and the construction of the administration building for The Pontiac Motor Division. In 1973, a close co-worker was selected for a promotion and was made Don's supervisor. Their relationship soon changed, and Don's new supervisor felt that he had to show him how to do his job, even though both had previously functioned in equal positions. After eight years with the company, Don left Walbridge. In July 1973, he opened The Emanuel Company.

THE EMANUEL COMPANY EARLY YEARS—1973 TO 1976

During the last five years at Walbridge, Don had begun to put together the initial components of his business concept. When the business started in 1973, he had already created a carefully worded business plan detailing how his company would operate, analyzing his targeted commercial and industrial markets, forecasting future revenues and planning on how the business would be staffed. He established himself as president, treasurer and chairman of the board, and set about building a corporate reputation of his own. His business would concentrate on commercial and industrial contracts, just like Walbridge. Friends and acquaintances helped to staff the business at the beginning, and hiring was done by word of mouth. The company began with three employees—Don as general manager, a secretary and an estimator.

Financing the business was not difficult for Don. He was able to secure a bank loan for $50,000, to be repaid over seven years. In addition, he received a $100,000 line of credit from the bank that was secured with actual contracts he expected to receive in the future. Motor Enterprises, a Minority Enterprise Small Business Investment Company (MESBIC), a special venture capital arm of General Motors, also loaned the company $25,000 under a seven year leverage arrangement. For equity, Don invested $28,000, made up of profit sharing money from his days at Walbridge, an automobile, books and other tangible items transferred to the corporation.

The motto in The Emanuel Company brochure said, "We're young. We're aggressive. We're talented. We're eager to work with you."

GETTING STARTED: THE FIRST PROJECTS

However, getting customers to generate needed revenue was not easy at first. One important prospect was The Ford Motor Company based on Don's relationship and project assignments with them while at Walbridge. However, Ford and other prospects were slow to commit themselves to this new firm for a number of reasons. First, Don had no established track record of his own—all of his business relationships had been a result of working for other architects and contractors. Ford and other companies were willing to do business with Walbridge because of their established reputation and impressive client base. Secondly, The Emanuel Company was new, and had not yet proved its ability to obtain, execute and complete. And finally, The Emanuel Company was partially financed by a venture capital segment of General Motors, a direct competitor of Ford.

Despite these start-up obstacles, the firm competitively bid, and was awarded its first contract in September, 1993—a $6000 storage pavement installment project at The Detroit Allison Division of General Motors in Redford, Michigan.

A $233,000 addition to The Lafayette Clinic in Detroit was their first reasonably large contract secured shortly after their first project. The Emanuel Company was officially in full operation. The Ford Motor Company finally awarded the firm a contract some three years later.

GROWTH, LARGER PROJECTS AND LABOR RELATIONS

The Emanuel Company continued to grow, securing contracts from such organizations as Michigan Bell Telephone Company, Chrysler Corporation, and The United States Army Corps of Engineers. The initial revenues of $650,000 in 1974 increased to $3 million in 1978 and $8.2 million by 1980. In 1981, the company sales topped $12 million and was listed as one of the top 100 black businesses in the United States in *Black Enterprise* magazine.

The largest contract awarded to The Emanuel Company was the East End Expansion of Hydra-Matic of Ypsilanti, Michigan. Totalling $7 million and broken into three phases, the final phase of this contract entailed gutting and then renovating the Chip Handling building. The project completely upgraded and replaced the conveyors and metal crushers without affecting the normal manufacturing process.

As the company grew, other contracts were won and completed. Clients included the following:

Veteran's Administration Hospital

Second Baptist Church Renovation

General Motors Training Center

National Bank of Detroit

Detroit Metropolitan Airport

Kresge Eye Institute

One difficult project to complete was the Hamtramck Deep Foundation Site. The project, awarded to several general contractors, called for some of the work to be subcontracted—which was The Emanuel Company's role in the project. By the end of the project, the original $400,000 estimate increased to $650,000. "The Emanuel Company, however, was only paid the original price, forcing them to eat the additional $250,000 unfairly," Don reflects. The company tried to negotiate a more reasonable solution to the problem, but was unsuccessful.

Early on Don joined The Association of General Contractors of America, "AGC," a large trade group. Company staffing swelled to over eighty employees during times of peak projects. Most of the office staff and construction laborers were black, while the majority of field employees and project managers were white. Many of his employees were members of one or more of the 31 construction unions in Michigan. His membership in AGC was important because the association actively negotiated with all of the unions during labor disputes. Since The Emanuel Company was a commercial and industrial firm doing business in a union town, they were required to hire union workers.

When strikes occurred, the unions struck AGC, not the individual companies who were members of the association. Negotiations and collective bargaining were handled through AGC, instead of being handled through individual companies within the organization.

FUTURE GROWTH OF THE EMANUEL COMPANY AND AFFIRMATIVE ACTION

"My corporate net worth is over $2 million. However, I am placed on the same level as the other black contractors in this town. The next strongest black contractor is somewhere in the neighborhood of $50,000 to $100,000. Since affirmative action is in vogue. . . I am immediately classified as a black contractor—not just a contractor." Even though Don Emanuel paid his dues, while benefitting from affirmative action in the 1970s, he struggles with its overall effectiveness. "[When I started this business], I was considered an exception. . . an integral part of the industry. . . and treated accordingly. Affirmative action has been good, but today. . . the way it's administered. . . it's bad for blacks in business. Affirmative action says we are all created equal, and we're not!"

Affirmative action policies have created the distribution of construction projects broken up into smaller pieces and parceled out to minority bidders. When divided up, corporate, non-profit and government projects can be spread around to accommodate a certain number/percentage of minority businesses. Many of these projects are a part of large mega-contracts, awarded first to the prime contractor, who in turn identifies the designated minority subcontractor(s). Some projects are simply apportioned and distributed among several minority companies. The development of Epcot Center in Florida exemplifies how this works. In the development of the Walt Disney site, a $15 million project was put out for bidding. Instead of one general contractor taking the entire project, it was divided into smaller pieces, so that six to twelve minority contractors could complete the project together as a joint venture. The Emanuel Company was asked to bid on the project, but declined. Don responded that he could have handled the entire project alone, did not like the idea of having it broken into smaller pieces, and certainly didn't want to participate in a joint venture with other companies. "My bonding company would have bonded me for $15 million without looking at me. [Parceling out these projects] may work for minority companies up to $200,000. But what happens if these firms can handle jobs for more than that all by themselves? Their growth is limited beyond that point."

On joint ventures, Don states, "at best, they are extremely difficult. At worst. . . .all types of catastrophes can happen. I remember a joint venture between Walbridge and Huber, Hunt and Nichols. The companies made a lot of money, but when all was completed, everyone was at each other's throat. My opinion is you joint venture when you have to. You don't joint venture because somebody wants you to."

STEPPING BACK INTO THE ARENA

The Relaunch of the Emanuel Company 1990–1993

Much had changed since 1986. Economic conditions had worsened since the mid-1980s. Many of the players in the industry had changed as well. And Don faced the struggles of re-entering an industry he had walked out of four years earlier. The difficulty of relaunching a once successful company would become one of Don Emanuel's greatest challenges.

Exploring different alternatives for four years had left its impression on Don. He immediately took piano lessons after closing his business in 1986, traveled throughout the world, and even thought of "sitting on the Left Bank contemplating the Seine." He had rearranged his life, making room for the things he had never been able to explore. However, four years of exploration had proved that he had actually left the one activity he enjoyed doing the most: being an entrepreneur by running a construction company. "What I really liked to do was what I stopped doing in 1986," Don reflects.

In July 1990, The Emanuel Company re-opened its doors for business with a $1 million unsecured line of credit and a $10 million bonding line. Don Emanuel owned 70 percent of the company's stock and John Rakolta, Sr. of Walbridge owned the remaining 30 percent. Scaled down in a tight economy, the company employed one office support employee, three project managers, four field superintendents and its founder, Don Emanuel. Eventually, Ford Motor Company and other previous clients renewed contracts with the firm.

BARRIERS AND OTHERS CHALLENGES FOR THE FUTURE

Not everyone was happy when Don relaunched his business. In addition to a soft, uncertain economy, there were those in the construction industry who did not welcome Don's return. To have left the business to pursue other interests was perceived by some as quitting—walking away from the industry. Some competitors, including other black contractors, had assumed positions of power within the AGC. Some buyers of construction were wary of the firm's re-entry into the industry. Among black contractors, many perceived Don as leaving the industry on top, making room for them to fill the gap in his absence. "My re-entry became a threat to them," he says, "and some even encouraged certain buyers not to work with my firm."

THE FUTURE

A reflective Don Emanuel looks back at his accomplishments as he contemplates the future. Business success for him had not always translated into personal happiness. A brief second marriage ended in 1992, producing one daughter. Michigan's economy has not yet turned around. The automobile industry, the mainstay for The Emanuel Company, awaits an uncertain future. However, the company's founder, Don Emanuel, re-energized at 54 years old, still looks forward to the challenges and opportunities of the future. Detroit's Renaissance Center was constructed in 1973, the same year The Emanuel Company was started. Just as the center symbolized the rebirth of a city, Don Emanuel carries that same spirit of rebirth forward as he fortifies his entrepreneurial efforts on the activity he enjoys the most in life.

Carole Copeland Thomas is publisher of the *Thomas Report*, currently in circulation in over 30 states and 11 foreign countries. It is the only minority-published news monthly of its kind in the United States, and is specifically targeted to reach a readership from a culturally diverse perspective. She is also a managing partner in C. Thomas and Associates, a training and development/management consulting firm in Woburn, MA. Ms. Thomas is an adjunct faculty member of Bentley College in Waltham, MA.

DISCUSSION QUESTIONS

1. How did race and Don's physical characteristics help his business pursuits? How did they add obstacles to his career and entrepreneurial path?
2. What affirmative action issues confront businesses like The Emanuel Company? Is affirmative action seen as positive or negative enforcement, or both?
3. What role did John Rakolta, Sr. have in Don's life? Is that role a critical factor in why Don become an entrepreneur? What may have happened if there had been no intercom incident?

General Dynamics in the Navajo Nation

Fairlee E. Winfield
Northern Arizona University

Mike Enfield sat at his desk and looked out across the 21,440-square-foot plant floor of the General Dynamics assembly and test facility in the Navajo Nation. As plant manager, he knew that the company was in the middle of negotiations with the Navajo Tribe to extend the company's lease for another 20 years. Given his experience with the facility, he wondered if it was worth it. "I'd describe us as a 'school bus'—a 1952 school bus! We continually put new engines in so that we don't have to buy a new body. We just never break down," said Enfield, when asked to describe his operation. "Around here everybody wears more than one hat. This is a utility vehicle. Maybe you can afford a new motor, but you can't afford the whole thing very often. I'm not a Masarati and I wouldn't want to be. That's for the snobs from somewhere else."

It was late 1984 and lease negotiations with the Navajo Tribal Council had been underway for over a year. General Dynamics wanted to expand the building by 15,000 square feet and to extend the existing long-term lease. Enfield continued: "I think business can operate here very well—if people running the business are willing to go into the Navajo culture and learn rather than trying to force the Navajo into our culture when they don't want to come in." He believed his Navajo employees, all 320 of them, could meet any trial.

BACKGROUND

In the mid-1960s General Dynamics needed to expand its electronic assembly capability to handle excess work at the Pomona Division Plant in California. New contracts with the Department of the Navy, the Department of the Air Force, and the U.S. Missile Command would require additional floor space and an expanded work force. Several sites were considered. For example, there were possibilities in Asia. Atari was moving a plant from California to the Far East to be more profitable, resulting in the loss of 1700 jobs in California. Mexico had a large available labor force. Canada seemed a possibility, but there were some problems with transportation.

After preliminary discussions with the Navajo Tribe and the Bureau of Indian Affairs in 1967, General Dynamics decided to pursue the possibility of locating near Window Rock, Arizona. It appeared to be an attractive business opportunity and a chance to play a positive role in Navajo economic development. The Navajo Nation

Reprinted with permission of the author and of North American Case Research Association (NACRA) from the *Case Research Journal*, Spring 1993.

is located in the four corners area of the Southwestern United States where the borders of Utah, Colorado, New Mexico, and Arizona meet.

THE NAVAJO NATION IN THE FOUR CORNERS REGION

Two factors seemed basic. First, General Dynamics believed that a socially responsive company would have to be committed to a positive role in Navajo economic development, reservation life, and the well-being of the people living in the area. Second, the company would have to operate more profitably in the Navajo Nation environment than at another location. This second factor would be a primary factor in the decision to open a plant in any location.

Initial Concerns

William H. Govette, Pomona's Vice President of Fabrication and Assembly, who was responsible for the operation of the Navajo Facility in 1984, recalls that General Dynamics had four initial concerns.[1]

1. Was there a plant site that offered sufficient available labor, ample housing, and adequate transportation service?
2. What type of building would be required to manufacture the product? Was the required building available or would the tribe be willing to build a facility that suited the company needs?
3. Was the Tribe willing to purchase the equipment necessary for production?
4. How would the training of employees be provided?

Beginning Operation of the Navajo Facility

In 1968, Navajo medicine men performed the traditional blessing ceremony at the dedication of the new General Dynamics Navajo Facility at Fort Defiance, Arizona. The blessing chants referred to beauty and harmony in an indefinite, intangible, time and space.

> May it be delightful my house;
> From my head may it be delightful;
> To my feet may it be delightful;
> Where I lie may it be delightful;
> All above me may it be delightful;
> All around me may it be delightful.

Enfield and the first fifty Navajo employees could now pass beyond the neat split rail fence and enter the new air-conditioned steel and concrete electronic assembly plant.

The Navajo Tribe had constructed a modern building to General Dynamics' specifications. The lease agreement had a 15-year term, with a guarantee that 75 percent of the construction cost would be paid back in 5 years and the remaining 24 percent over the next 10 years. The tribe had also agreed that major repairs and modifications would be negotiated. To equip the plant, the tribe agreed to purchase all required equipment. General Dynamics then leased the equipment and agreed to repay the cost of the items over a 10-year period.

The site was 5 miles from tribal headquarters at Window Rock and 35 miles from Gallup, New Mexico, on interstate highway I-40. Major truck, bus, and scheduled airline routes pass through Gallup. Window Rock has a 6700-foot paved, lighted private landing strip.

The partnership between General Dynamics and the Navajo Nation was the result of fortunate timing. In 1968, the Bureau of Indian Affairs was encouraging industry to locate on Indian land, and Pomona needed to expand its electronic assembly capability to provide missile components to Navy and Air Force contracts. By 1984, the population of the Navajo Nation was rapidly approaching 200,000; 33.9 percent were unemployed, and about 18,000 Navajo people were actively seeking work.[2]

STATE OF AFFAIRS IN 1984

The Labor Pool

Dennis Hardy, the Navajo superintendent of Standard Missile, talked about the early days of training the Navajo employees. "General Dynamics originally entered into an agreement with the Manpower Development and Training Act Federal Funding Program to train employees in electronic assembly through a 6-week course. Later we moved to a 40-hour concentrated course. Did all our own screening and training." Hardy has his white shirt sleeves turned up at the cuffs. The coat to his gray suit was draped over a chair and his vest was open. Outside the window of the Navajo facility a dog howled and an answering yowling seemed to come from nearby. Hardy stopped to listen. Then he talked for a while about the full-grown German shepherd he recently brought back from the Flagstaff Animal shelter for his 4-year old son.

After a detailed description of the Flagstaff trip, Hardy straightened his tie and returned to the discussion of training:

Employees are now given detailed training at the time of hiring—usually in basic soldering, welding, and assembly. On-the-job training lasts from a few weeks to several months, depending on the job complexity. Anyway, under the old Manpower Development courses we were producing 40 percent rejects. That had to change. With our own training program, rejects are now less than 10 percent.

By 1984, the facility was involved in assembly work all the way from insertion of electronic components into circuit boards to final assembly of the Standard Missile and Phalanx Missile lines.

Art Stockdale, who conducted professional development activities both on-site at Fort Defiance and at the Pomona division headquarters, reported on the Navajo facility trainees:

> I have not found a more attentive and appreciative group. . . . Each participant is willing to relate both work and cultural experiences to the concepts that are presented. I found that as a group they are dedicated employees. The mutual respect that they have for one another is something all organizations would do well to emulate.

"I was QA manager for years," said Enfield. "We're on a par with anybody. I'm a great believer in these Navajo people. I'm betting my butt on them. They have something going that doesn't go on anywhere else. That is, this isn't simply General Dynamics, this is *The Navajo Facility*!"

Over the years, the Fort Defiance, Arizona, plant generally met or exceeded established cost, quantity, and quality requirements for each product. The on-site managers consistently reported that quality control simply wasn't needed. This cut expenditures and made the product both high quality and low cost.

Affirmative Action and Labor Costs

General Dynamics realized a definite affirmative action advantage through the employment of Native American Indians, who were underrepresented in the general work force. This gave the company an advantage in bids on U.S. government contract work. Additionally, with the high unemployment rate on the Navajo Nation, most of the company's new employees began work at federal minimum wage pay rates or only slightly higher than current rates. Job progression in the Navajo facility began with basic assembly and moved on to more advanced assembly techniques with increases in pay at each progression. In spite of minimum wage rates, Enfield believed the employees were the best in the aerospace industry. "I have never heard one person who works for me tell me 'you can't do it that way.' You give them the work, and they do it—they are superproductive. Our high productivity is related to the 90 percent acceptance rates."

Enfield reported that turnover rates were about the same as in the surrounding states, but he said he didn't count statistics. "If they fail school, that's not job-related turnover." By 1984, nine of the employees had 15 years of service, thirty had 10 years, and thirty-three had more than 5 years. Turnover rates had averaged about 10 percent per year. Enfield insisted that the average to low turnover rates were evidence of Navajo employees' satisfaction with both their wages and their jobs.

Mattie Singer, a Navajo production supervisor for Standard Missile, said that there was always the need to learn to operate new equipment. Singer started work at the Navajo facility about the same time as Hardy. "I like it when there's a lot of challenge," confided Singer. "In the 16 years I've been here, I've enjoyed every minute. There are so many things I have benefitted from. Dineh [the Navajo people] have a skilled crafts tradition. We take what someone shows us, and then we make it better." Mattie Singer's picture is in the entryway next to the perfect attendance chart. Her team recently won a trophy in the bowling tournament.

Cultural and Traditional Considerations

Because the Navajo Nation is located within U.S. borders, the temptation was to adopt a business and management model appropriate to California, or Michigan, or Georgia. It was difficult to think of the Navajo Nation as a foreign country. Shouldn't companies here be able to operate as they would in any domestic location? General Dynamics said "no," and the General Dynamics management team adjusted to the customs of the host culture as in an international setting.

A smile appeared across Mike Enfield's suntanned features when he talked about cross-cultural considerations.

> Corporate life for most means that if you're not in the intensive care ward, you're not a success. You've got to be able to scream and intimidate. The Navajo will simply refuse to do it if you order them around. I get just bristling mad cause I can't force my will upon them. Pretty soon when you get beat up as much as I have you say, "maybe if I just ask them to do it, they'll do it."

> We're going for a twenty-year lease right now and expanding the building, but none of those things would have happened if we didn't produce *our* way, the Navajo way. Our philosophical way. I lean toward the Navajo peacefulness not toward the traditional corporate grind, not toward U.S. business practices.

Enfield believed that without knowledge of, and respect for, the Navajo culture the General Dynamics operation would have collapsed. To avoid this, General Dynamics took great care to ensure that the culture was respected.

First, before making the decision to locate in the Navajo Nation, the company made extensive studies of Navajo culture and traditions. Table 1 contains a Navajo adaptation of Edward T. Hall's cultural primary message systems researched by Bill Strasen at General Dynamics in the mid-1960s and made available to General Dynamics staff.

The company's Industrial Relations Educational Services produced a thirty-page monograph to assist personnel who visited or worked in the Navajo

TABLE 1 The Navajo: Primary Message System Navajo Traits

1.	Interaction	Very precise language in description and meaning. All communication is face-to-face, verbal, with unanimous agreement of everyone a vital requirement.
2.	Association	No formal "tribe." Family organization based on "clan" of wife's relatives. Richer men may have more than one wife (in separate hogans).
3.	Subsistence	Primarily an agrarian culture. Sheep are very important to the Navajo.
4.	Gender Status	Women are equal of men, and often are the key decision makers.
5.	Territoriality	Within hogan women sit only on south side, men only on north side. Grazing land and "sacred" salt areas are shared by all.
6.	Temporality	Time is measured by the season or task to be accomplished, not by white man's minutes and hours.
7.	Learning	All teaching is verbal; learning is by mimic and rote. Instructors are the oldest, hence wisest, members of the clan. Until 1960 there were no Navajo writings from which to learn.
8.	Play	Navajo enjoy humor. Recreation is geared to noncompetitive games.
9.	Relationships	The "medicine man" is the supreme authority. The entire "clan" is responsible for a wrong doing by one of its members.
10.	Resource Exploitation	Hogans constructed of mud, grass, and logs. Adapts to environment.

Source: Adapted from a framework of Edward T. Hall by Bill Strassen, General Dynamics Corporation, Pomona, CA, 1976.

Nation. The monograph, with an extensive bibliography, contained information on geography, history, economy, religion, social structure, belief system, and education.

Second, the company took pains to assure respect and acceptance of Navajo traditions by careful screening and briefing of non-Indian employees before visits to the Navajo facility. Candidates for positions had to show a willingness to relocate to a totally different type of environment.

Third, non-Indian candidates for managerial positions spent several days in the Fort Defiance area with their families. They met members of the Navajo tribe with whom they would work on a regular basis. Housing, schools, and employment of the entire family were discussed. Frequently, non-Indian candidates decided they might not enjoy, or even tolerate, being a visible, white European American minority person within the dominant American Indian culture.

Fourth, General Dynamics continued the screening process until suitable non-Indian candidates were found. In the Navajo culture, family and religious responsibilities truly predominated and were respected by the organization even when those customs were at odds with traditional U.S. business practice. A balance had to be achieved between the company's production needs and a unique tribal culture.

Absenteeism

"In California or Arizona you would discipline someone who was gone nine days, but here we put them on leave of absence. You've got to recognize their right to go to the nine-day Yeibichai healing ceremony, and you've got to recognize that their job is second to that—not first," said Enfield when asked about absenteeism. The Yeibichai healing rite is only one of many ceremonials.

Dennis Hardy agreed, "You know, we have no separate word for 'religion.' The white man turns his religion on and off. With us, each and every daily act is influenced by the supernatural."

In such circumstances, absenteeism can easily become a problem. Enfield said he planned for absenteeism by overstaffing. There were then enough people on hand to perform day-to-day tasks, and there were no large fluctuations in the work force. Nevertheless, a major concern was a work force unaccustomed to coming to work every scheduled work day.

Ability of Navajos to Accept Leadership Responsibility

The long-range goal of General Dynamics was to adequately train Navajos to take over the operation of the facility. Navajos identified as having management potential were brought to the Pomona, California, plant for management and technical training. Management training was also carried on at Fort Defiance. The Navajo Nation facility opened with a management team of 26 non-Indians. By 1984 the facility had over 300 employees, and 14 of the 22-member management team were Navajos. Enfield said:

> Amy Allen is a Navajo in production control being trained by Carl Gentry. Edna Yazzie, Donald Young, Ernest Tso—they're all being trained for various disciplines. All we've got to do is be smart enough to put them to work. That's what I'm doing. We now have two production superintendents, and both are Navajos. The personnel and cost person is a Navajo being trained for all the finance administration. . . . What do you do with a guy like me who's been here 15 years. My wife's a Navajo. Throw me out? You've got three of us like that. I think we consider ourselves Navajos. We're probably closer to that than our own society. But, we have a neat thing in that we recognize both. We prefer one over the other, but we know how to deal with both.

Alcohol-Related Problems

While alcohol-related problems exist in industry located in all areas, such problems have been extensive and acute on American Indian Reservations, where high unemployment has exacerbated an already serious alcoholism rate. General Dynamics needed to be informed in detail in order to cope with the situation adequately. With tribal agency cooperation, plant management worked with families to reduce or correct alcohol-related difficulties. General Dynamics looked upon their relationship with the tribe as a partnership. They were partners, working together to solve mutual problems and improve local economic and social conditions.

Continuing-Education Facilities

An industrial environment demands that all employees, regardless of position, keep current with the "state of the art" in their occupation. In 1984, continuing-education facilities in the Navajo Nation were minimal or non-existent. The Navajo Tribe was considering this factor and moving toward consensus to create the necessary educational facilities so that their employees could advance and ultimately move into management. However, to date nothing concrete had been done.

Housing and Medical Facilities for Non-Indians

Because all land belongs to the tribe, neither Navajo nor non-Indian employees could simply go out and buy a lot and build a house. There were no apartment complexes, townhouses, or condos until you reached Gallup, New Mexico, 35 miles to the southeast. Housing for Navajo employees was not readily available, especially if the employee was from another part of the reservation. Navajo Indians were accustomed to waiting 6 years to get a home site lease. The limited housing provided for Indians was not available to non-Indian personnel.

Medical help for non-Indians on the Navajo Nation was almost non-existent. The large Indian Health Service hospital at Fort Defiance was for Indians only, since Indian hospitals are operated as part of Indian treaty agreements with the federal government. For non-Indians, the closest medical facilities were in Gallup. General Dynamics managers felt this was a serious problem, especially for non-Indian families with children. (In 1984, only eight non-Indian families with children remained on the Navajo Facility staff.)

Negotiating with the Tribal Government

The Navajo Tribe was governed by a Tribal Council composed of seventy-four elected members and presided over by a chairman and vice chairman. The seventy-four delegates represented the number of districts, called "chapters," spread across the Navajo Nation. Meetings were held every three months, and unanimous decisions were preferred. Consensus building took time. Everyone had to approve or disapprove, so things moved slowly. Fourteen different committees with from three to eighteen members advised the Tribal Council on matters such as health, education, alcohol, resources and welfare. Chapter officers and grazing committees also advised the Tribal Council as did the judiciary.

Tribal officers had an "official" vested interest in encouraging business investment and development. However, nonofficial people, both Indian and non-Indian government bureaucrats, displayed a greater diversity of opinions about such investment. Corporate representatives needed to seek out a variety of people to gain a fuller comprehension of the total environment. Bureau of Indian Affairs officials, local business persons, teachers, editors of local newspapers, and other members of the Indian population needed to be consulted.

Lease negotiations were frustrating and time-consuming because tribal officials sometimes could not reconcile the needs of industry with tribal needs. "If it's a question of Janie Tso's sheep grazing on a particular corner lot versus an electronic assembly facility employing a hundred people, those sheep are probably going to have first priority," said Dennis Hardy. "And, maybe they *should* have priority. The dineh have been here a long time. We'll still be here when the industries are gone."

Building improvements and modifications were extremely complex because many tribal and government committees had to give approval. Both the Navajo Tribal Council and the Bureau of Indian Affairs must approve all lease agreements. In the years between the mid-1960s, when General Dynamics began operations at the Navajo Facility, and the mid-1980s new layers were added to both of these bureaucratic structures. Each of these new offices had to supply its approval, and what little centralization had existed in the past became nonexistent. Lease agreements requiring 10 years of negotiation were not infrequent. Enfield estimated that the lease agreement necessitated that a company representative be at tribal headquarters in Window Rock almost daily to complete the sixty-seven-step site lease process and receive archaeological clearance and governmental assessment under seven separate federal laws.[3]

Additionally, tribal elections, which were conducted every four years, could bring lease negotiations to a standstill. In the past, negotiations that had been under way for as long as three years and were nearing completion had been scrapped when the election of a new tribal chair put things back to square one. Historically, a new tribal chair changed tribal government personnel completely. Everyone was replaced—from top administrators, to clerical staff, to janitorial services. Long-standing animosities frequently developed among tribal political factions, preventing implementations of planned development.

In 1972, the Navajo 10-Year Plan for industrial development on the Navajo Nation was promulgated by Tribal Chairman Peter MacDonald. The following were the objectives of the plan.

1. What is rightfully ours, we must protect; what is rightfully due us, we must claim.
2. What we depend on from others, we must replace with the labor of our own hands and skills of our own people.
3. What we do not have, we must bring into being. We must create for ourselves.[4]

The original General Dynamics lease negotiated in 1967 required a year for initial approval under Tribal Chairman Raymond Nakai. However, as the original 15-year lease neared completion in the early 1980s, the corporation seeking a new 20-year lease and expanded plant, found itself dealing with officials who could not reconcile the corporation's and tribe's needs. Unrealistic demands were made and time was lost. In addition to renegotiating the original lease, the General Dynamics Pomona Division was seeking to expand to a second off-site assembly facility in the Navajo Nation.

The Navajo Tribe had land, a highly stable, dedicated work force, and a proud heritage of craftsmanship, productivity, and quality. However, the tribe also had a multilayered bureaucracy that was slow to respond to private industry.

The federal government's Overseas Private Investment Corporation encouraged economic development programs in foreign countries through direct loans, loan guarantees, and insurance against political risk, but these programs were unavailable to private industry seeking to locate on sovereign American Indian nations.

SUMMARY

Back in the Navajo facility at Fort Defiance, Arizona, Mike Enfield wondered how the tribe could achieve government centralization and stability to facilitate economic development. He wondered whether or not General Dynamics should continue with negotiations for the second facility in the Navajo Nation. Even the needed approval for lease extension and expansion of the present plant was still circulating through the layers of Navajo bureaucracy. He sat down to list both the advantages and the disadvantages of operating on the Navajo Indian Reservation. How long could he keep the old 1952 school bus going? How should General Dynamics react to the objectives in Peter MacDonald's 10-Year Plan? Certainly there were some concessions General Dynamics might try to get from the tribe after 16 years of successful operation. A mutually beneficial partnership forged from respect and understanding now existed. Enfield wanted to keep that partnership alive and growing, but it was an ethical dilemma. Were employee pride and favorable public image enough? Should a company seek to establish a viable business operation for purely ethical reasons?[5]

NOTES

1. William H. Govette. Address at the American Indian National Bank Enterprise and Resource Development Seminar, Albuquerque, New Mexico, March 22, 1983.
2. Edward T. Hall. *The Silent Language*, Fawcett Publications, Greenwich, Conn., 1959.

3. Navajo Economic Development Program 1988 Annual Progress Report, *The Navajo Tribe*, Window Rock, 1988.
4. "Business Site Lease Procedures," Navajo Reservation and Tribal Trust Land, final draft, August 23, 1991.
5. *A Study to Identify Potentially Feasible Small Business of The Navajo Nation,* vol. 2, Center for Business and Economic Research, Brigham Young University, Provo, Utah, 1975.

Fairlee E. Winfield is a professor of Organizational Behavior and International Management at Northern Arizona University. She received her Ph.D. in Psycholinguistics from the University of New Mexico. Her major research areas include comparative management, cross-cultural management, and work family issues. She began doing research in the Navajo Nation in 1978. During 1989 and 1990 she was a visiting professor at Miyagi Gakuin University in Japan. She is the author *Commuter Marriages: Living Together, Apart* (Columbia University Press) and *The Work and Family Sourcebook* (Panel Publishers).

DISCUSSION QUESTIONS

1. What opportunities and advantages are present for General Dynamics in the Navajo Nation External Environment?
2. What threats and disadvantages are present for General Dynamics in the Navajo Nation External Environment?
3. As a General Dynamics manager, how do you react to tribal Chairman Peter MacDonald's objectives in the 10-year plan?
4. What is the General Dynamics cultural position on important management strategies, policies, and programs?
5. Are there differences between non-Indian and Navajo work related attitudes? Consider, if possible, any of Geert Hofstede's dimensions.
    Power Distance
    Individualism/Collectivism
    Uncertainty/Avoidance
    Masculinity/Femininity
    Temporality
    Decision Making
6. Is there an emerging or well-defined cultural synergy composed of shared beliefs, expectations, and values that has defined past performance and that will probably affect future performance?

7. As a General Dynamics manager, would you continue to pursue expansion of the Navajo Nation? If so, what concessions might you try to get from the Navajo Tribal Council?

8. As Tribal Chair of the Navajo Nation, would you want to pursue additional manufacturing opportunities with private industry? If not, what other means of economic development would you seek?

9. Negotiation is one of the single most important international business skills. Divide into two groups, General Dynamics and Navajo Nation. Use the following dimensions to complete a stakeholders' analysis to clarify your group's negotiating perspective on the economic and ethical issues.

	Negotiate	Bargain	Take-it or Leave-it
Values of Exchange	high ◀------------------------------▶ low		
Power/Status	high ◀------------------------------▶ low		
Trust Level	high ◀------------------------------▶ low		
Commitment	important ◀------------------▶ unimportant		
Relationship	important ◀------------------▶ unimportant		
Time	important ◀------------------▶ unimportant		

Optional Activity

Your instructor will divide the class into two groups.

Group One:
As members of a corporate-responsibility planning service for a major organization, answer the following questions.

1. What are the advantages of locating on Native American Indian lands?
2. What are the disadvantages of locating on Native American Indian lands?

Group Two:
As members of an American Indian Nation Economic Development Committee, answer the following questions.

1. What are the advantages of attracting private industry to locate on your sovereign lands?
2. What are the disadvantages of private industry locating on your sovereign lands?

Groups One and Two:
Discuss what the U.S. industry policy should be towards the 1.4 million Native American Indian labor force—the nation's oldest minority group.

Mail Management Systems: The Karin Hazam Case

Becky DiBiasio

Assumption College

Small business success stories are common. However, a small business whose founder and CEO spent her childhood in a state institution, is legally deaf, has travelled with Rosalynn Carter and Coretta Scott King as an advocate for the handicapped, was president of the local AFL-CIO, was the first handicapped woman in the Navy, has won prestigious awards for her work with the disabled and whose work force is 80 percent disabled, presents an unusual success story.

The key to the success of Mail Management Systems is to be found in the remarkable story of its owner, Karin Hazam. Karin was put in a state mental institution when she was five years old and stayed there for many years. She watched the night supervisor play chess and learned to play herself. The nursing supervisor realized that Karin was not retarded and began to get testing for her. It took three more years before Karin was correctly diagnosed as being deaf. She was then sent to a school for the deaf and learned to sign and to speak.

She had implant operations beginning about 18 years ago and now has 28 percent hearing ability. After years of training, she speaks perfectly. You cannot tell that Karin is deaf unless she tells you. However, that was not always true; the hard work necessary to succeed and the prejudice and obstacles she faced both in the institution and once she left the school for the deaf have made her a fighter. She said that she never heard the word "no" so she never knew that failure was even a possibility.

During an interview before Massachusetts Governor William Weld who presented her with an award for her work with the deaf, Karin said, "I'm getting more people saying negative things, now that I can understand them. Before, I couldn't hear it." Being able to hear "no" hasn't made her any more likely to listen to it.

The way Karin started her first business is a case in point. Her first job was in a fish-packing plant in Gloucester, Massachusetts. She was the only deaf woman working in the union and she met with a lot of prejudice and hostility. Her job was packing fish sticks in boxes, the lowest paying job in the plant. She put up with the prejudice, but didn't put up with the job; she looked around to see what else she could do, and began studying. She even took up weightlifting to be strong enough to do one of the jobs she was going to bid on. She also examined federal laws affecting minority hiring, which she has become an expert on; and she had a great advantage—she wasn't prejudiced. As she pointed out, "Being prejudiced is a handicap."

She was chosen to be a union representative for the handicapped and served as a deaf interpreter during Jimmy Carter's last bid for re-election. She did a great deal of public relations work and became acquainted with Rosalynn Carter, Coretta Scott King, and many other influential people. She learned more about business laws regarding women and the disabled. She also began to work very hard to learn to speak well because she was determined to be able to speak in a hearing world.

Karin tells a story about learning to speak that shows how she has taken advantage of every opportunity. When she was on tour with the Carter Administration, she met the President of General Motors and his wife, Edith. Learning to speak was very difficult, so Edith made a deal with Karin that she would give Karin a silver spoon for every new word that she pronounced correctly. "Now," said Karin," I have a complete set of Gorham Chantilly service for twelve. The last time I saw Edith, she brought me a silver sugar bowl. I couldn't think of a new word to say to her, so I just said, 'Edith, you've been holding out on me!'"

Karin is grateful for the help she has received. "I've always been very fortunate that I've always met somebody along the way." But she has created her opportunities, she doesn't wait for fortune to shine on her. When she returned to Gloucester after her political tour, she brought a lot of knowledge back. Within months of her return, she had a prospectus drawn up, gotten a loan, gone independent and underbid the union for the fish packing job. She even hired her old union boss to work for her. Eventually, she was elected president of the Gloucester AFL-CIO.

She went from the bottom to the top in a few short years and she was ready for another challenge. She asked a career diplomat in the Carter Administration if he could think of any job that she could not do. He answered, "The Navy." So, sure enough, with some more help from the Carter Administration, she became the first deaf woman in the Navy. She spent several valuable years receiving training in production control and public relations and continued to extend her network of friends and co-workers around the world.

Karin made contacts in all corners of the world. Thanks to her time in the Navy, Karin said, "When anyone from Algiers is coming to do work in this area, they call me." Mail Management Systems has just begun packaging and shipping biomedical supplies to France and Algiers. As she said, "I never know when information may come in handy down the road." Once Karen left active duty, she joined the Navy Reserves and has been active in advocating for the handicapped in the Armed Services.

One begins to wonder if Karin's deafness is a handicap. "I look at it as a blessing. Would I have been this way if I was born in a hearing world?" she said in an interview in 1990. "I never knew where to draw a line at what I couldn't do, but it took me a lot of years to realize that."

In 1988 Karin decided to combine her interests and her training. She wanted to be able to take advantage of the legal knowledge she had, so she went to the state publishing house and bought everything that might apply to her situation: needs of the handicapped; equal opportunity advantages; tax advantages for women and the handicapped; small business administration and certification. She took all of it and looked at what she wanted. Karin wanted to make a profit and employ the handicapped. Her brother was in a wheelchair and she had a lifetime of living with deafness. She knew she could provide work for many handicapped people if she developed a company that had a variety of products or services that could be made in a sheltered environment. She immediately thought of stuffing envelopes because, she said, "It's one of the first things they teach you in an institution. It involves repetition."

She went to a local credit union and offered to stuff their invoices in envelopes. The credit union sent her to the post office to learn to pre-sort for zip codes and then sent her the first batch of 1500 statements. Karin, her brother, their kids and the neighbors folded and stuffed 1500 envelopes by hand. With the profits from her first job she bought a used table top folder. Then she went to other credit unions to get their jobs. Labels are heat activated and Karin had a folding machine but no labelling machine. Every month Karin and her neighbors were ironing on thousands of labels. She quickly realized that the key to growth was investment in machinery. She took her profits and bought a labelling machine for $47,000.

Her first priority once she had steady work was to hire handicapped workers. After a year and a half and a loan, Mail Management Systems had 87 employees and was housed in a 30,000-square-foot plant with specialized equipment and facilities that were accessible to the handicapped workers. The company had about 15 clients, including the local credit union and DEC. All of Karin's equipment was paid for and she was able to create flexible schedules for all of her employees.

In order to get the first job with DEC, Karin and two employees got jobs in the mail room at DEC. For two weeks, Karin studied every aspect of cost and production. Two years later, DEC bid out their mailing and MMS got the job. Karin said, "I was the only one who understood what I was really bidding on." Because she thinks visually, rather than verbally, Karin always wants to see all the aspects of a job before taking it. Once she successfully bid for DEC's mailing job, she began to see other jobs her company could do for DEC. Now, in addition to mailing and packaging, MMS does assembly work, printing, binding and recycling.

She also consolidated the mailing at DEC—they used three sites, three machines, and lots of equipment. MMS reduced it all to one site. She followed a similar pattern in putting together a mailing bid for Milipore.

Currently, Hazam's company has five sheltered environments for workers, 187 employees and dozens of clients including Burpee Seed Company, Cains Foods, Polaroid, and the Federal Deposit Insurance Corporation. MMS also has begun expanding into international assembly and shipping services, packaging, recycling and shipping biomedical supplies to France and Algeria.

Hazam took advantage of the fact that most companies do not want to devote employee time or space to nonprimary business. More and more companies, large and small, are willing to contract out to independents for a variety of jobs—and packaging, mailing, shipping, and recycling are high on the list of jobs most companies do not do themselves in a cost-efficient manner.

In addition, Karin has taken full advantage of everything the federal, state, and small business administration offers for women and the handicapped, which includes Disabled Access Tax Credits. Karin gets jobs through the disadvantaged work coordinator of a company. MMS is owned by a woman who is deaf. Most of the workers are handicapped. The government gives out tax advantage points to large corporations that do business with the government or with school systems if they employ disadvantaged workers or contract out work to disadvantaged employers. Karin, as a woman and a deaf person, automatically offers double tax advantage points and the companies receive additional points for each disadvantaged worker. So companies meet their EEO quotas and meet Federal Americans with Disabilities Act regulations. The ADA regulations also involve tax credits for both Karin's company and the company that contracts out to her.

In addition, MMS gets tax write-offs for many of its workers, plus it is eligible for a number of tax points as a small business owned by a woman who is deaf. So Karin can charge less and make more.

MMS can do all of this cost efficiently and Karin Hazam has also recently added equipment that has allowed her to expand her operation to include printing jobs and assembly work. But MMS is not just a small business on the fast track.

Karin has a true commitment to the handicapped and gears every step of her company's growth to ensuring that her workers are respected. Karin gets about four hours sleep a night; she says the deaf don't need much sleep, so she has extra time to devote to her ideas. She is the sales force, the job trainer, and the management rolled up in one.

Eighty percent of her workforce is handicapped and she trains each person to work at several jobs. She will stay with a new worker and figure out what job they would be best at. "I don't want to hear what you can't do," she said. "Tell me what job you can do best." She points out that all too often employers don't bother to ask the employees what they can do well.

"One girl only uses two fingers. We bent a spoon for her and she presses a button on a shrink-wrap machine all day. And she puts out more shrink-wrap material in one day than any other person with two arms and two legs does. She takes her job very seriously," said Karin, and made the point that all of her employees care more than most about doing their jobs. She says that their abilities are only limited by the slowest person on the job. So she mixes ordinary workers, retarded workers and disabled workers in order to speed up the slowest and as a confidence builder.

Karin Hazam's hard work and innovation as an advocate for the handicapped have won awards from local civic groups, the Navy, the State of Massachusetts, international organizations and the U.S. government. Karin cares about each person who works for her and about each job she bids on. Her dream is to make independent living quarters near the plant available for her workers. She is sure to succeed—she still won't hear "No."

BIBLIOGRAPHY

"Classroom Interview with Karin Hazam." videotape, Spring 1993, Women, Minorities and Diversity in the Workforce course.

Disabled Access Tax Credit. (Title 26, Internal Revenue Service, Section 44).

Federal Americans with Disabilities Act; Part I: Buildings and Facilities. *Federal Register,* July 26, 1991. corrected January 14, 1992.

Federal Americans with Disabilities Act: Part II: *Federal Register,* September 6, 1991. corrected January 14, 1992.

Fitchburg Sentinel and Enterprise, July 23, 1989; August 4, 1989; August 18, 1989.

Journal Express, November 2, 1988.

"Personal Interview with Karin Hazam." audiotape, August 26, 1993.

Worcester Telegram and Gazette, 1989; 1990; D5 February 13, 1992.

Dr. Becky DiBiasio is an assistant professor of English at Assumption College, Worcester, MA. She writes about speech, rhetoric, writing groups, and narrative theory.

DISCUSSION QUESTIONS

1. In this case, was it an advantage, a disadvantage, or both for Karin Hazam to be physically challenged?
2. List the specific ways in which Karin Hazam "manages diversity" at Mail Management Systems.
3. Discuss Karin Hazam's management style in terms of planning, organizing, motivating, and controlling this business.
4. What are your major concerns for the future of this business?

The Cracker Barrel Restaurants

John Howard

DeKalb University

Employment discrimination against lesbians and gays is common in the workplace. Sole proprietors, managing partners, and corporate personnel officers can and often do make hiring, promoting, and firing decisions based on an individual's real or perceived sexual orientation. Lesbian and gay job applicants are turned down and lesbian and gay employees are passed over for promotion or even fired by employers who view homosexuality as somehow detrimental to job performance or harmful to the company's public profile. Such discrimination frequently results from the personal biases of individual decision-makers. It is rarely written into company policy and thus is difficult to trace. However, in January 1991, Cracker Barrel Old Country Store, Inc., a Tennessee-based chain of family restaurants, became the first and only major American corporation in recent memory to expressly prohibit the employment of lesbians and gays in its operating units. A nationally publicized boycott followed, with demonstrations in dozens of cities and towns.

THE COMPANY: A BRIEF HISTORY OF CRACKER BARREL

Cracker Barrel was founded in 1969 by Dan Evins in his hometown of Lebanon, Tennessee, 40 miles east of Nashville. Evins, a 34-year-old ex-Marine sergeant and oil jobber, decided to take advantage of the traffic on the nearby interstate highway and open a gas station with a restaurant and gift shop. Specializing in down-home cooking at low prices, the restaurant was immediately profitable.

Sensing the opportunity, Evins, with neither food service experience nor a college education, began building Cracker Barrel stores throughout the region, gradually phasing out gasoline sales. By 1974, he owned a dozen restaurants. Within five years of going public in 1981, Cracker Barrel doubled its number of stores and quadrupled its revenues; in 1986, there were 47 Cracker Barrel restaurants with net sales of $81 million. Continuing to expand aggressively, the chain again grew to twice its size and nearly quadrupled its revenues during the next five years.

By the end of the fiscal year, August 2, 1991, Cracker Barrel operated over 100 stores, almost all located along the interstate highways of the Southeast and, increasingly, the Midwest. Revenues exceeded $300 million, nearly 20 percent of which came from gift shop sales of toys, handicrafts, memorabilia, candies, preserves, and other items. Employing roughly 10,000 non-unionized workers, Cracker Barrel ranked well behind such mammoth family chains as Denny's and Big Boy in total sales, but led all U.S. family chains in sales per unit for both 1990 and 1991.

As of 1991, Cracker Barrel was a well-recognized corporate success story, known for its effective, centralized, but somewhat authoritarian, leadership. From its headquarters, Cracker Barrel maintained uniformity in its store designs, menu offerings, and operating procedures. Travelers and local customers dining at any Cracker Barrel restaurant knew to expect a spacious, homey atmosphere, an inexpensive, country-style meal, and a friendly, efficient staff. All were guaranteed by Dan Evins, who remained as president, chief executive officer, and chairman of the board.

THE POLICY: NO LESBIAN OR GAY EMPLOYEES

In early January 1991, managers in the roughly 100 Cracker Barrel operating units received a communiqué from the home office in Lebanon. The personnel policy memorandum from William Bridges, vice president of human resources, declared that Cracker Barrel was "founded upon a concept of traditional American values." As such, it was deemed "inconsistent with our concept and values and . . . with those of our customer base, to continue to employ individuals. . . whose sexual preferences fail to demonstrate normal heterosexual values which have been the foundation of families in our society."

Throughout the chain, individual store managers, acting on orders of corporate officials, began conducting brief, one-on-one interviews with their employees to see if any were in violation of the new policy. Cheryl Summerville, a cook in the Douglasville, Georgia store for three and a half years, was called in by her supervisor, who read the policy aloud. When asked if she were a lesbian, Summerville knew she had to answer truthfully. She felt she owed that to her partner of ten years. Despite a history of consistently high performance evaluations, Summerville was fired on the spot, without warning and without severance pay. Her official separation notice, filled out by the manager and filed with the state department of labor, clearly indicated the reason for her dismissal: "This employee is being terminated due to violation of company policy. The employee is gay."

Cracker Barrel fired as many as 16 other employees across several states in the following months. These workers, mostly waiters, were left without any legal recourse. Lesbian and gay antidiscrimination statutes were in effect in Massachusetts and Wisconsin and in roughly 80 U.S. cities and counties, but none of the firings occurred in those jurisdictions. Federal civil rights laws, the employees learned, did not cover discrimination based upon sexual orientation.

Under pressure from a variety of groups, the company issued a statement in late February 1991. In it, Cracker Barrel management said, "We have re-visited our thinking on the subject and feel it only makes good business sense to continue to employ those folks who will provide the quality service our customers have come to expect." The recent personnel policy had been a "well-intentioned over-reaction." Cracker Barrel pledged to deal with any future disruptions in its units "on a store-by-store basis." Activists charged that the statement did not represent a retraction of the policy, as some company officials claimed. None of the fired employees had been rehired, activists noted, and none had been offered severance pay. Moreover, on February 27, just days after the statement, Dan Evins reiterated the company's antagonism toward nonheterosexual employees in a rare interview with a Nashville newspaper. Lesbians and gays, he said, would not be employed in more rural Cracker Barrel locations if their presence was viewed to cause problems in those communities.

THE BOYCOTT: QUEER NATIONALS VS. GOOD OL' BOYS

The next day, when news of Cracker Barrel employment policies appeared in the *Wall Street Journal*, *New York Times*, and *Los Angeles Times*, investment analysts expressed surprise. "I look on [Cracker Barrel executives] as pretty prudent business people," said one market watcher. "These guys are not fire-breathing good ol' boys." Unconvinced, lesbian and gay activists called for a nationwide boycott of Cracker Barrel restaurants and began a series of demonstrations that attracted extensive media coverage.

The protest movement was coordinated by the Atlanta chapter of Queer Nation, which Cheryl Summerville joined as co-chair. Fellow co-chair Lynn Cothren, an official with the Martin Luther King, Jr. Center for Non-Violent Social Change in Atlanta, helped plan many of the demonstrations, which were modeled after the civil rights protests of the 1960s. Committed to nonviolent civil disobedience, lesbian and gay activists and supporters staged pickets and sit-ins at various Cracker Barrel locations, often occupying an entire restaurant during peak lunch hours, ordering only coffee.

Protesters were further angered and spurred on by news in June from Mobile, Alabama. A 16-year-old Cracker Barrel employee had been fired for effeminate mannerisms and subsequently was thrown out of his home by his father. Demonstrations continued throughout the summer of 1991, spreading from the Southeast to the Midwest stores. Arrests were made at demonstrations in the Detroit area, while Cothren and Summerville were among several people arrested for criminal trespass at both the Lithonia and Union City, Georgia stores. Reporters and politicians dubbed Summerville the "Rosa Parks of the movement," after the woman whose arrest sparked the Montgomery, Alabama Bus Boycott of 1955–1956.

Support for the Cracker Barrel boycott grew, as organizers further charged the company with racism and sexism. Restaurant gift shops, they pointed out, sold Confederate flags, black mammy dolls, and other offensive items. The Cracker Barrel board of directors, they said, was indeed a good ol' boy network, made up exclusively of middle-aged and older white men. In addition, there was only one female in the ranks of upper management. Among the numerous groups that joined in support of the protests were the National Organization for Women (NOW); Jobs with Justice, a coalition of labor unions; The National Rainbow Coalition founded by Reverend Jesse Jackson; and the American Association of Public Health Workers. By early 1992, Summerville and Cothren had appeared on the television talk shows "Larry King Live" and "The Oprah Winfrey Show." The two were also featured in a segment on ABC's "20/20," after which Barbara Walters declared that she would refuse to eat at Cracker Barrel restaurants.

THE RESOLUTION: NEW YORK ATTEMPTS TO FORCE CHANGE

Meanwhile, New York City comptroller, Elizabeth Holtzman, and finance commissioner, Carol O'Cleiracain, at the urging of the National Gay and Lesbian Task

Force, wrote a letter to Dan Evins, dated March 12, 1991. As trustees of various city pension funds, which owned about $3 million in Cracker Barrel stock, they were "concerned about the potential negative impact on the company's sales and earnings which could result from adverse public reaction." They asked for a "clear statement" of the company's policy regarding employment and sexual orientation, as well as a description of "what remedial steps, if any, [had] been taken by the company respecting the employees dismissed."

Evins replied in a letter of March 19 that the policy had been rescinded and that there had been "no negative impact on the company's sales." Unsatisfied, the City of New York officials wrote back, again inquiring as to the status of the fired workers. They also asked that the company put forth a policy that "would provide unequivocally" that discrimination based on sexual orientation was prohibited. Evins never responded.

Shortly thereafter, Queer Nation launched a "buy one" campaign. Hoping to gain additional leverage in company decision-making, activists became stockholders by purchasing single shares of Cracker Barrel common stock. At the least, they reasoned, the company would suffer from the relative expense of mailing and processing numerous one cent quarterly dividend checks. More importantly, they could attend the annual stockholders meeting in Lebanon, Tennessee.

In November 1991, company officials successfully prevented the new shareholders from participating in the annual meeting, and they used a court injunction to block protests at the corporate complex. Nonetheless, demonstrators lined the street, while inside, a representative of the New York City comptroller's office announced the submission of a resolution "banning employment discrimination against gay and lesbian men and women," to be voted on at the next year's meeting. The resolution was endorsed by the Philadelphia Municipal Retirement System, another major stockholder. Cracker Barrel refused any further public comment on the issue.

THE EFFECT: NO DECLINE IN CORPORATE GROWTH

The impact of the boycott on the corporate bottom line was negligible. Trade magazines reiterated the company's claim that neither sales nor stock price had been negatively affected. Indeed, net sales remained strong, up 33 percent at fiscal year-end 1992 to $400 million, owing in good part to continued expansion; there were now 127 restaurants in the chain. Though the increase in same-store sales was not as great as the previous year, Cracker Barrel at least could boast growth, while other chains blamed flat sales on the recession. Cracker Barrel stock, trading on the NASDAQ exchange, appreciated 18 percent during the first month after news of the scandal broke, and the stock remained strong throughout the next fiscal year, splitting three-for-two in the third quarter.

Dan Evins had good reason to believe that the firings and the boycott had not adversely impacted profitability. One market analyst said that "the feedback they get from their customers might be in favor of not hiring homosexuals." Another even ventured that "it's plausible . . . the majority of Cracker Barrel's local users support an explicit discriminatory policy." Such speculation was bolstered by social science surveys indicating that respondents from the South and from rural areas in particular tended to be less tolerant of homosexuality than were other Americans.

Queer Nationals looked to other measures of success, claiming at least partial victory in the battle. Many customers they met at picket lines and inside restaurants vowed to eat elsewhere. Coalitions were formed with a variety of civil rights, women's, labor, and peace and justice organizations. Most importantly, the media attention greatly heightened national awareness of the lack of protections for lesbians and gays on the job. As the boycott continued, increasing numbers of states, counties, and municipalities passed legislation designed to prevent employment discrimination based on sexual orientation.

THE OUTCOME: STAND-OFF CONTINUES

As the November 1992 annual meeting approached, Cracker Barrel requested that the Securities and Exchange Commission make a ruling on the resolution offered by the New York pension fund administrators. The resolution, according to Cracker Barrel, amounted to shareholder intrusion into the company's ordinary business operations. As such, it should be excluded from consideration at the annual meeting and excluded from proxy ballots sent out before the meeting. The SEC agreed, despite previous rulings in which it had allowed stockholder resolutions regarding race or gender based employment bias.

Acknowledging that frivolous stockholder inquiries had to be curtailed, the dissenting SEC commissioner nonetheless expressed great dismay: "To claim that the shareholders, as owners of the corporation, do not have a legitimate interest in management-sanctioned discrimination against employees defies logic." And a noted legal scholar warned of the dangerous precedent that had been set: "Ruling an entire area of corporate activity (here, employee relations) off limits to moral debate effectively disenfranchises shareholders."

Thus, the stand-off continued. Queer Nation and its supporters persisted in the boycott. The Cracker Barrel board of directors and, with one exception, upper management, remained all-white, all-male bastions. The company still had not issued a complete retraction of its employment policy, and those employees fired had yet to be offered their old jobs back.

Lynn Cothren, Cheryl Summerville, and the other protestors arrested in Lithonia, Georgia were acquitted on charges of criminal trespass. Jurors ruled that the protestors' legitimate reasons for peaceably demonstrating superseded the company's rights to deny access or refuse service. Charges stemming from the Union City, Georgia demonstrations were subsequently dropped. Meanwhile, within weeks of the original policy against lesbian and gay employees, Cracker Barrel vice president for human resources William Bridges had left the company. Cracker Barrel declined comment on the reasons for his departure.

As of Cracker Barrel's fiscal year-end, July 30, 1993, a total of seven states and the District of Columbia offered protections for lesbians and gays on the job, both in the public and private sectors. Cracker Barrel had opened new stores in one of those states, Wisconsin, in 1992 and 1993. Moreover, plans for expansion seemed destined to take the company into areas even less receptive to employment discrimination. "Cracker Barrel isn't going to be in the South and Midwest forever," said one business editor. "Eventually they will have to face the issue—like it or not."

BIBLIOGRAPHY

Atlanta Journal-Constitution, 6, 11 July 1993; 2, 3 April 1992; 29 March 1992; 4, 18, 20 January 1992; 9 June 1991; 3, 4, 5 March 1991.

Carlino, Bill. "Cracker Barrel Profits Surge Despite Recession." *Nation's Restaurant News*, 16 December 1991, 14.

———. "Cracker Barrel Stocks, Sales Weather Gay-Rights Dispute." *Nation's Restaurant News*, 1 April 1991, 14.

Cracker Barrel Old Country Store, Inc. *Third Quarter Report* 30, April 1993.

———. *Second Quarter Report*, 29 January 1993.

———. *First Quarter Report*, 30 October 1992.

———. *Annual Report* 1992.

———. *Securities and Exchange Commission Form 10-K*, 1992.

———. *Annual Report* 1991.

———. *Securities and Exchange Commission Form 10-K*, 1991.

———. *Annual Report* 1990.

Cheney, Karen. "Old-Fashioned Ideas Fuel Cracker Barrel's Out-of-Sight Sales Growth and Profit Increases." *Restaurants & Institutions* 22 July 1992, 108.

Chicago Tribune, 5 April 1991.

"Cracker Barrel Hit by Anti-Bias Protests." *Nation's Restaurant News*, 13 April 1992, 2.

"Cracker Barrel's Emphasis on Quality a Hit with Travelers." *Restaurants & Institutions*, 3 April 1991, 24.

Dahir, Mubarak S. "Coming Out at the Barrel." *The Progressive*, June 1992, 14.

Farkas, David. "Kings of the Road." *Restaurant Hospitality*, August 1991, 118–122.

Galst, Liz. "Southern Activists Rise Up." *The Advocate* 19 May 1992, 54–57.

Greenberg, David. *The Construction of Homosexuality*. Chicago: University of Chicago Press, 1988.

Gutner, Toddi. "Nostalgia Sells." *Forbes* 27 April 1993, 102–103.

Harding, Rick. "Nashville NAACP Head Stung by Backlash from Boycott Support." *The Advocate*, 16 July 1991, 27.

———. "Activists Still Press Tennessee Eatery Firm on Anti-Gay Job Bias." *The Advocate*, 9 April 1991, 17.

Hayes, Jack. "Cracker Barrel Protesters Don't Shake Loyal Patrons." *Nation's Restaurant News*, 26 August 1991, 3, 57.

————. "Cracker Barrel Comes Under Fire for Ousting Gays." *Nation's Restaurant News*, 4 March 1991, 1, 79.

"Investors Protest Cracker Barrel Proxy Plan." *Nation's Restaurants News,* 2 November 1992, 14.

"Larry King Live." CNN television, aired 2 December 1991. 28 February 1991.

New York Times, 11 November 1992; 22 October 1992; 9 April 1992; 20 March 1991; 28 February 1991.

"Oprah Winfrey Show." Syndicated television, aired January 1992. Queer Nation. Documents on the Cracker Barrel Boycott. N.p., n.d.

"SEC Upholds Proxy Ruling." *Pensions & Investments*, 8 February 1993, 28.

Star, Marlene Givant. "SEC Policy Reversal Riles Activist Groups." *Pensions & Investments*, 26 October 1992, 33.

The (Nashville) *Tennessean,* 27 February 1991.

"20/20." ABC television, aired 29 November 1991.

Walkup, Carolyn. "Family Chains Beat Recession Blues with Value, Service." *Nation's Restaurant News,* 5 August 1991, 100, 104.

Wall Street Journal, 9 March 1993; 2 February 1993; 26 January 1993; 28 February 1991.

Wildmoon, KC. "QN Members Allowed to Attend Cracker Barrel Stockholder's Meeting." *Southern Voice,* 10 December 1992, 3.

————. "Securities and Exchange Commission Side with Cracker Barrel on Employment Discrimination." *Southern Voice*, 22 October 1992, 1.

————. "DeKalb Drops Most Charges Against Queer Nation." *Southern Voice*, 9 July 1992, 3.

John Howard holds degrees from the University of Alabama, the University of Mississippi, the University of Virginia. He is a doctoral candidate in American studies at Emory University in Atlanta, and he teaches American history at DeKalb College in Decatur, Georgia. He is the editor of *Carryin' On: An Anthology of Southern Lesbian and Gay History*, forthcoming from New York University Press.

DISCUSSION QUESTIONS

1. How could Cracker Barrel's initial policy statement have been "well-intentioned"? What benefits did Cracker Barrel achieve by ridding itself of lesbian and gay employees? What were the disadvantages?

2. How should the perceived values of a customer base affect a company's person-
    nel policies? In a large, national corporation, should personnel policies be uni-
    form across all operating units or can they be tailored by region according to lo-
    cal mores?

Mobil Oil Corporation

Eileen Hogan
Valdosta State University

INTRODUCTION

By 2000, the American workforce will be comprised of 39 percent white, non-Hispanic males; 47 percent women; 12 percent blacks; 10 percent Hispanics; and 4 percent Asians and others.[1] In 1986, corresponding figures were 44 percent white, non-Hispanic males; 45 percent women; 11 percent blacks; 7 percent Hispanics; and 3 percent Asians and others. For organizations, these statistics provide evidence of a changing labor force, and a consequent need to recognize and adapt to different value systems, life-styles, backgrounds, and preconceptions.

The increasing diversity of America's workforce has sparked heightened concern over how organizations can best manage their human resources. Increasingly, today's philosophy is directed toward how an organization can best take advantage of diversity—not only correcting the attitudes that lead to problems of different people working together, but creating environments in which diversity can flourish and create richer solutions to an organization's problems.

REJECTING AFFIRMATIVE ACTION

At Mobil Corporation, an executive provokes discussion by asking, "Look at our executive dining room. Do you ever see four blacks sitting together? You see four white males all the time. Why is that?"[2] No longer is the answer that there aren't enough blacks to fill a table; it is because blacks hesitate to gather in public because they'd believe, perhaps correctly, that others were thinking that they were excluding whites, or even plotting together.

The executive asks this question in order to make others more conscious of how diversity affects perceptions, attributions, and judgements. Often occurring in management training programs, these and similar efforts raise awareness of both positive and negative stereotypes of races, genders, ages, physical conditions, and ethnic groups.

Discussions occur in both cross- and same-culture groups. In same-culture groups, people discuss both the stereotypes they hold of others as well as the stereotypes others may hold of them. In cross-culture groups, members openly describe

Development of this case was made possible by a grant from the Funds for Excellence Program of the State Council of Higher Education for Virginia.

the preconceptions they hold of other groups, as well as those they believe are held of their own group. Discussions such as these are a prelude to helping people to a new, higher comfort level with their differences with others.

NO MORE IGNORING DIFFERENCES

Past efforts at eliminating discrimination—spurred largely by Equal Employment Opportunity (EEO) legislation—urged organizations to treat everyone basically the same. However, the new recognition is that everyone is *not* the same—and, in fact, this diversity is something that can add value to an organization. Therefore, while recognizing that diversity sometimes creates problems, organizations should value the diversity by managing people differently, but fairly.

The first step of this process is recognizing and discussing stereotypes. While experts recognize that there is some danger of perpetuating stereotypes by such a process, most believe that trying to ignore them is part of why organizations fail to get the most value from their human resources. Given the decreasing rate of growth of the labor force and the greater number of so-called minorities that will be entering employment in the nineties, coupled with greater competitiveness in the marketplaces of many organizations, firms that can take advantage of diversity should attain a competitive edge on their industry fellows.

After raising awareness of differences and stereotypes, programs then attempt to change attitudes. Key is that individuals cease to view those who are different from themselves as somehow deficient, but instead possessing different perspectives, strengths and weaknesses. Programs urge participants to become more aware of their own behavior, acknowledge their biases and stereotypes, focus on job performance, and avoid assumptions.

CREATING DIVERSITY—VALUING CULTURES

Mobil Corporation—A Case Study in Managing Diversity

The most forward-thinking organizations attempt to create diversity-valuing attitudes not only through training programs but also through multiple-pronged approaches that are aimed at creating diversity-valuing cultures. One organization that has been highlighted repeatedly for its proactive efforts toward managing diversity is Mobil Corporation.

Mobil Corporation is a vertically integrated oil company that operates globally. Now 125 years old, Mobil explores for and produces oil and gas in the United States and abroad; refines these raw materials into gasoline, lubricants, and other products, and markets them worldwide; and makes petrochemicals, fabricated plastics, and synthetic lubricant base stocks. In addition, divisions of Mobil mine phosphate, develop communities, and are involved in developing environmental protection technologies.[3]

TABLE 1 Selected Financial Results

	1989	1990	1991
Revenues			
Sales and Services	$55,432	$63,521	$62,359
Interest, dividends, and other	756	941	868
Total Revenues	$56,188	$64,472	$63,227
Costs and Expenses			
Crude oil, products, supplies, expenses	$31,839	$38,249	$35,735
Exploration expenses	529	686	779
Selling and general expenses	4,157	4,398	5,010
Depreciation, depletion, amortization	2,502	2,682	2,589
Interest and debt discount expense	771	700	713
Taxes other than income taxes	12,636	13,313	14,376
Income taxes	1,845	2,515	2,105
Total Costs and Expenses	54,379	62,543	61,307
Net Income	$ 1,809	$ 1,929	$ 1,920
Net Income per common Share	$ 4.40	$ 4.60	$ 4.65
Key Financial Indicators			
Common Stock Dividends per share	$ 2.55	$ 2.825	$ 3.215
Debt-to-Capitalization Ratio	30%	30%	32%
Total Debt	$ 6,962	$ 7,314	$ 8,229
Shareholders' Equity	16,274	17,072	17,534
per Common Share	39.84	42.44	43.74

Mobil employs over 67,000 people worldwide (down from 101,000 in 1983[4]) in a large number of locations. Twenty-six thousand six hundred of these employees are located in the United States. As of the summer of 1990, 3,300 of these employees work at Mobil's corporate headquarters, located just outside the Washington, D.C. Beltway in Fairfax County, Virginia.

Sixty percent of Mobil's refining capacity lies outside the United States, in 16 oil refineries in which Mobil owns operating interests, including operations in Africa and Australia. Mobil operates 47 chemical facilities in eight countries.

In a rough year for the industry, Mobil managed to earn $1.9 billion in 1991, about equal to the previous year. Summary financial data appear in Table 1.

MOVING CORPORATE HEADQUARTERS

In 1988, Mobil relocated its corporate headquarters from its long-time location in Manhattan to Fairfax County, Virginia, for "compelling economic and social reasons."[5] Motivations included saving money—Mobil estimated savings of $40 mil-

TABLE 2 Women and Minority Employee, Mobil and Other Firms*

Group	Mobil Corporation	Ten Oils	Nine Non-Oils
Women	15%	13%	22%
Blacks	5%	3%	5%
Hispanics	1%	1%	2%

* This information was contained in the previously referenced speech by Rex Adams, Vice President of Administration for Mobil Corporation, July 27, 1990. Figures are approximate.

lion annually, even after paying for the move; improving the quality of life for employees; and easing accessibility for executives.

Mobil chose to relocate to Fairfax County, Virginia, a suburban area outside of Washington, D.C., for several reasons. Virginia's corporate tax rate is 6 percent, compared with 19.35 percent in New York. Personal income taxes are also lower. Crime rates, housing costs, public schools, adult education programs, and availability of cultural opportunities were life-style aspects where the Fairfax County area rated well. Yet the area is not so geographically distant nor culturally dissimilar from New York to cause major culture shock problems such as those faced in J.C. Penney's corporate headquarters' move to Texas.

In addition, Mobil already owned a large tract of land just outside the Washington, D.C. Beltway, which it had purchased in the 1970's when land prices were more reasonable. It was able to sell its New York headquarters—which had developed significant vacant space due to the decline in the number of employees—to a Japanese investor.

The employees who moved included not only executives, but secretaries and other clerical workers. Overall, about 65 percent of corporate staff moved. Mobil called on its extensive experience in international moves of executives to smooth this transition.

Mobil's move included approximately 2,000 employees in two waves: one of 500 in 1989, followed by 1,500 employees in 1990. Mobil invested extensively in making the move as comfortable and convenient as possible, reimbursing employees for all expenses of relocation, helping them sell their homes and even guaranteeing sales of houses in the New York area, organizing and financing homefinding trips to the Fairfax County area, and providing financial and career counseling and help for spouses. Mobil offered assistance on getting car loans, specifically tailored to New Yorkers who may never have owned a car, as well as driver training classes.

Some employees who moved are happy they did. They enjoy the suburban life-style, the flexibility of commuting by automobile, the lower cost of living. However, many employees miss New York City: walking to myriads of shops or restaurants for lunch, the pace of life, the variety of experiences.

THE FIVE-YEAR PLAN IN 1986

In 1986, Mobil developed and implemented a five-year plan for improving both the diversity of its workforce and the upward mobility of minority groups and women within that workforce.

In 1986, the oil industry was facing a turbulent environment. Oil companies were consolidating, restructuring and downsizing. Mobil's number of employees was decreasing through normal attrition and planned processes. Organizational processes were being streamlined to increase efficiency.

In this type of environment, increasing diversity and promotional opportunities in a workforce can be a problem. For example, Mobil hired over 300 new college graduates in the United States in 1981[6]; in 1986, that number declined to 169. Women made up 30 percent of the professional hires in 1986—a group composed of 17 percent women—contributing to recognition of the importance of work and family issues in management.

Politically, the Reagan administration was in power, with decreased emphasis on affirmative action and equal employment opportunity. However, Mobil recognized that its commitment to obtaining and retaining qualified minority and female employees should not diminish.

Mobil's culture is one of loyalty to its employees, but also one of strong leadership. Management felt that a continued commitment to managing diversity required a strong stance on the issue, as well as specific strategies to fulfill its goal of a diversity-valuing culture. These were stated in Mobil's 1990 Five-Year Plan, developed in 1986.[7]

The plan was based on three premises. First, diversity in the workforce was inevitable. Second, a fast-track strategy for obtaining the goal of a cultural-diverse, diversity-valuing culture was not feasible due to current business conditions. Third, to be successful, the effort would have to go deep within the company, merely setting goals and/or increasing recruiting efforts would not accomplish the goal.

Based on these premises, Mobil launched five upward-mobility strategies in 1986:

1. Outreach: Encouraging minority and female students to pursue careers in technical fields, and enhancing Mobil's reputation as a diversity-valuing organization through community involvement.
2. Recruiting: Attracting quality minority and female applicants.
3. Training: Increasing awareness among managers of the challenges of managing a diverse workforce, and enhancing the career development of minorities and women.
4. Career development: Identifying and developing high potential females and minority employees.
5. Targets: Establishing specific targets for representation at all levels.

STATUS IN 1991

By the end of the five-year period, Mobil was able to assess its progress in achieving these five strategies.

OUTREACH

Mobil attempted to operationalize its outreach strategy by forming working partnerships with outside organizations in order to enhance its public reputation and encourage students to pursue technical disciplines. For example, Mobil contributed funds and time to Adopt-A-School, the National Action Council for Minorities in Engineering, the American Indian Science & Engineering Society, and the National Urban League, to name a few. Mobil sponsored awards at conferences, as well as actively recruited minority candidates.

RECRUITING

Mobil recognized that hiring top quality minority students meant getting involved with them far before their last year of college. So Mobil concentrated on identifying and mentoring talented individuals as early as high school. Fifty college sophomores were selected yearly to spend a week with Mobil during the school year, then intern the following summer, along with 450 other college students. Mobil also sponsored scholarships. Overall, Mobil involves over 10,000 students a year in some type of program.

In 1989, Mobil hired nearly three times as many blacks and Hispanics as in 1986, and nearly twice as many women, at a rate substantially higher than their proportion in the relevant population. Mobil's perception of the quality of these hires is positive.

TRAINING

In the area of training, Mobil, with the aid of a consulting social psychologist from Harvard, developed two programs. One, "Managing Diversity," is designed to help managers and supervisors become better managers of diverse groups. The second, "Efficacy Program," is designed for black and Hispanic professionals to provide guidance on career planning and self-development. Over 1200 managers attended the first class; over 450 professionals the second. These programs are considered a beginning at the tough issue of grappling with bias, sexism, and racism in a positive way.

CAREER DEVELOPMENT

The career development strategy was aimed at optimizing the contribution and potential of minority and women employees already in Mobil's workforce. Mobil sought to provide these people with "aggressive developmental experiences" in order to assess each individual's potential and developmental needs. Some promotions resulted, but attempts to shift employees at senior levels from staff to line positions were more difficult.

TARGETS

In 1986, Mobil set targets for increasing the representation of women, blacks, and Hispanics in the professional workforce by 10 percent, 30 percent, and 30 percent, respectively, by 1990. In addition, Mobil sought to raise representation of these groups in each salary band by the same percentages. The same goal applied to all corporate staff groups as well as all operating divisions. Six months before the end of the target period, Mobil had met all of these goals.

MOBIL VERSUS THE COMPETITION

Wondering how they stacked up against other corporations, Mobil conducted a survey to see how well they compared to the other oil companies as well as companies in other industries. Much to Mobil's delight, they did quite well. Mobil performed best of all but one other oil company, and favorably with other industries.

WORK AND FAMILY

Not only is the workforce in America becoming more diverse, some of the characteristics of the individuals that make up that workforce are also changing. More and more people are involved in dual career families, single parent families, or have significant responsibilities for elder care. Recognizing this, Mobil made a commitment to address work and family conflicts among employees. Efforts included elder and child care referral services, a spouse employment assistance program, flexible hours in many locations, a dependent care leave policy, a part-time return to work option, and an employee assistance program.

LOOKING AHEAD

As Mobil prepared to develop its next five-year plan, covering 1991–1995, executives recognized several facts about its workforce.

First, racial, ethnic, and gender tensions continue to exist and continue to provide potential problems for organizations. However, diversity can be both a challenge and an opportunity for organizations.

Second, educational standards in the American workforce are very low among industrial nations. Most American 17 year olds cannot summarize a newspaper article, write a letter, calculate the cost of a meal, or follow a public transit schedule. Of 1.8 million 18 year olds in 1988, 700,000 had dropped out of school, while another 700,000 were so illiterate that they could not read their own high school diplomas. Recognizing that the organization it wishes to build requires that each employee be able to take responsibility for his or her own performance on the job, Mobil worries whether its potential workforce can do the job, or what it will have to do to get these employees productive.

Of the new employees Mobil hires, values will differ. Rather than seeing themselves as company employees, they are more like self-managed independent contractors, viewing a career more as a series of contractual arrangements than as a long term commitment to a particular organization. Personal definitions of "success" will vary widely, and may not mean moving up the corporate hierarchy. Employees being requested to transfer may be more likely to ask, "What's in it for me?"

DECENTRALIZATION

Already organized into a divisional structure, Mobil Corporation decentralized even further in the late eighties and early nineties. The reasons for this increased decentralization stemmed from the realization of Mobil's needs to be responsive to particular customer bases, market needs, and geographical areas. Executives felt that the best way to stay responsive to its various environments was to delegate increased planning and decision making authority to its product divisions.

Thus, when the time arose to formulate the new five-year plan, top management was no longer willing to provide a standard, overarching plan for divisions to come to valuing diversity. Instead, the need for such an approach was made clear by top management, but each division was left to formulate and implement its own plan for accomplishing the goal. In response to this corporate approach, divisions at Mobil did indeed take different approaches to managing diversity.

EXPLORATION AND PRODUCING DIVISION

Before Paul Hoenmans became president of the E & P Division of Mobil (the "upstream" side of the business) in 1988, its culture was much like the rest of Mobil: paternalistic, loyal to its employees, top-down. Hoenmans saw E & P's culture as a barrier to achieving its goal of being the best and most profitable in the industry. Hoenmans felt that a traditional top-down management style could inhibit the creativity and flexibility needed for E & P to adapt to a rapidly changing environment. Therefore, Hoenmans implemented a major strategy to create a more participative, responsible culture within the division.

Hoenmans accompanied this change of philosophy with a restructuring of the entire division. Instead of the functional organization previously in place, the division would now operate in teams. For example, exploration teams now consist of as many as eighteen geologists, geophysicists, and engineers as parts of specific asset teams responsible for particular sites. The team leader might be of any of the specialties. Two layers of management were cut out; team leaders report directly to division management in Dallas. E & P's new culture was described: — *group goals*

> . . . a new environment in which employees have a greater sense of freedom in getting their jobs done, and in which our entire organization is more responsive, more flexible, and better able to seize new opportunities. In the new culture, a strong sense of individual participation, combined with teamwork and improved communications. . . should make employees' individual jobs more rewarding and professionally fulfilling, which in turn will promote profitability and growth.
>
> . . . All employees at every level have a role in this effort, and will be encouraged to participate by doing the following:
>
> - Communicate—that is, inform others, both up and down the line, about what we are each doing. Exchanging ideas can spark creativity; sharing information helps eliminate duplication of effort.
> - Show and encourage initiative and contribute new ideas as a regular part of the job.
> - Work as a team. Eliminate the tendency toward 'turf protection' and encourage participation by everyone who can contribute.
> - Be open-minded, flexible and receptive to change; tolerate and try new ideas; accept some risk as inherent to success in our business.

too work focused

- Focus on our core activities and place emphasis on major tasks. Move rapidly through essential but low-priority work.
- Accept responsibility. Increased authority and delegation affords more individual scope, but also means being more accountable.[8]

In keeping with its culture, E & P adopted a team approach to developing a plan for managing diversity. A work team, composed of people from diverse geographic locations, salary levels (from top to entry level), both women and men, various minority groups—a true snapshot of the division—attacked the problem. Using a team had several advantages. First, diverse points of view on the problem were brought together. Second, broad participation would make selling the plan easier. Third, the diversity of the group got away from the notion that efforts to manage diversity were something that white males could do for women and minorities.

The team deliberated for four months, a long and agonizing process. The key focus of the team was on how to change attitudes within the division. The solution they arrived at was multi-faceted. First, awareness training would raise consciousness about the issues of managing diversity. Second, managers would be trained in techniques of coaching, dealing with hostility, and managing differences.

Past training programs often tried to involve everyone in the organization; more often than not, the results of such programs were not sustainable because of the length of time it took to train everyone. Instead, this time the team recommended that a vertical slice of the organization be taken, with ten people selected to partake in one of 15 one- to two-week sessions off-site. Because not everyone was being selected to participate, the organization could afford to take people off their regular jobs for this considerable period of time. People having attended the sessions then had the responsibility to return to their own workplaces and run focus groups discussing and passing along what they learned.

At the end of this deliberations, the team presented its recommendations to the division's top management—a five and a half hour job. The team gained management's credibility through their meticulous preparation and "homework." Senior management's first reaction was somewhat negative—"What's all this touchy-feely stuff?"—but the team succeeded in convincing them that their recommendations were consistent with the division's new culture and would be effective.

MARKETING AND REFINING DIVISION

As E & P is responsible for providing the products of Mobil's petroleum operations, the M & R division is responsible for the "downstream" side.

By contrast to E & P, the M & R division of Mobil did not go through intentional cultural change. In addition, other differences exist. The M & R division is composed largely of sales people and marketers, as contrasted with E & P's technical workforce; following the stereotype of marketers, M & R employees tend to be more aggressive and oriented toward being responsive to their market. M & R professionals pride themselves on seeing the "big picture," as opposed to focusing on only one aspect of the business. M & R is results oriented and more focused on individual performance, as the jobs within the division tend not to be as interdependent on each other as in the E & P division.

M & R approached its development of the new five-year plan differently from E & P. Decentralization at the corporate level had made the "boilerplate" method used five years ago inappropriate. This time division management didn't tell each unit what its plan for managing diversity should be, but let each unit develop its own plan. Responsibility was assigned to the Employee Relations manager within each unit—a refinery, or a subsidiary company—whose role it then became to involve his or her peers in the development of a plan to fit that unit. The approach empowered the units to come up with a plan that was geared to their own particular status and needs, but also insured their commitment to the plan.

Plans developed within each unit then went to the division's employee relations staff. At times, division staff found themselves in the situation of telling units they were being too ambitious in their plans or goals, in order to ensure that top management of the division bought into the overall plan. Units were not forced into strict compliance with each other, however, because executives recognized and accepted the idea that units facing different situations required different responses.

1992 AND BEYOND

In the turbulent and problematic economy of 1992, Mobil faces the continued need to carefully manage its human resources. Substantial layoffs and retrenchments of the past 10 years have reduced its workforce. However, a downsizing firm—particularly one that has traditionally employed its people for life-long careers—faces great challenges both in creating diversity in its workplace and managing that diversity once it's in place. Mobil provides an interesting quasi-experiment; which of its divisions will succeed best in its attempts to integrate both its present workforce and its future employees into an effective organization?

NOTES

1. Braham, Jim, "No, You Don't Manage Everyone the Same," *Industry Week*, February 6, 1989, pages 28–30, 34–35. Note that figures for women and minorities overlap, and Hispanics may be of any race.
2. ———, "Firms Address Workers's Cultural Variety," *Wall Street Journal*, February 10, 1989, pp. 5–6.
3. Much of the information in this section was contained in Mobil Corporation's 1991 Annual Report.
4. Sweeney, Paul, "Escape from New York: Mobil Sets Up Shop in Suburban Fairfax County," *Washington Business Journal*, February 13, 1989, pp. 24–26, 28–29, 66–67.
5. Information in this discussion was obtained through personal interviews and from the following article: Sweeny, Paul, "Escape from New York: Mobil Sets

Up Shop in Suburban Fairfax County," *Washington Business Journal Magazine*, February 13, 1989, pp. 24–26, 28–29, 66–67.

6. ———, "Equal Employment Opportunity Update," (text of a speech by Rex D. Adams, Vice President of Administration, at a Public Issues Committee meeting of the Mobil Corporation Board of Directors, July 27, 1990).

7. This information was obtained from "Equal Employment Opportunity Update," text of a speech by Rex D. Adams, Vice President of Administration of Mobil Corporation, July 27, 1990.

8. ———, "Strategies for the 90's: Working Together Toward a Common Goal," a report produced by the Exploration and Producing Division of Mobil Oil Corporation, undated.

Eileen Hogan is an Assistant Professor at Valdosta State University in Valdosta, GA. Since receiving her MBA and Ph.D. from the University of California at Berkeley in 1983, she has served on the faculties of the University of Virginia, George Mason University, and the University of California at Berkeley. Her research interests focus on the ability of large organizations to manage change.

DISCUSSION QUESTIONS

1. Briefly contrast the approaches for managing diversity taken by the Exploring & Producing (E&P) Division and the Marketing & Refining (M&R) Division. What do you see as the strengths of each approach? Which approach do you think will result in the greatest commitment among current employees? Why?

2. Which division do you think used the most participatory system of devising their plans for managing diversity? Why?

3. How do you think Mobil's plans for managing diversity will make it more competitive?

4. In some cultural groups, employees do not take the initiative nor do they talk casually with their supervisors. How might members of these groups feel in a participative management environment?

C H A P T E R

FIVE

On Experiencing Diversity: Exercises

It is not enough just to value and understand differences. A caring, knowledgeable co-worker who is inept is just not helpful. Ultimately, teaching about diversity must be about teaching students how to become more skilled at working with people who are different.[1]

The way we see people and groups and the way that we act towards them is learned behavior, which means that we can learn new ways. The changing demographic composition of the workforce, the different styles and values of these workers, and the increasing emphasis on global business will require that we develop an increased sense of self-awareness and innovative approaches to working with people who may have attitudes and ideas quite different from our own.

In the same way that only reading about college really does not prepare you for the experience, only reading about diversity is not sufficient. Understanding diversity in the workplace requires us to examine our attitudes and perceptions, acquire new knowledge about members of diverse groups, and put this combination of internal and external knowledge into practice. As a result, the exercises in this section follow the three-level structure for diversity training advocated by Gardenschwartz and Rowe: becoming aware of differences and stereotypes, learning about others, and applying new skills.[2]

Initially, you will be asked to participate in exercises that increase your awareness of what it is like to be different. Exercises such as *I AM. . .* , and *Exploring Diversity on Your Campus* ask you to consider how your life experiences have shaped your attitudes and assumptions about differences; *Musical Chairs*, and *The Multicultural Negotiations Exercise* are designed to produce a higher level of awareness by simulating feelings of what it is like to be different.

Short questionnaires such as *Workforce I.Q.*, *Women and Work*, *Cultural-Diversity I.Q.*, *Test of Management Knowledge/The Navajo Culture*, *The Older Worker* etc., give you additional knowledge about specific types of differences. Other exercises require more involvement on your part. Experiences such as *Increasing Multicultural Understanding*, the *Invisible Volleyball Game*, and *Gender and Participation* are structured to help you to gain knowledge about differences through a deeper level of involvement.

The third level of exercise requires you to apply the skills that you have learned. Here, *Is This Sexual Harassment*, *Creating Your Own Culture*, *Trancendus Exercise*, *The In-Basket Dilemma*, and *Create an Exercise* allow you to practice the skill of managing a diverse workforce.

These exercises require you to be an active participant who is highly involved in the learning process and reflective about your experience. These exercises offer you an opportunity to build upon the readings and cases by internalizing new ideas, trying out new behaviors, and developing the new skills that will be needed to manage the new workforce.

Sometimes the purposes of these exercises may not be initially apparent to you. Sometimes they may seem complex and unrelated to understanding diversity. Be patient. Because diversity is a highly charged subject, the process of learning about diversity often involves feelings of confusion and frustration along the way.

The exercises range from short questionnaires to longer role plays and experiences. They were chosen to provide a wide range of opportunities for individuals to identify and investigate the sources of their ideas about diversity, to learn more about how others experience the world, and to provide multiple opportunities to practice new ways of communicating and working with diverse individuals and groups. Understanding diversity and acquiring the skills to manage a diverse workforce requires us to change many of our attitudes and behaviors, which can be a complex process.

NOTES

1. Gracia, Joseph E., Frost, Peter, Nkomo, Stella, and White, Judith. "Teaching About Diversity Within a Diverse Learner Environment." *Mastering Management Education*, Charles M. Vance, ed., Newbury Park, CA: Sage, 1993, pp. 253–262.
2. Gardenswartz, Lee, and Rowe, Anita. "Experiential Exercises for Diversity Training." *Managing Diversity*, vol. 2, 11 (August, 1993): pp. 7–8.

I AM. . .

M. June Allard
Worcester State College

GOALS
1. To help you learn about yourself by examining your group memberships, i.e., dimensions of culture, by which you define yourself.
2. To further examine your self descriptors for indications of your most important group memberships.

INSTRUCTIONS
1. Think about how you would describe yourself to someone you have never met. On each line below, write a single-word description.

I AM a (an). . . .

1. _____	11. _____
2. _____	12. _____
3. _____	13. _____
4. _____	14. _____
5. _____	15. _____
6. _____	16. _____
7. _____	17. _____
8. _____	18. _____
9. _____	19. _____
10. _____	20. _____

2. Put a star by the three most important descriptors.

What Is Your Workforce I.Q.?

American Version

Carol P. Harvey
Assumption College

Read each of the following statements and mark them **T** for true or **F** for false.

_____1. During the 1990s the number of people in the United States who are age 65 or older is projected by the Census Bureau to increase 42 percent, six times the rate of overall population growth.

_____2. One American in four is either Hispanic or nonwhite.

_____3. Today the population of Detroit is 63 percent black, Miami is 66 percent Hispanic, Washington is 70 percent black, and more than 30 percent of New York's residents are foreign born.

_____4. In the United States, total minority markets for goods and services are larger than our exports to any one country.

_____5. In 1990, nonwhites had a combined spending power of $424 billion. By the year 2000 this is projected to increase to $650 billion.

_____6. Women and nonwhites will comprise 85 percent of the new entrants into the workforce by the year 2000.

_____7. Three percent of the top management positions in the Fortune 500 companies are held by women.

_____8. Approximately 2.8 million United States men are single heads of households. This group is the fastest growing family unit in the United States.

_____9. Disabled people are the most likely demographic group to be unemployed.

_____10. Between 5 percent and 10 percent of the United States population is estimated to be gay or lesbian.

Total number of true answers _____

Total number of false answers _____

What Is Your Workforce I.Q.?

Canadian Version

Gerald Hunt

Nipissing University, Ontario, Canada

Read each of the following statements and mark them **T** for true or **F** for False.

_____1. Twenty percent of the new enrollments in Canadian university engineering programs are female.

_____2. Between 5 percent and 10 percent of the Canadian population is estimated to be gay or lesbian.

_____3. Close to 80 percent of Canadian women between the ages of 25 and 44 work outside the home.

_____4. Visible minorities will make up almost half of the population of Metropolitan Toronto by the year 2001.

_____5. Visible minorities will be responsible for at least a fifth of Canada's gross domestic product by the year 2001, an amount equal to $311 billion.

_____6. Disabled people are the most likely group to be unemployed.

_____7. Three percent of the top management positions in the Fortune 500 companies are held by women.

_____8. Study after study has found that immigrants are less likely than Canadian-born workers to end up on welfare.

_____9. At least 10 large organizations in Canada, such as IBM and the Metro Toronto Police Force, now have gay and lesbian employee support groups.

_____10. Canada is home to at least 4.3 million first generation immigrants.

Total number of true answers _____

Total number of false answers _____

Exploring Diversity on Your Campus

Herbert Bromberg
Carol P. Harvey
Both of Assumption College

GOALS
1. To understand how diversity enriches learning/living experiences.
2. To understand how lack of diversity contributes to limited perspectives.

INSTRUCTIONS
1. Describe your college's faculty and administration in terms of its aspects of diversity and/or demographics.

2. Describe your college's student body in terms of its aspects of diversity and/or demographics.

3. What are the similarities and differences between the two groups?

4. How does the degree of diversity in the faculty affect your learning experience?

5. How does the degree of diversity in the student body affect the classroom experience, dorm life, and extra-curricular activities? What are its advantages and disadvantages?

6. What could be done in terms of diversity to enrich your college experience?

———————————

Herbert Bromberg is an associate professor at Assumption College. He has worked for W.R. Grace, Celanese Corporation, and was director of the Chemical and Agricultural Products Division of Abbott Laboratories.

———————————

Increasing Multicultural Understanding:
Uncovering Stereotypes
John Bowman

GOALS
1. To help individuals become aware of their own values.
2. To show individuals how their culture programs them to react to and judge others in automatic and stereotypic ways.
3. To discover the types and sources of stereotypes about others.
4. To provide an opportunity for participants to see how their stereotypes create barriers to appreciating individual differences.

INSTRUCTIONS
1. Form groups of 4–6 students each. Members of each group should sit in a circle and face each other.
2. Turn to the Uncovering Stereotypes: Worksheet.
3. Follow your instructor's directions for completing the blank category boxes to reflect different special populations.
4. Working Individually

   - Complete the First Thought/Judgment column by writing your first thought about or judgment of each category. Refer to the example given on the worksheet.
   - Rate each thought/judgment as positive (+), negative (–), or neutral (0).
   - Complete the Sources column by indicating the source of your judgment for each category.

5. As a Group

   - Turn to the Uncovering Stereotypes: Group Summary Sheet.
   - Five categories (family, media, experience, work experience, friends) have already been listed on the summary sheet. Add additional categories (derived from your group discussions) to the sheet.
   - Take a quick count of the number of positive, negative, and neutral thoughts/judgments made by your group for each of the Source Categories and enter totals on the last line.

6. As a Class

   - Discuss which sources lead to positive, which to negative, and which to neutral judgments.
   - Discuss the implications of having negative or positive stereotypes/judgments from different perspectives; for example, among workers, between managers and workers, and at the corporate level.

Adapted from Dr. John Bowman, Pembroke State University of the University of South Carolina.

Uncovering Stereotypes Worksheet

Category	First Thought/ Judgment	Rating*	Sources
Working Mother	Neglects children, busy, tired		Own experience, movies
Southerner			
AIDS Carrier			
Smoker			
Hispanic			
African-American Male			
Female President of the United States			

* (+) = positive

  (−) = negative

  (0) = neutral

Uncovering Stereotypes Group Summary Sheet

Source Categories	Positive (+) Thoughts/ Judgments	Negative(−) Thoughts/ Judgments	Neutral (0) Thoughts/ Judgments
Family			
Media			
Experience			
Work Experience			
Friends			
Total			

Invisible Volleyball Game

Barton Kunstler
Lesley College School of Management

GOALS

This activity is designed to help explore the following themes:

1. That males and females in our society may experience sports differently from one another
2. How this sports experience tends to reinforce and exaggerate gender-associated differences in managerial behaviors, attitudes, and values
3. Whether managerial culture often self-selects for advancement those people familiar with the values and vocabulary of sports culture
4. Whether understanding and even changing the role of sports in our society, especially in regard to gender-related values and behaviors, can be a source of societal and organizational reform.

INSTRUCTIONS

The following instructions will be reviewed with you by the instructor and will be accompanied by activities and discussion as noted.

1. We are going to play a volleyball game—two games, actually. The women will play one game among themselves, as will the men. We will use an invisible ball and invisible net. As each group plays, the other will observe and take notes. Will either group volunteer to go first? If not, let's flip a coin.
2. Now that we know who is going first, organize a game and start playing. Members of the other group, observe and keep notes on your observation sheets.
3. Now that we have played the game, how did the two groups differ in how they approached, organized, and played the game? Start by making a list of your observations of the other group and then make a separate list of your perceptions of your own group as well. Include such aspects as playing style, teamwork, and organization of the game.
4. Imagine now that each of these two lists represents a profile of someone up for a management job. The person can be male or female. You are the committee deciding this person's future. The instructor will play devil's advocate for either side that you argue. Start with why the person on the women's list would not make a good manager. After giving a few reasons, start defending this person so that a debate will get going on the pros and cons of each of the two profiles.
5. Now do the same with the person on the men's list.
6. How does this argument reflect:
   a. how managers are viewed and evaluated in the workplace?
   b. how these traits and our attitudes toward them reflect current trends and theories in managerial style, behavior, and function?

c. the actual experiences you have had in the workplace, in terms of how people are perceived, how they are promoted, attitudes toward men and women, and the behaviors considered appropriate for each?

7. In what ways do childhood experiences with sports contribute to the pattern that emerged in our volleyball game? What do you remember growing up, or observe in kids today, that is similar to or different from what you observed in our game?

Optional Role Play

The class breaks into groups of at least four people and develops a role play using the following roles: a male acting according to the male team's profile as described by the class; a female acting according to the female team's profile; a male acting out the female profile; and a female acting out the male profile. After the role play, each group relates the points it intended to demonstrate and a class discussion ensues.

Invisible Volleyball Game Observation Sheet
for the Other Group

Use this sheet to note your observations of the invisible volleyball game. The questions below are intended to suggest what you might watch for. Feel free, however, to include any ideas that come to you as you observe.

1. What do you notice about the attitudes of the players towards the game? Be specific about the behaviors that lead you to your conclusions.

2. How would you describe the way the group organized the game?

3. Please note any aspects of teamwork or competition among the players or between the teams.

4. Other observations:

Invisible Volleyball Game Observation Sheet
for Your Own Group

Use this sheet to note your observations of the invisible volleyball game. The questions below are intended to suggest what you might watch for. Feel free, however, to include any ideas that come to you as you observe.

1. What do you notice about the attitudes of the players towards the game? Be specific about the behaviors that lead you to your conclusions.

2. How would you describe the way the group organized the game?

3. Please note any aspects of teamwork or competition among the players or between the teams.

4. Other observations:

INVISIBLE VOLLEYBALL GAME SUGGESTED WRITING ASSIGNMENTS

1. Write a one page discussion of your past sports experiences and how they affected your view of the opposite sex and of your own sex. What kind of gender-related values were promoted in these sports or games programs? Consider some of the details of the experience. For instance, did name-calling or put-downs seem to delineate attitudes about one sex or the other? Did the values that were promoted give you positive or negative ideas about what it was to be a girl or boy, woman or man?

2. Write a one page response to any or all of the following questions:

   - Do you think men and woman at work relate differently to team work, leadership, and strategizing?
   - Are managerial skills truly learned to some extent on the playing field?
   - Are the lessons of the playing field really designed to produce effective managers, or just those who know how to get ahead?

3. Write a response to the following idea from *The Managerial Woman,* by Margaret Hennig and Anne Jardim. Pocket Books, NY, 1977, p. 90: Successful women have always been aware of "the inconsistencies in traditional [sex] role definitions." In what ways in your life did sports reinforce or undermine (or both) such traditional definitions?

Barton Kunstler, Ph.D., is an assistant professor and program director at the Lesley College School of Management, where he has developed extensive curricular materials in such fields as ethics and management, sports and society, communications strategies for managers, and professional writing and problem solving. As a consultant, he specializes in business communications, creativity and problem solving, diversity issues, and the facilitation and organization of symposiums, meetings, and retreats. Dr. Kunstler earned his doctorate at Boston University, in the field of classics, and his articles on scholarly and professional topics have appeared in a variety of publications.

Women and Work Opinion Questionnaire

Gerald D. Klein

Rider College

This questionnaire consists of a series of opinions or statements that deal largely with women and working. You are asked to carefully read each statement and to indicate next to each the extent to which you agree or disagree with the view expressed. Please circle the letter next to each statement which most accurately reflects *your* personal opinions or beliefs. For each statement select one of four answers:

Strongly Agree	(A)
Agree	(a)
Disagree	(d)
Strongly Disagree	(D)

Please consider each statement separately from the others and try to make *some* response to every statement.

A a d D   1. I think that it is unnecessary for women to go outside of the home to find challenge because there is plenty of challenge for women in child rearing and in running a home.

A a d D   2. I believe that when a husband and wife both work it is important that the husband make the larger salary.

A a d D   3. I believe that women experience physical and emotional changes throughout the month that make them less suitable for positions of responsibility than men.

A a d D   4. I believe that women with children should not work outside of the home.

A a d D   5. I have no objection to women attempting to obtain jobs like truck driver or steel worker which in this society are traditionally performed by men.

A a d D   6. I believe that in a period of high unemployment, a male applicant for a job should be given preference over a female applicant.

A a d D   7. I would rather not work for a woman.

A a d D   8. The popular belief that women are too emotional for high level positions is a fallacy.

A a d D   9. A woman would be a liability on a construction crew because she couldn't contribute her fair share.

Reprinted with permission of Gerald D. Klein, Rider College, Lawrenceville, New Jersey, 08648 and Kathryn B. Klein.

Strongly Agree   (A)

Agree   (a)

Disagree   (d)

Strongly Disagree   (D)

A a d D   10. A woman who uses Ms. is trying to cover up the fact that she is not married.

A a d D   11. Even when she is paying her own way a woman should let the man she is with handle the money.

A a d D   12. I believe that the women's liberation movement will probably help the women more than hurt them.

A a d D   13. I believe that hiring single women into management trainee positions represents a poor investment for an organization.

A a d D   14. I think that married women who are eager to leave the home and enter the world of work full-time don't realize how good they have it.

A a d D   15. Women possess the aggressiveness and decisiveness necessary for leadership positions.

Is This Sexual Harassment?

Carol P. Harvey
Assumption College

GOALS
1. To help students to understand what is and what is not sexual harassment on the job.
2. To apply the federal government's sexual harassment guidelines to workplace situations. The Equal Employment Opportunity Commission's Guidelines define sexual harassment as:

   unwelcome sexual advances, requests for sexual favors, and other physical and verbal contact of a sexual nature when it affects the terms of employment under one or more of the following conditions: such an activity is a condition for employment; such an activity is a condition of employment consequences such as promotion, dismissal, or salary increases; such an activity creates a hostile working environment.

INSTRUCTIONS
1. Given the guidelines, which of the following incidents are examples of sexual harassment?
2. Explain your reasons for your answers.

1. While teaching Gary how to run the new spreadsheet program on the computer, Lois, his supervisor, puts her hand on his shoulder.

   Not sexual harassment untils Gary expresses dislike and Lois continues to touch him.

2. Julie, the new secretary to the vice-president of manufacturing, frequently has to go out into the plant as part of her job. Several of the machinists have been whistling at her and shouting off-color remarks as she passes through the shop. One of the other women in the company found Julie crying in the ladies room after such an incident.

   yes, this is a hostile environment for Julie, it makes her job more difficult

3. Paul and Cynthia, two sales reps, are both married. However, it is well known that they are dating each other outside of the office.

Could create a hostile environ. if (adultry) it makes other employees uncomfort.; - But as long as it is outside of work and consenual....

4. Jeanne's boss, Tom, frequently asks her out for drinks after work. She goes because both are single and she enjoys his company. On one of these occasions, he asks her out to dinner for the following Saturday evening.

- Consenual ?-...

5. Steve's boss, Cathy, frequently makes suggestive comments to him and has even suggested that they meet outside of the office. Although at first he ignored these remarks, recently he made it clear to her that he had a steady girlfriend and was not available. When she gave him his performance appraisal, much to his surprise, she cited him for not being a team player.

Definate sexual harassment, both types

6. Jackie received a call at work that her father died suddenly. When she went to tell her boss that she had to leave, she burst into tears. He put his arms around her and let her cry on her shoulder.

NO

7. Marge's co-worker, Jerry, frequently tells her that what she is wearing is very attractive.

Does it make marge uncomfortable?

8. While being hired as a secretary, Amanda is told that she may occasionally be expected to accompany managers on important overnight business trips to handle the clerical duties at these meetings.

NO – /uncomfortable to Amanda?

9. Joe, an elderly maintenance man, often makes suggestive comments to the young females in the office. His behavior has been reported to his supervisor several times but it is dismissed as, "Don't be so sensitive, old Joe doesn't mean any harm."

Old Joe's gotta go—

10. Jennifer frequently wears revealing blouses to the office. Several times she has caught male employees staring at her.

Is Jennifer creating a hostile environ. for them, or for herself?

– maybe she likes it.

Cultural-Diversity Quiz: How's Your "Cultural I.Q."?

Sondra B. Thiederman

This quiz will give you an idea of how much you already know about cultural diversity. In some cases, there is more than one correct response to each question. Your instructor will give you the correct answers along with an evaluation of your "Cultural I.Q."

_____1. On average, how long do native-born Americans maintain eye contact?
a. 1 second
b. 15 seconds
c. 30 seconds

_____2. *True or false:* One of the few universal ways to motivate workers, regardless of cultural background, is through the prospect of a promotion.

_____3. Learning to speak a few words of the language of immigrant clients, customers, and workers is:
a. Generally a good idea as the effort communicates respect for the other person
b. Generally not a good idea because they might feel patronized
c. Generally not a good idea because they might be offended if a mistake is made in vocabulary or pronunciation

_____4. *True or false*: American culture has no unique characteristics; it is composed only of individual features brought here from other countries.

_____5. When communicating across language barriers, using the written word:
a. Should be avoided; it can insult the immigrant or international visitor's intelligence
b. Can be helpful; it is usually easier to read English than to hear it
c. Can be confusing; it is usually easier to hear English than to read it

_____6. *True or false*: Behaving formally around immigrant colleagues, clients, and workers—that is, using last names, observing strict rules of etiquette—is generally not a good idea as it gives the impression of coldness and superiority.

Reprinted with the permission of Lexington Books, an imprint of Macmillan, Inc., from PROFITING IN AMERICA'S MULTICULTURAL WORKPLACE: How to Do Business Across Cultural Lines by Sondra B. Thiederman, Ph.D. Copyright © by Sondra Thiederman.

_____ 7. In times of crisis, the immigrant's ability to speak English:
   a. Diminishes because of stress
   b. Stays the same
   c. Improves because of the necessity of coping with the crisis
   d. Completely disappears

_____ 8. The number of languages spoken in the U.S. today is:
   a. 0–10
   b. 10–50
   c. 50–100
   d. 100+

_____ 9. *True or false*: Immigrant families in the United States largely make decisions as individuals and have generally abandoned the practice of making decisions as a group.

_____ 10. When you have difficulty understanding someone with a foreign accent:
   a. It probably means that he or she cannot understand you either.
   b. It probably means that he or she is recently arrived in this country.
   c. It is helpful if you listen to all that he or she has to say before interrupting, the meaning might become clear in the context of the conversation.
   d. It is helpful for you to try to guess what the speaker is saying and to speak for him or her so as to minimize the risk of embarrassment.

_____ 11. When an Asian client begins to give you vague answers before closing a deal, saying things like "It will take time to decide," or "We'll see," the best thing to do is:
   a. Back off a bit, he or she may be trying to say "no" without offending you.
   b. Supply more information and data about your service or product, especially in writing.
   c. Push for a "close." His or her vagueness is probably a manipulative tactic.
   d. State clearly and strongly that you are dissatisfied with his or her reaction so as to avoid any misunderstanding.

_____ 12. Apparent rudeness and abruptness in immigrants is often due to:
   a. Lack of English-language facility
   b. A difference in cultural style
   c. Differing tone of voice

_____ 13. *True or False*: Many immigrant and ethnic cultures place greater importance on how something is said (body language and tone of voice) than on the words themselves.

_____14. The avoidance of public embarrassment (loss of face) is of central concern to which of the following cultures?
a. Hispanic
b. Mainstream American
c. Asian
d. Middle Eastern

_____15. *True or False*: One of the few universals in etiquette is that everyone likes to be complimented in front of others.

_____16. In a customer-service situation, when communicating to a decision maker through a child who is functioning as interpreter, it is best to:
a. Look at the child as you speak so that he or she will be certain to understand you.
b. Look at the decision maker.
c. Look back and forth between the two.

_____17. Which of the following statements is (are) true?
a. Most Asian workers like it when the boss rolls up his or her sleeves to work beside employees.
b. Taking independent initiative on tasks is valued in most workplaces throughout the world.
c. Many immigrant workers are reluctant to complain to the boss as they feel it is a sign of disrespect.
d. Asians are quick to praise superiors to their face in an attempt to show respect.

_____18. *True of False*: The "V" for victory sign is a universal gesture of good will and triumph.

_____19. Which of the following statements is (are) true?
a. It is inappropriate to touch Asians on the hand.
b. Middle Easterner men stand very close as a means of dominating the conversation.
c. Mexican men will hold another man's lapel during conversation as a sign of good communication.

_____20. Building relationships slowly when doing business with Hispanics is:
a. A bad idea; if you don't move things along, they will go elsewhere
b. A bad idea; they will expect native-born professionals to move quickly so will be disoriented if you do not
c. A good idea; it may take longer, but the trust you build will be well worth the effort

Private Industry on American Indian Reservations

Test of Management Knowledge in the Traditional Navajo American Indian Culture

Fairlee E. Winfield

Northern Arizona University

DIRECTIONS

Imagine you are the manager at a manufacturing facility on the Navajo Indian Nation. Place an X beside the best answer in each set of answers below.

1. If Navajo employees ask permission to be absent from work for a ceremony, you should
   - _____a. give them work to take home.
   - _____b. ask them to tell you all about it.
   - _____c. grant permission without question.
   - _____d. threaten them with dismissal.

2. If Navajo employees go to a medicine man, the employees are to respect all tabus for
   - _____a. 12 hours.
   - _____b. 24 hours.
   - _____c. 4 days.
   - _____d. 7 days.

3. How should you react when you see corn pollen or ashes on Navajo employees' heads?
   - _____a. Quietly tell them to wash it off.
   - _____b. Joke about it. (Navajos enjoy jokes.)
   - _____c. Ignore it.
   - _____d. Ask them to tell you about it so you can learn about the culture.

4. If you visit a traditional Navajo employee's family at home, how should you greet them?
   - _____a. No greeting, just talk of the business at hand.
   - _____b. Trade small chunks of turquoise for Indian corn before getting to the business at hand.
   - _____c. Stand quietly until spoken to.
   - _____d. Give them a slight handshake.

Reprinted with permission of the author and of North American Case Research Association (NACRA) from the *Case Research Journal*, Spring 1993.

5. What does getting up before sunrise mean to your Navajo employees?
   _____a. The obtainment of something valuable
   _____b. Tabus are nullified for the day.
   _____c. Insomnia
   _____d. The early bird gets the worm.

6. How is wealth recognized in the traditional Navajo culture?
   _____a. Medicine man—his wisdom, knowledge, and skill
   _____b. Pickup truck
   _____c. A house instead of a hogan
   _____d. Livestock

7. Which way do Navajo employees' homes face if they live in traditional hogans?
   _____a. Any direction as long as it meets the sunrise
   _____b. East
   _____c. West
   _____d. South

8. Which bird is tabu in Navajo culture?
   _____a. The golden eagle
   _____b. The roadrunner
   _____c. The owl
   _____d. The black crow

9. Which animal is tabu in Navajo culture?
   _____a. The bear
   _____b. The mountain lion
   _____c. The wild boar
   _____d. No animal is tabu

10. What is the horned toad considered as in Navajo culture?
    _____a. Grandfather
    _____b. Uncle
    _____c. Brother
    _____d. Kind stranger

11. When a young woman pulls at a young man's arm at a traditional social dance where there is a large gathering of people, the man should
    _____a. start running
    _____b. dance with her, and give her money.
    _____c. start a conversation.
    _____d. take her home.

12. A social dance ceremony (squaw dance) lasts about
    _____a. 3 hours.
    _____b. 12 hours.
    _____c. 4 days.
    _____d. 9 days.

13. Children of your traditional Navajo employees are silent around adults because
    _____a. they are stupid.
    _____b. they are shy.
    _____c. it is a social custom.
    _____d. adults are usually very cruel to them.

14. If Navajo employees refuse to eat fish or water birds in the company dining room, it is probably because
    _____a. they have never developed a taste for those foods.
    _____b. the food is tabu to them.
    _____c. the symbol of a fish and the symbol of a water bird are sacred.
    _____d. they are just being finicky.

15. The baking of a 10-pound cornmeal cake means
    _____a. a birthday celebration.
    _____b. a healing ceremonial.
    _____c. a puberty event.
    _____d. a wedding celebration.

16. If there is a death in a traditional Navajo family, the Navajo employee may
    _____a. attend the funeral and return to work the next day.
    _____b. continue in work as usual.
    _____c. stay at home for 1 to 2 weeks but will not attend the funeral.
    _____d. stay at home for 1 to 2 weeks but will attend the funeral.

17. When Navajo employees return to work after the death of a traditional family member, it is best to
    _____a. offer your condolences.
    _____b. make no reference to the death.
    _____c. offer them the Christian hope of the resurrection.
    _____d. cheer them with some poetry explaining the beauty in death.

18. When raw vegetables or fruit, especially melons, are served to Navajo employees, the carver of the food should
    _____a. turn the food on end before cutting it.
    _____b. seize the food firmly, and stab it vigorously.
    _____c. gently poke the knife, point first, into the food.
    _____d. lay the knife flat on the food to begin cutting, blade down.

19. According to Navajo custom, a Navajo cannot tell a lie after being asked the question
    _____a. one time.
    _____b. two times.
    _____c. three times.
    _____d. four times.

20. A manager of Navajo employees should not wear a ring on the index finger because

_____a.   only medicine men wear rings on the index finger.
_____b.   only the dead wear rings on the index finger.
_____c.   only witches wear rings on the index finger.
_____d.   only clan leaders wear rings on the index finger.

21. If a traditional Navajo wanders about your lawn before coming to the door, he or she is probably

_____a.   "sizing up" the place.
_____b.   trying to attract evil spirits to your house.
_____c.   trying to distract evil spirits from your house.
_____d.   showing reluctance to visit you.

22. Which type of discussion may not be considered appropriate by traditional Navajo employees?

_____a.   Talk about what they did last summer.
_____b.   Talk about what they plan to do next summer.
_____c.   Talk about the most enjoyable experience of their life.
_____d.   Talk about death and dying.

23. The best way to warn traditional Navajo employees of possible danger is to

_____a.   tell them the truth, about the ghastly results of failure to mind you or to exercise caution.
_____b.   make positive statements if possible, and don't go into all the ghastly details or negative aspects of the situation.
_____c.   threaten to withdraw your friendship if they don't observe your warning.
_____d.   warn them of the punishment that may await them in the next life.

24. If Navajo employees respond to a question by raising their eyebrows, they are

_____a.   surprised.
_____b.   perplexed.
_____c.   answering "yes".
_____d.   acting impolite.

25. If Navajo employees purse (pucker) their lips, they mean

_____a.   that direction.
_____b.   they are nothing.
_____c.   they are ashamed.
_____d.   they are angry.

Creating Your Own Culture

Art Shriberg
Xavier University

GOALS

1. To identify some of the elements of culture by creating and becoming part of a new culture.
2. To simulate the stress and confusion of a cross-cultural business contact.
3. To develop an appreciation of diverse cultural behavior and its impact on business transactions.

INSTRUCTIONS

This exercise has three components:

1. The class will be divided in half and each group will "create" their own culture. Your culture will have a wide variety of rules of behavior that you write on your worksheets, or that a "scribe" will write on newsprint for your section.
2. You will then send visitors to the other culture to learn about the culture and to attempt to sell the other culture a product you make.
3. The class will reassemble to discuss the exercise.

Creating Your Own Culture Worksheet

In this exercise each group will create their own culture. There are no rights and wrongs; your culture can have any rules that the group decides, *but* the group is expected to follow the rules it creates throughout the exercise.

Your instructor will appoint a guide for each group. The group should choose one student to be the scribe and to write down your rules. For each of the following questions you might have several answers.

1. In your culture, who are the most respected people (females, males, light skin, dark skin, tall, short, bald, very hairy, other, etc.)?

2. How is this respect shown (bowing, avoiding eye contact, constant eye contact, never speaking to the person unless spoken to, other, etc.)?

3. What does your culture value (religion, the earth, truth, productivity, relationship, beauty, other, etc.)? (There should be several answers to this question.)

4. What are the favorite topics of conversation (politics, religion, only about grandparents, only about children, other, etc.)?

5. What happens at social events (people dance only with their own gender, people are always in groups of at least four, men do most of the talking, etc.)?

6. How is business conducted (you get right to the point, never in front of women, only after eating, other, etc.)?

7. What will your culture sell? (Choose one product that is consistent with your cultural values.) At what price?

8. How does your culture treat strangers (very friendly, very unfriendly, only friendly to women, no eye contact, other, etc.)?

9. How does your culture deal with people who don't know or don't follow its rules?

10. How do members of your culture greet each other?

11. How does your culture use non-verbal behavior? What are some of your non-verbal cues?

12. What other unique elements does your culture have?

13. What is the name of your culture?

Musical Chairs

M. June Allard
Worcester State College

GOAL

To experience how it feels to be physically challenged; that is, unable to communicate with people in the traditional way.

INSTRUCTIONS

1. Form a group of four to six members and arrange your chairs in a circle.
2. Read the passage below to yourself.

> Fifty students reported for a class which had 35 student desk-chairs: 30 RH (right hand) and five LH (Left Hand). Fifteen RH students then volunteered to transfer to an honors section down the hall, thereby leaving everyone in the original class seated.
>
> After class, six RH students and one LH student reported their chairs were broken and needed replacing. Later that afternoon the honors instructor called saying eight of the transfer students were not eligible for the honors class and were, therefore, returning to the original class. How many additional RH and LH desk-chairs did the original instructor need for his class?

3. **Working as a group**, use **one** worksheet to come to some consensus on the answer to the question posed in the passage.
4. Your instructor will give you further *special* instructions on how your group will conduct the exercise.

Musical Chairs Worksheet

Additional Chairs Needed:_____RH_____LH

The Older Worker

Stella M. Nkomo
Myron D. Fottler
R. Bruce McAfee

GOALS

1. To familiarize you with typical stereotypes toward older workers and the managerial implications of these stereotypes.
2. To provide you with factual information regarding older workers.

TIME REQUIRED

Out of Class   15 minutes to complete the Older Worker Questionnaire

In Class   45 minutes for group and class discussion of all items on the Older Worker Questionnaire.

INSTRUCTIONS

Prior to the class meeting in which this exercise will be discussed, you should read any material on older workers assigned by your instructor and complete the Older Worker Questionnaire. Record your answers in the Individual Answer column on the left.

At the start of the exercise, the class will be divided into groups of three to five by your instructor. Your group's task is to discuss each item on the questionnaire and arrive at a consensus regarding the correct answer (20-minute time limit). Record the group answer in the column on the right. After all groups have finished, the instructor will present the correct answers in the margin along with an explanation. Each group should record these answers in the margin along side the group's own answers and then compare the two to determine the number right and wrong.

Reprinted from *Applications in Human Resource Management,* 2nd ed., by Stella M. Nkomo, Myron D. Fottler, and R. Bruce McAfee, Reprinted with permission by Wadsworth Publishing Company.

The Older Worker Questionnaire

Individual Answer	Mark the statements **T** for true and **F** for false.	Group Answer
	1. Younger workers tend to have higher job satisfaction than older ones.	
	2. A worker's creativity peaks between the ages of 55 and 65.	
	3. The life expectancy of the average U.S. citizen has been increasing.	
	4. The proportion of people 65 and over is expected to decline between now and 2030.	
	5. Since 1948, employees have been retiring later in life.	
	6. Job switching (quitting one job and getting another) tends to decline dramatically with age.	
	7. One's level of education is the major influence affecting the probability of staying in the workforce vs. retiring.	
	8. About one third of all older employees work after receiving a pension.	
	9. Older workers generally require less light for performing a task than do younger workers.	
	10. The majority of old employees are set in their ways and are unable to adapt to changing conditions.	
	11. In general, older workers are less healthy than younger ones.	
	12. Older employees experience no more work disabilities than younger workers.	
	13. Older employees usually take a longer period of time to learn something new than do younger employees.	
	14. Studies have universally found that older workers are less productive than younger ones.	

Individual Answer	Mark the statements **T** for true and **F** for false.Answer	Group Answer
	15. Younger workers have higher injury frequency rates than do older workers.	
	16. Older workers have more serious injuries and lose more time per injury than do younger workers.	
	17. Older workers are increasingly becoming all or nothing employees in the labor market, i.e., they either work full time or not at all.	
	18. Older employees tend to react more slowly than younger employees.	
	19. Less than half of the heads of households stay in career jobs (positions with a single employer) for 15 years or more.	
	20. One's ability to taste and smell tends to improve with age.	

Transcendus Exercise

Carole G. Parker
St. Michael's College

Donald C. Klein
The Union Institute

GOALS

1. To identify individual differences that may not be apparent among participants with respect to the nature and value of conflict.
2. To increase awareness of participants' assumptions, beliefs, values, biases, concerns, and preferences in relation to conflict that results from their experiences with differences.
3. To enable participants to manage more effectively their experience of diversity and conflict.

INSTRUCTIONS

1. Selection of Transcendents and Earthlings—the class is divided into small groups of 6–8, from which two persons will be identified as Transcendents and the rest as Earthlings. The instructor will provide more information about this process.
2. Planning and Role Preparation—approximately 10–15 minutes. Members of each group of Earthlings and pair of Transcendents meet separately to discuss their assignment and get into their role. Role assignments and information are provided by the instructor.
3. Meetings between groups of Earthlings and Transcendent pairs (approximately 10–15 minutes)
4. Small groups of Earthlings and pairs of Transcendents in their assigned roles come together to explore the nature and purpose of conflict.
5. Entire class is re-formed for a discussion

The original version of the Transcendus Exercise was created by Donald Klein in June 1984 for the use at the Beyond Conflict Training Laboratory in Bethel, Maine, conducted by the NTL Institute for Applied Behavioral Science.

INTRODUCTION TO TRANSCENDUS

In another galaxy, far, far away, there is a planet called "Transcendus." The inhabitants on this planet are physically very similar to the people on Earth and differ from one another, just as Earthlings do. There is one major difference, however, between Transcendents and Earthlings, on Transcendus: there is no conflict.

Word has spread to Transcendus that Earth is a planet on which there is conflict that pervades relationships between individuals, groups, nations, and many other aspects of life. The Transcendent Governing Council has decided to send a team of anthropologists/sociologists to Earth to learn about conflict. Their instructions are to decide whether it would be advantageous to bring conflict, whatever it is, back to their home planet.

The Transcendents work in pairs as they meet with small groups of Earthlings to carry out their study.

Carole G. Parker, Ph.D., is an assistant professor of Business Administration at Saint Michael's College. She is responsible for teaching courses in management and organizational behavior. She also functions as a management consultant to health care systems, human service agencies, and business and industry. Among the organizations for which Dr. Parker has served as consultant or trainer are such firms as General Electric Co., General Motors Corporation, Touche Ross, Canada, University Hospitals, Cleveland, EG&G Idaho, Inc., National Training Laboratories, Neighborhood Centers Association, Mt. Sinai Medical Center, and Evangelical Health Systems. She has also served as a member of the Visiting Staff, The Gestalt Institute of Cleveland, and is a member of NTL Institute.

Donald Klein, a community and organizational psychologist, has served as consultant and trainer since 1953 with business, government, and nonprofit organizations. A core faculty member of the Graduate School of The Union Institute and a member of NTL Institute for Applied Behavioral Science, he has published books and articles on organizational diagnosis, transformative change, power, systems simulation, consultation and training, community development, mental health, and the dynamics of humiliation.

Instructions for Observers

The task of the observer is to watch the behavior of group members and note how the group works together. Guidelines on what to look for include, but are not limited to the following:

Observations	Transcendents	Earthlings
1. Who speaks most and least? In what order do people talk?		
2. Does everyone contribute? What happens to the contributions of different members?		
3. What occurs when the Transcendents arrive? To what extent does the group stick to its original plan for interacting with the visitors? Does the plan change? If so, how does the change occur?		
4. What is the level of tension in the group before the Transcendents arrive and after they join the group?		
5. What kinds of emotions are expressed by group members and exhibited in their posture, facial expressions, and actions?		
6. What were your thoughts as an individual sitting on the sidelines observing?		
7. What, if any, emotions were stirred in you as an observer?		

Gender and Participation: An Exploration of Differences

Joan V. Gallos
University of Missouri-Kansas City

GOALS

1. To explore the connections between gender and task group participation.
2. To examine perceptions about gender-based behaviors in task and discussion groups.

INSTRUCTIONS AND OVERVIEW

1. A small number of students will be selected by the instructor to participate in a designated group task.
2. Each of the students participating in this group task will be given a character description with assigned role behaviors. These students will not share information about their characters or roles with each other or with the larger class, but will use the information to inform their involvement in the group task. The character and role descriptions are based on research about gender differences in participation styles, involvement, and comfort levels in mixed-gender task and discussion groups.
3. Students participating in the group task will be given time alone to study their roles and become comfortable with their characters. The group will then begin working on the designated task in a "fishbowl" setting.
4. Students who have not been assigned characters will observe the task group in action and record on the provided worksheets their observations of (a) what is happening in the group and (b) how individuals are behaving.
5. At the end of the observed task group activity, observers will be given time alone to review their observations and to record possible explanations for the dynamics observed.
6. Student observers will share their recorded observations and explanations with the large group.
7. Students who participated in the group task will reveal their assigned roles and characters.
8. The instructor will then lead a general discussion of gender and group participation.

Jean V. Gallos is associate professor in the Division of Urban Leadership and Policy Studies at the School of Education, University of Missouri-Kansas City. She has a B.A. from Princeton University, and a masters and doctorate in organizational behavior from the Harvard Graduate School of Education. As a consultant and educator, Dr. Gallos has worked in the U.S. and abroad on issues of professional effectiveness, on the design and management of collaborative work systems, and on gender in the workplace. She has published widely on issues of individual performance, gender, and management education and is the editor of the *Journal of Management Education.*

———————————

Gender and Participation—Observer Worksheet

Name of observed participant	What do I see happening? What do I see the participant doing?	Why do I think this is happening?
Brandi	waited for a good opportunity	Brandi's temperament
	not interrupting	logical thinking pattern.
	at the opportune time - focused on next question	Politeness, focus on task at hand.
	Is that leadership? Keeping group on track, not giving opinion.	Fairness; speaking without over elaborating.
	professional opinion	

Gender and Participation—Observer Worksheet

Name of observed participant	What do I see happening? What do I see the participant doing?	Why do I think this is happening?

Gender and Participation—Observer Worksheet

Name of observed participant	What do I see happening? What do I see the participant doing?	Why do I think this is happening?

The In-Basket Dilemma

Alice L. O'Neill
University of Scranton

GOALS
1. To examine the effects of multicultural issues on the practice of management.
2. To learn how to prioritize management decisions and actions which are compounded by multicultural considerations and legal implications.

DESCRIPTION
This in-basket exercise (refer to Table I for a list of participants) consists of several telephone messages or memos that a manager might find waiting in the office upon return from a three-day seminar. Discussion should focus on the multicultural and legal aspects of each situation and on establishing a priority for handling the messages (See Table II).

DIRECTIONS
1. You are Mike Flynn, the administrator of Birch Acres, a 200-bed long-term care facility.
2. You have just returned from a three day seminar entitled "The Importance of Understanding Cultural Diversity in Health Care Administration." You are ready to get back to work and are thankful that Birch Acres doesn't have some of the administrative problems that were discussed at the seminar. Gerald Jones, your secretary, greets you with "Welcome back! There are lots of messages you will need to check out right away."
3. Read the following background information and prioritize the order in which you should act (i.e., what should you do first, second, third, etc.).

MIKE FLYNN

Mike Flynn had been an assistant administrator at Northwood Community Hospital/Skilled Nursing Facility (SNF), a 100-bed nonprofit acute care facility with a 30-bed SNF for three years. He had enjoyed working at Northwood, which was near Scranton, Pennsylvania, where he had lived all his life. Several West-European ethnic groups had settled in the area, their ancestors having come to the area to mine the coal fields, and everyone knew one another or at least someone's relative. There were few minorities, and the families were close-knit and had a real "work ethic," as Mike's father used to say.

Mike's main responsibilities as assistant administrator at Northwood included directing the Employee Relations Department, Joint Commission on Accreditation of Health Care Organizations (JCAHO) preparedness of Northwood, plant operations, and hospital-community relations. He had been involved in two union contract negotiations as well as budgetary preparation for his departments and the entire facility. He had also obtained his nursing home administrator's (NHA) license, following the

Board's request that each assistant administrator be so licensed (Pennsylvania state law requires that nursing home administrators be licensed although hospital administrators are not required to be licensed).

Mike was 31 years old and eager for more administrative challenges. He realized that there would be no upward mobility at Northwood for a few years, so he decided to search for a position that would offer him a chance to prove his administrative capabilities. He applied to Birch Acres for the administrator position and was hired following his first interview. Mike was certain that he could handle the job and he would have no problem relocating on short notice.

Birch Acres

Birch Acres, a 200-bed proprietary long-term care facility, is located in a suburb of Scotsville, Pennsylvania, which has a significant black population, a small Asian population, and over the past three years, an influx of Hispanics into the area. Both the employee component and the residents are representative of the regional population (see Table I). The facility is not unionized. A majority of the employees are female; several are single parents. One problem that the facility is having is retaining nursing assistants; just as soon as the orientation period is completed, many of the new hires quit and go to work at the local hospital. Two years ago, the facility advertised for an administrator, following the resignation of an administrator who had been there for ten years. Mike Flynn was hired by the owners following his first interview.

TABLE I List of Participants

Mike Flynn	Administrator, Birch Acres
Gerald Jones (GJ)	Mike Flynn's Secretary
Ms. Jackson	One of the best day shift RNs.
Mr. Rivesio	Hispanic roommate of Mr. James
Mr. James	Black roommate of Mr. Rivesio
Bob French	President, Nursing Home Board
Miss Rodriguez	New Hispanic nursing assistant
Ms. Roth	Director of Nursing (DON)
Ms. Bankroll	Assistant Director of Nursing
Mr. Bascombe	Plant Engineer
Mary Jones	Dietitian recruited by Mike Flynn from Northwood when last dietitian retired
Ombudsman	Overseer of resident rights; not a facility member
Department of Health	Inspects and recommends licensure/ relicensure; makes unannounced visits and inspections

TABLE II   Telephone Messages and Memos

Rate priority of action on the line next to the letter from 1 to 15 with 1 being first priority and 15 being last.

A._____	**Wednesday—8:30 AM/GJ** Ms. Jackson (day RN) called; she wants to see you ASAP. Having baby-sitter problems; can she either come in 1/2 hr later on her days to work or can she bring in her children (ages 3 and 4) until somebody can come by to pick them up.
B._____	**Wednesday—11:00 AM/GJ** Mr. James' (Room 202) family wants to talk to you as soon as you get back. They are VERY upset! They claim that Mr. James' roommate, Mr. Rivesio, is stealing his clothing and a sum of money is missing from his bedside stand. If you don't transfer Mr. Rivesio out of that room immediately they will transfer their father out of the facility (he has private insurance).
C._____	**Wednesday—11:30 AM/GJ** Mr. Rivesio's wife stopped in to see you. She says that Mr. James' family is discriminating against her husband because he is Hispanic and on welfare, and that Mr. James is hiding his money and telling his family that somebody stole it. She said that the nurses were searching her husband's dresser for the money that Mr. James said was stolen and she's going to sue us.
D._____	**Thursday—6:00 AM/GJ** Message left on your answering machine that the nursing assistants are talking about unionizing with 1199. Lady's voice—didn't identify herself. Seems that they are unhappy about the nurses here getting a raise when the nursing assistants are the ones that do all the work around here.
E._____	**Thursday - 9:00 AM/GJ** The Ombudsman called. She has received complaints about the food. Nobody seems to care whether the residents like or dislike the food they are served. She will be visiting the facility Monday and will meet with the Residents' Council.
F._____	**Thursday - 1:00 PM/GJ** Carol Roth, Director of Nursing (DON) wants you to have Social Services check about transferring Mrs. Belacastro to another facility. All she does is complain and is abusive to the staff. Why can't she be like Mrs. Chen—the sweet little 80 year old Chinese lady never complains, even though she has severe pain from terminal bone cancer—in fact,

TABLE II (continued)

	she denies having pain when the nurses ask her about it. If the facility admits any more residents like Mrs. Belacastro, the nurses would revolt—they are already short-staffed.
G._____	Thursday - 1:00 PM/GJ Mary Jones, the dietitian called. She's upset about the complaints about the food and that the Ombudsman never notified her that she was coming. Nobody ever complained about the food when she was the dietitian at Northwood, she said. She wants to know what should she do?
H._____	Thursday - 2:30 PM/GJ Ms. Roth left a message for you. She wants to talk to you about the hiring policies around here. The new Hispanic nursing assistants have adequate work skills, but they speak Spanish all the time and from now on it would be better if only English speaking employees were hired. She says they should learn to speak English just like everybody else around here; she's afraid that communication problems will cause problems with patient care quality.
I._____	Thursday - 7:00 PM/GJ A group representing the nursing assistants called to make an appointment with you to meet with you ASAP about the rumor that one of the residents has AIDS. If it's true, they said, they would refuse to take care of that resident if they are assigned to do so. "Let the nurses do it," they stated.
J._____	Friday - 8:00 AM/GJ Urgent message from Bob French, Board President "Call me as soon as you get back about the AIDS patient. Transfer the patient to another facility ASAP because we don't need this type of publicity out in the community."
K._____	Friday - 8:30 AM/GJ Miss Rodriguez (one of the new Hispanic nursing assistants, day shift) called and said that she *must* have her working hours changed. She can't work with Ms. Roth (DON) who is always complaining about not being able to understand what she is saying and that she should learn to speak English or leave Birch Acres, and she can't say anything back to Ms. Roth because Ms. Roth is her supervisor.
L._____	Friday - 9:00 AM/GJ Message on answering machine from unknown person: "One of your employees is a homosexual who has tested positive for HIV." (I didn't tell anyone about this-G.J.)

TABLE II (continued)

	Friday - 2:00 PM/GJ
M.____	Ms. Roth (DON) heard that the Department of Health paid a surprise visit to one of the other nursing homes in the area this morning. They are zeroing in on employee personnel records, staffing ratios, infection control and patient abuse. FYI - Our annual Department of Health inspection is due any day now.
	Friday - 4:00 PM/GJ
N.____	Mr. Bascombe called. The fire alarm went off three times today; the girls on third floor called him (sounded angry) and said they were too busy to go through the fire plan routine all day long and we'd better get those alarms fixed or else get them some more help for third floor. Mr. Bascombe says that he thinks that someone is setting them off deliberately just to scare the residents and get more help on the nursing unit floors.
	Friday - 4:30 PM/GJ
O.____	Ms. Bankroll, the assistant DON, called. She wanted you to know that she interviewed a great nursing assistant applicant but couldn't hire her to fill that vacant position on 11-7 because of the applicant's unavailability to travel after sundown Friday through Sunday due to some kind of religious reason.

QUESTIONS FOR DISCUSSION

Although this in-basket exercise is based in a health-care setting, problems such as those stated are ones that can occur in any setting. Managers face issues of diversity frequently, many times not realizing the causes or extent of some of those problems. The issues are real and point to the fact that managers must be aware of the need to understand the effects of multicultural diversity on organizational administration.

1. What are the diversity issues in this in-basket exercise?
2. What diverse groups are represented?
3. What legal problems may arise from some of the diversity issues presented?
4. What are some major differences between Northwood Community Hospital/SNF and Birch Acres?
5. What might Mike Flynn have failed to do before he accepted the job at Birch acres?
6. What are the board's responsibilities in the issues presented?
7. What are Mike Flynn's responsibilities to the board in relation to the issues presented?
8. Why are so many of the newly trained nursing assistants going elsewhere to work following the orientation period?

9. What are Carol Roth's (DON) responsibilities as far as the nursing department staffing problems?
10. What actions should be taken to help overcome staffing problems and employee concerns? Who should take these actions?
11. What can be done to address the evident problem of residents who are room-mates and who cannot get along satisfactorily?

––––––––––––

Alice L. O'Neill is Director, Health Administration Program at the University of Scranton, Scranton, PA.

––––––––––––

Multicultural Negotiations Exercise

Egidio A. Diodati
Assumption College

Student Instructions

GOAL
To experience, identify, and appreciate the problems associated with negotiating with people of other cultures.

INSTRUCTIONS
1. Eight student volunteers will participate in the role play: four representing a Japanese automobile manufacturer and four representing an American team which has come to sell micro-chips and other components to the Japanese company. The remainder of the class will observe the negotiations.
2. The eight volunteers will divide up into the two groups and then separate into different rooms, if possible. At that point they will be given instruction sheets. Neither team can have access to the other's instructions. After dividing up the roles, the teams should meet for 10–15 minutes to develop their negotiation strategies based on their instructions.
3. While the teams are preparing, the room will be set up using a rectangular table with four seats on each side. The Japanese side will have three chairs at the table with one chair set up behind the three. The American side of the table will have four chairs side-by-side.
4. After the preparation time is over, the Japanese team will be brought in, so they may greet the Americans when they arrive. At this point, the Americans will be brought in and the role play begins. Time for the negotiations should be 20–30 minutes. The rest of the class act as observers and will be expected to provide feedback during the discussion phase.
5. After the negotiations are completed, the student participants from both sides and the observers will complete their feedback sheets. Class discussion of the feedback sheets will follow.

Egidio A. Diodati is currently an assistant professor of Management at Assumption College in Worcester, Massachusetts. His research specialty is International Marketing and he has published in that area. In 1990, he was selected as International Visisting Colleague at the University of Hawaii's Pacific-Asian Management Institute.

Feedback Sheet for the Japanese Team

1. What was your biggest frustration during the negotiations?

2. What would you say the goal of the American team was?

3. How would you rate the success of each of the American team members in identifying your team's needs and appealing to them?

Mr. Jones, Vice-President and Team Leader

Mr./Mrs. Smith, Manufacturing Engineer

Mr./Mrs. Nelson, Marketing Analyst

Mr./Mrs. Frost, Account Executive

4. What would you say the goal of the Japanese team was?

5. What role (e.g., decider, influencer, etc.) did each member of the American team play?

Mr. Jones

Mr./Ms. Smith

Mr./Mrs. Nelson

Mr./Mrs. Frost

6. What strategy should the American team have taken?

Feedback Sheet for the American Team

1. What was your biggest frustration during the negotiations?

2. What would you say the goal of the Japanese team was?

3. How would you rate the success of each of the American team members?

   Mr. Jones, Vice-President and Team Leader

   Mr./Mrs. Smith, Manufacturing Engineer

   Mr./Mrs. Nelson, Marketing Analyst

   Mr./Mrs. Frost, Account Executive

4. What would you say the goal of the American team was?

5. What role (e.g., decider, influencer, etc.) did each member of the Japanese team play?

   Mr. Ozaka

   Mr. Nishimuro

   Mr. Sheno

   Mr. Kawazaka

6. What strategy should the American team have taken?

Feedback Sheet for the Observers

1. What was your biggest frustration during the negotiations?

2. What would you say the goal of the Japanese team was?

3. How would you rate the success of each of the American team members?

   Mr. Jones, Vice-President and Team Leader

   Mr./Mrs. Smith, Manufacturing Engineer

   Mr./Mrs. Nelson, Marketing Analyst

   Mr./Mrs. Frost, Account Executive

4. What would you say the goal of the American team was?

5. What role (e.g., decider, influencer, etc.) did each member of the Japanese team play?

   Mr. Ozaka

   Mr. Nishimuro

   Mr. Sheno

   Mr. Kawazaka

6. What strategy should the American team have taken?

Create an Exercise

M. June Allard
Worcester State College

GOAL
To gain greater information about and understanding of physical and mental disabilities.

INSTRUCTIONS
1. Form groups of five or six members. List the members of your group on the worksheet.
2. Create an exercise to demonstrate/experience a physical or mental disability. Your instructor will provide more information on the specific disability to be addressed by your group.
3. The exercise can take the form of a demonstration, role play, game, trivia, or whatever. It can be designed for individuals, small groups, or large groups. Be sure that it covers a *broad range of information pertinent to the topic.*
4. Create all appropriate materials such as: introduction, rules, game board and pieces, props, scoring sheets, note-taking sheets, forms, or whatever is needed for the exercise.
5. The criteria to be used to grade the exercise include:
    a. accuracy of information
    b. breadth of coverage
    c. evidence of organization and relevance (e.g., development of meaningful categories or roles)
    d. evidence that additional research has been done and more material has been obtained on the disability
    e. neatness, completeness, and coherence of materials (e.g., readable instructions, meaningful introduction, usable game or observational materials, etc.).
6. Due date: _____ Plan to play/demonstrate your exercise on this date.

Create an Exercise Worksheet

Group Members: _____   _____

_____   _____

_____   _____

Topic (Disability):   _____

Title of Exercise: _____

Nature of exercise
(check):   _____ demonstration   _____ role play

_____ game   _____ other: _____

(please explain)

_____

_____

Brief Description of Exercise:

Materials Needed:

Procedure (steps):

INDEX

NOTES

NOTES

NOTES